Great
Golf Quotes

Great
Golf Quotes

Michael McDonnell

**ROBSON
BOOKS**

First published as *Classic Golf Quotes* in 2002

This edition published in Great Britain in 2007 by
Robson Books
10 Southcombe Street
London
W14 0RA

An imprint of Anova Books Company Ltd.

ISBN 9781905798070

10 9 8 7 6 5 4 3 2 1

A CIP catalogue record for this book is available from the
British Library.

Typeset by SX Composing DTP, Rayleigh, Essex
Printed and bound by MPG Books Ltd, Bodmin,
Cornwall.

This book can be ordered direct from the publisher.
Contact the marketing department, but try your bookshop first.

www.anovabooks.com

Contents

Acknowledgements

Acknowledgements are due to the following for their kind permission to reproduce quotations.

Alliss, Peter, *Peter Alliss: An Autobiography,* William Collins Sons & Co, 1981.

Azinger, Paul with Abraham, Ken, *Zinger: A Champion's Story of Determination, Courage and Changing Back,* Zondervan, 1995.

With the permission of Zondervan; copyright Paul Azinger 1995.

Gough, Darren with Norrie, David, *Dazzler: The Autobiography,* Michael Joseph, 2001. With the permission of Penguin Books

Ltd; copyright Darren Gough 2001.

Hitchcock, Jimmy, *Master Golfer,* Stanley Paul, 1967. With the permission of Random House Group Ltd.

Kahn, Liz, *The LPGA: The Unauthorised Version,* Group Fore Productions, Inc, 1996.

Laidlaw, Renton, *Golfing Heroes,* Century Benham Ltd, 1989.

Menzies, Gordon (ed.), *The World of Golf.* With the permission of BBC Worldwide Ltd; copyright the BBC and contributors 1982.

Palmer, Arnold & Dodson, James, *A Golfer's Life,* Century, 1999.

With the permission of Random House Group Ltd.

Wodehouse, P G, *The Heart of a Goof,* Hutchinson, 1963. With the permission of Random House Group Ltd.

Thanks also for assistance from the Oxford and Cambridge Golfing Society.

Introduction

There is a common belief that golfers are strong, silent types who let their clubs do the talking and never vent their feelings in public. They are held to be calm and contained and slow to boil. The truth, however, is rather different.

There is as much passion and emotion in the seemingly genteel, royal and ancient pursuit of golf as can be found in any heavyweight title fight, and golfers are driven by a multitude of personal motives – ambition, jealousy, defiance, belligerence and many others – in the pursuit of success. There is humour too, sometimes self-deprecating, often impish. But above all there is an honesty that is shared by the greatest player and the most feeble hacker because they are both in the same boat. Victims of the game, never its complete master.

This book is a catalogue of the thoughts and sayings of campaigners and commentators stretching over past centuries to the present day. They define the human condition common to all golfers, whether it be Simon Hobday looking heavenwards in a crowded clubhouse and crying out: 'Why don't you come down and fight like a man?' or Seve Ballesteros telling his caddie: 'It's not your fault. It's my fault because I listen to you.'

But there are priceless personal insights too, from such as Catherine Lacoste who after winning the US Women's Open reflected: 'Each time you win, you lose a little of your sensitivity and that's a bad thing for a girl.' Or Brian Huggett admitting: 'It hurts to win. In my case my stomach tightens like a knot and stays like that till it's all over.'

Anger also plays its part in this collection. Lee Trevino, dismissing his defeated US Ryder Cup team thus: 'They're a bunch of cry-babies. I can't play for them, they got the socks beaten off them.' Or Jack Nicklaus clashing with the referee and growling: 'I would like to have one who knows the rules.'

Humour too. Jose Maria Olazabal addressing the 2000 PGA European Tour annual dinner and saying: This speech is a bit like my tee shot. I don't know where it's going.' Or Peter Alliss's comment on BBC television when a player made the sign of the cross before playing a bunker shot and then left the ball in the sand: 'You can't trust anybody these days.'

Personal animosity has its place in such a pageant; there's the unashamed coolness between Gary Player and Tom Watson as the South African says: 'I would hate to have won two world championships knowing I had used illegally grooved clubs.' Or Arnold Palmer's pointed remark about Peter Thomson: 'We Americans take particular pleasure in beating Peter.'

And then there are the wordsmiths who follow their heroes. Leonard Crawley on Jack Nicklaus: 'He plays like a beautifully proportioned field gun, automatic with perfect range.' Bernard Darwin on Harry Vardon: 'He raised the general conception of what was possible in his game.' Pat Ward-Thomas on Ben Hogan: 'The glorious swing flashes and a long iron pierces the wind like an arrow.. .we shall never see his like again.' David and Patricia Davies on Tiger Woods: 'He is helping to drag the game out of the country clubs and introduce it to the tenements and the streets.'

There are poignant moments too. Cape Coloured golfer Sewsunker 'Papwa' Sewgolum's explanation for being made to wait outside the whites-only clubhouse to receive the Natal Open Trophy he had just won: 'There would have been no fuss if it hadn't rained.' Or Bruce Crampton after finishing second to Jack Nicklaus in a major championship for the fifth time: 'I shall appear next year in my customary role as defending runner-up.'

This is the world of golf, its charms, challenges and frustrations, as seen by its leading characters who down the years were brave – or daft – enough to voice their thoughts in front of a camera, notebook or tape recorder. Bernard Darwin, the great golf essayist, once walked out of a press conference grumbling that he was not interested in what the golfer was saying, only how he played. Bernardo, you don't know what you missed.

Pleshey, 2002

1

'The Best Feeling of All?'
A Reason for Golf

Golf is essentially a battle with self. And a solitary one too, across unforgiving countryside where character and skill are both challenged to the limit. Yet curiously, this inner conflict provides a wealth of profound insights and perceptions from campaigners who have pondered on their way of life and why they play their game.

For Tony Jacklin the supreme moment comes when he is alone and can savour the memory of beating everybody. For Catherine Lacoste there is an awareness that she loses some of her sensitivity every time she wins. For both Jack Nicklaus and Tom Watson there is the sheer joy of trying to triumph over each other. 'This is what it's all about,' remarked Watson in the 1977 Open championship. 'You're damn right, it is,' replied Nicklaus even though he lost to Watson.

Each contender acquires their own personal reason as a means of motivation; a way of sticking to the task despite the vagaries of fate. Perhaps some are sustained by the hope that success is just around the corner. Others feel a constant need for the fulfilment of victory or are inspired by an ambition to be acknowledged by their peers. And there are those for whom competition is the air they breathe and they cannot live without it. Whatever the lure, they have come to their own conclusions on their fascination for the game.

The best feeling of all? When it's all over – the excitement, the pressure, the presentation, the interviews, the autographs, the party back at the hotel with all your friends. You are in your room on your own and you stare at the ceiling and say to yourself: 'By God, I beat the lot of them. I really DID beat them all.' That's the real moment to savour.

Tony Jacklin on winning the 1969 Open championship (Ryder Cup magazine, 1985).

The competitor in me says: 'Jack, I don't care what age you are and I don't care who's out in front of me. I'm a competitor who can still play and still win. That may not be realistic but it's the way I have to think or else there's no sense being here.

Jack Nicklaus, aged 59, at the 1998 US Masters.

I have seen champions come and go like short-lived daffodils and bluebells. Wine, women and song, and various other extravagances, have helped some on their way out of the headlines but for most, the decline has been due simply to a lack of understanding of how to protect their talents from the ravages of time.

Sir Henry Cotton (*Thanks for the Game,* 1980).

All men are created equal. I'm just one stroke better than the rest.

Gene Sarazen on winning the 1922 US Open (*Golf World* magazine, 1995).

There was no major reason for our defeat. No giant flaw. This contest just ebbed and flowed and it's whether you catch it coming in or going out. We just caught it going out.

Tony Jacklin explaining Europe's narrow defeat in the 1983 Ryder Cup match.

She's asked me to call her Judy but I always call her Madam.

Sunningdale caddie **Ron Mullins** on working for American professional Judy Rankin (Colgate LPGA Championship magazine, 1979).

All I know is I've seen Nicklaus watch Hogan practise. I've never seen Hogan watch Nicklaus practise.

US Open champion **Tommy Bolt** on the comparative merits of Ben Hogan and Jack Nicklaus, as told to Pulitzer Prize-winning sports columnist Dave Anderson (*Golf World* magazine, 1997).

One of these days I'm gonna win this bitch of a tournament. It can't keep getting away from me like this. Can it?

John Mahaffey after narrowly missing two successive US Open titles. He never did win, but captured the 1978 US PGA championship instead.

About a hundred and twenty years.

Sandy Lyle's reply in 1987 to an American journalist who asked him to define the difference between winning the Tournament Players championship which began in 1974 and the Open championship, founded in 1860.

Most people thrive on winning. I don't. Hell, if I finish second, I consider it a victory. If I finish third, I feel great.

> US Open and Masters champion **Fuzzy Zoeller**
> (the official US Open magazine, 1985).

🏌

We are not trying to catch out the best player. We are trying to seek him out.

Sandy Tatum, US Open championship official, responding to criticisms by players that the Inverness course had been set up too severely for the 1979 event.

🏌

You've got to know when it's time to say goodbye.

Tony Jacklin confirming that he had relinquished the European Ryder Cup captaincy after the tied 1989 match.

🏌

Sometimes I don't understand why I'm sitting here. I think I was given a gift to play golf and to be mentally strong. You know, I don't see a sports psychologist. I've somehow just known what to do in that situation.

> **Karrie Webb** on winning the 2000 US Women's Open
> championship.

🏌

The greatest obstacle to his building the greatest championship record of all time will be himself. If he fails to win many more of golf's crowns he will not be the first sportsman to succumb to the easy life, or the champagne circuit as Lee Trevino calls it. I can think of Tom Weiskopf and Tony Jacklin who opted out before they realised their true potential.

Peter Thomson talking about Greg Norman to Australian golf writer Tom Ramsey (*the International* magazine, 1987). Norman won two Open championships.

This is the first time I've retired in mid-round but it's ridiculous to miss two-foot putts. Throw it [the bag] in the lake. I think the lake by the first hole is the deepest. Make it disappear.

Peter Alliss on withdrawing from an Italian tournament at the start of his putting troubles. (Piero Mancinelli in *The Golfers*, 1982).

When you are a champion, if you win *c'est normal;* once you lose everybody says you're over the hill.

Catherine Lacoste to Peter Ryde (*Golfer's Bedside Book*, 1971).

To anyone else, perhaps the fact that I had beaten Cecil Leitch was unimportant – an off-day for the champion. To me it was the beginning of a successful career. I had gained confidence I needed so badly. My nerves became steadier, my shots bolder. No opponent held any terror for me.

Gienna Collett on defeating the leading woman golfer, Cecil Leitch, in 1921.

It's like diving off a high board or skiing down a steep mountain. It's always easier to do something once you've done it.

Lee Trevino talking to American writer Steve Hershey about winning the US Open for a second time.

The time she missed a putt during a championship, she moaned 'Knickers!' and having been rebuked, changed the expletive to 'bee's knees' and still got told off.

Golfing magazine on Vivien Saunders, 1969.

The difference between a sand trap and water is the difference between a car crash and an airline crash. You have a chance of recovering from a car crash.

Bobby Jones (Sidney L Mathew, *Life and Times of Bobby Jones*).

I don't autograph new ones. Get an old one. It's the same autograph.

Sam Snead to an Australian fan who asked him to sign a golf ball during the 1959 World Cup in Melbourne.

I am a perfectionist. I knew I had a lot of work to do before I could rely on my swing absolutely.

Nick Faldo explaining to golf writer Mark Wilson the reason for his self-imposed exile from the top rank of European golf for two years (*PGA European Tour Yearbook,* 1988).

By one inch, America's stars of golf regained their stripes on Sunday. The confounded game was invented in Scotland, a British seed merchant conceived the event, a German missed the putt, so the Spanish cried while the Yankees bathed in bubbles on the beach.

Sports columnist **Bob Verdi,** in the *Chicago Tribune,* on US victory in the 1991 Ryder Cup match after Bernhard Langer missed a putt on the last green.

The players look to Monty for inspiration and leadership. He sets the tone, no question.

European captain **Mark James** on Colin Montgomerie before the 1999 Ryder Cup match against the United States.

The Ryder Cup brings out the best in me and I'm glad it does.
Colin Montgomerie in reply.

I felt like his father. I had to look after him.
Seve Ballesteros on partnering newcomer Paul Way, six years
his junior, in the 1983 Ryder Cup match.

Sometimes, my dear Grantland, I think, with our marvellous
modern development of clubs, stepped up ten yards at a step,
and a lively ball that travels so far, we have lost a little something
in golf, especially when I remember how Harry Vardon with six
clubs played six consecutive rounds of 68 or better. Perhaps that
may have been because Vardon was an artist and not an artisan.
(O B Keeler in *The American Golfer* magazine, 1932).

Tell me, do you chaps actually play this hole? Or do we just
photograph it?
Former Walker Cup amateur **Edward Storey** on seeing the
awesome second hole at Pine Valley in New Jersey for the first
time (Charles Price in the *International* magazine, 1987).

You start playing for money instead of trophies and golf becomes
a job.
Danielle Ammaccapane in 1991 on winning her first event as a
professional.

I don't play for the money. I only play for the victories.
Tommy Armour III on receiving a massive cheque after
losing a play-off for the 1999 Tucson Open.

The golf world is overpopulated with persons who wish they had commenced to play in the proper way.

James Braid (*Golf Guide and How to Play,* 1906).

Choker is the charmingly cruel American sporting term for a player who, when it comes to the crunch, crumbles. They also call it taking the gas, easing back into the comfort zone. In Britain for some curious reason we call it losing one's bottle. Whatever it is called, it adds up to the same thing, a loss of nerve when faced with the final challenge and it is a terrible tag to pick up and an even harder one to lose.

(Renton Laidlaw, *Golfing Heroes,* 1987).

I thought my legacy to the tour would be as a player. You might say that's changing now. I still think this whole thing can be bigger and better. It's incredible. And the best is yet to come.

Tony Jacklin on how his captaincy transformed European fortunes against the United States (Ryder Cup magazine, 1987).

What I've learned is that I wanted to be remembered as a golfer. To do that, I've got to go out and win tournaments.
Peter Jacobsen after winning the 1995 Buick Invitational.

The US GA does not retaliate.
Bill Campbell, President of the United States Golf Association, replying to media who wanted to know whether the Winged Foot course had been toughened up for the 1983 US Open, because of low scoring in previous events (John Radosta in the official US Open magazine, 1984).

I'll be better for this tournament. After all, a smooth sea never produced a skilful sailor.

Mac O'Grady after scoring 80 in the Bing Crosby Pro-Am (*Sports Illustrated,* 1984).

And then, oh! weary soul, what joys await the faithful. The putting off of mud-caked shoes, the brisk plunge or shower-bath and the warm glow thereafter; the immaculate shirt front that crackles at your touch, the glad joy of dinner and the utter relaxation of content 'with just a wee drappie of guid Scotch to follow.'

Scribner's Magazine on winter golf, 1895.

You look at all the great players and they've travelled well and won everywhere in the world. That's what I want to do.

Lee Westwood after scoring his first US Tour win in 1998.

People say it is too bad that I won all those events when the prize money was so small but I am not envious. You can only beat the competition that is around at the time and you can only compete when you feel well enough to do so. It was fun when I played, much more fun I fancy than it is now.

Byron Nelson, who won eleven consecutive US Tour events in 1945. (Renton Laidlaw, *Golfing Heroes,* 1987).

The partisans among us know it already. The outsiders will never be persuaded that things can be other than they appear in the record books. To those who cannot get away from the record books, the secret of these matches can never be revealed.

Peter Ryde of *The Times* commenting on the eve of the 1971 Walker Cup match at St Andrews.

I also learned from Gerald that it was important that, if the captain has to drop a member of the team, he does so in such a way that the player still feels part of the team.

> **Sir Michael Bonallack** on being dropped from the entire 1957 Walker Cup match by his skipper Gerald Micklem.

ʃ

I love match play. It is the essence of golf. It is what golf was meant to be. It is golf in its purest form.

> US Open champion **Corey Pavin,** 1994.

ʃ

. . . as all souls are equal before their Maker, a two-inch putt counts the same as a 250-yard drive. There is a comedy in this and a certain unfairness even, which makes golf an even apter mirror of reality.

> American author **John Updike** (*Golf: The Greatest Game*).

ʃ

In all games, and especially in golf, we have seen players possessed of a style seemingly borrowed from the angels; endowed also with health and ambition; blessed, indeed, with all the paraphernalia of invincibility. And yet we know, and I suppose they come in the end to have an inkling, that they will never win the glittering prize. They are strong and elegant runners but they never break the tape.

> **R C Robertson-Glasgow** (*The Oxford and Cambridge Golfing Society* 1898–1948).

ʃ

He was a fascinating personality. Outwardly so gentle, so intelligent and pleasingly charming in a remarkably mature way; underneath lay concealed a furious often uncontrolled temper. In the young Bobby Jones, the emotions, the temperaments were a chaotic mixture with the fiercely choleric threatening to take control at times.

American sports writer **Al Laney** on the early years of failure in Bobby Jones's competitive career.

I feel like a million bucks – minus tax.

Corey Pavin on winning the 1995 Million Dollar Challenge.

The story of the 1930 British championship seems to me to confirm, or at any rate strongly support, a sort of hypothesis that had been forming in the back of my head for years – that golf tournaments are matters of destiny and that the result is all in the book before a shot is hit. Looking back over Bobby's eight matches, you may see crisis after crisis in those furious encounters with Tolley, Johnson and Voigt where the least slip of nerve or skill or plain fortune would have brought defeat to Bobby's dearest ambition. Yet at every crisis he stood up to the shot with something I can only define as inevitability and performed what was needed with all the certainty of a natural phenomenon.

O B Keeler on the Grand Slam of Bobby Jones (*The Bobby Jones Story*).

Well, they all have to start somewhere, don't they?

The response of 46-year-old Barrow-in-Furness crane operator Maurice Flitcroft's **mother** when asked why he had entered the qualifying event for the 1976 Open championship and scored a first round 121 – 49 over par – at Formby Golf Club.

They inspired each other. There was a lot of Spanish pride too. So when you get such fierce pride and immense respect for each other, it can be a lethal cocktail.

Bernard Gallacher, European Ryder Cup captain, on the reasons why Seve Ballesteros and Jose Maria Olazabal were such a formidable partnership (Ryder Cup magazine, 1999).

Luck plays a huge role in deciding every tournament. I'm not crying about it and I hope it doesn't sound like I'm saying that's why Vijay won but somebody's going to get the bounces.

David Duval on losing the 2000 US Masters to Vijay Singh (Mark McCormack, *The World of Professional Golf 2001 edition*).

I don't care what anybody says. The first tournament is not the hardest to win, it's the second.

John Daly after winning the 1992 BC Open.

When I drive into the rough, let me not blame the club – maybe I am the sinner and need more discipline. If by pure luck I make a hole in one, let me not boast but think of all the exercise ! missed. And finally teach me that the way I play golf, I would be better off in church on Sunday.

Part of a prayer composed by the **Reverend Fulton Sheen** for the 1976 US PGA championship.

The knack for scoring can go at any moment. It can go while you're walking from the second green to the third tee. But it's like worrying about an atom bomb hitting you. You can't worry about it.

Howard Twitty at the 1980 US PGA championship.

I did it more with the heart and the stomach than anything else.
Jose Maria Olazabal explaining how he controlled his indifferent form to win the 1994 PGA championship.

Serenity is knowing your worst shot is still going to be good.
Johnny Miller (*The Art Spander Collection*).

Me? Unlucky? I came through the war didn't I? That's a lot better than many did who were at St Andrews the day I won.
Richard Burton, the 1939 Open champion, on whether he felt the Second World War had deprived him of the chance to earn a lot of money. (Robert Sommers, *Golf Anecdotes,* 1995).

The least thing upset him on the links. He missed short putts because of the uproar of butterflies in adjoining meadows.
P G Wodehouse (*The Clickings of Cuthbert,* 1921).

You have to remember that the Ryder Cup was the players' idea. It came from them. Even before Sam Ryder became involved we had played two matches between the professionals of the United States and Great Britain. But in those first matches we paid our own expenses. We came over for the Open and stayed on to play the match. I think there was more spirit, more of a will to win. That's what we were there for.
Gene Sarazen before the 1989 Ryder Cup match.

There is nothing new about the ideas of the so-called Golf Architect; he simply wishes to produce the old ideas as exemplified in the old natural courses like St Andrews, those courses which were played on before over-zealous committees demolished the natural undulations of fairways and greens and made the greens like lawns for croquet, tennis or anything except golf, and erected eyesores in the shape of straight lines of cop bunkers instead of emphasising the natural curves of the links.

In the old view of golf, there was no main thoroughfare to the hole: the player had to use his own judgement without the aid of guide posts or other adventitious means of finding his way.

Dr Alister Mackenzie, creator of Augusta National, Cypress Point, Royal Melbourne and many other classic courses worldwide (*Golf Architecture,* 1920).

The real battle at Muirfield Village is not between the best United States professionals and their European counterparts but with American public opinion and interest. In short, this is the best and possibly last chance this traditional event may have of moving out of its esoteric category and on to the wider stage of a major sporting occasion to become the focus of national interest.

Comment in the *PGA of America* magazine before the 1987 Ryder Cup match in which the Europeans scored an historic first win on American soil.

I tried for years to slow my swing. Then all of a sudden it came – like whistling.

Tony Jacklin after fellow professional Tom Weiskopf left a note with the word TEMPO written on it in the Englishman's locker before the final round of the 1969 Open championship.

It's a heck of a lot harder to stay on top than it is to get there.

Tom Kite after winning the 1991 Tournament of Champions. When all is said and done, it isn't the score that really matters, and surely, it does not matter whether you beat anybody, because you don't play people, you play the course; but it does matter whether you come off the course with your dignity and integrity intact.

Dexter Westrum (*Elegy for a Golf Pro*).

Behind every genius is a frustrated understudy. Cast in the role as golf's Dr Watson, the mystery of David Duval's missing major is one of the longest-running stories on the fairways. It is not so much the Baskervilles the American has been hounded by as a Tiger.

James Corrigan (*Independent on Sunday*) on the morning Duval went on to win the 2001 Open championship.

You get four chances at the majors each year and a lot of things have to go right just to get into position to win. But you have to do it. There's no way around it.
David Duval after winning the 2001 Open championship – his first major title (*Golf World* magazine).

The results of games should never matter too much. But if they don't matter at all nobody should bother to play. That surely is the case with the Ryder Cup.

Hugh McIlvanney in the *Sunday Times* on the debate about whether the 2001 match should go ahead following the New York terrorist outrage.

When Jacklin was winning the British Open championship at Royal Lytham, down the road about a mile away, a course full of completely oblivious addicts were enjoying their own kind of thrilling golf. This does not reflect lack of patriotic support. It merely illustrates golf hunger. Watching can only be second best to playing because golf is more a sensation than a game.

George Houghton (*How to Be a Golf Addict,* 1971).

I open the driving range and I close it. I thought you ought to know that I work hard. I like practising. I enjoy it. If I did not enjoy it I would not do it. What is the point of going back to the hotel, having a drink and talking a load of bull?

Vijay Singh to his new caddie as reported by the *Independent* newspaper during the 1992 World Match Play championship.

I had this course by the scruff of the neck then put two shots out of bounds, played another backhanded to get away from a tree and holed a very good fifteen footer to stay out of double figures. But I'm a reformed character. No more outbursts from me.

Ken Brown on staying calm after taking nine shots at a hole during the 1980 French Open.

I think Arnold and I are adversarial friends or friendly enemies. All our lives we've competed against each other. Arnold and I fight like the devil about different stuff. There are things I don't like about Arnold and I am sure there are things Arnold doesn't like about me.

Jack Nicklaus on his rival Arnold Palmer.

We had a lot of fun being the centre of all that attention. But most of all we wanted to beat each other to pulp. That's the nature of healthy sportsmanship and the spirit of tournament golf.

Arnold Palmer on his rivalry with Jack Nicklaus (Mark McCormack, *The World of Professional Golf,* 2000).

I don't think any player is afraid of me. The thing is they are afraid of the trophy more than me. The trophy means so much.

Seve **Ballesteros** before the final round of the 1991 Open championship.

I realised that your legacy is your children, your friends, not the trophies you have in your trophy case. I don't want to be the richest guy in the cemetery. It doesn't matter who has the most toys. As you get older you can still gain wisdom.

Joe Inman on winning the Pacific Bell Senior Classic soon after Payne Stewart died in an air crash.

The golf ball may represent the flight of imagination but the driver reflects the baser instincts of man, the animalistic passion to dominate. I am totally addicted to my driver. It's bombs away, bombs away, bombs away.

American professional **Mac** O'Grady.

I extol not only the virtues but also the nonsense of the game; the silliness and bitchiness of it all. I mean all that these grown men are doing is knocking a ball round a beautiful place. Although these players think it's the real world, it's not.

Peter Alliss on modern professionals.

I think it more engrossing than any game I have played in the open air and most beneficial to health. I regret to say that at present I have just gone far enough with it to find it on occasions very trying to the temper.

Cartoonist **Leslie Ward,** alias 'Spy' in *Vanity Fair,* quoted in *Golfing* magazine, 1907.

I think when I play golf, yes, I think I have to make the world revolve around me. If you want to be the best at something you have to make it revolve around what you are doing. Is that clear?
Jack Nicklaus to *Golf Digest* magazine, 1991.

*

There would have been no fuss if it hadn't rained.
Cape Coloured golfer **Sewsunker 'Papwa' Sewgolum** who was drenched while he was obliged to wait outside the whites-only clubhouse to collect the 1963 Natal Open trophy.

*

Campbell tends to call golf penalties on himself when he has the slightest cause to believe he has breached a rule. Endowed with a lively imagination, he carries his self-abnegation to a fault.
Joe Dey on American Walker Cup golfer Bill Campbell (the official US Open magazine, 1988).

*

It means what every little boy dreams about when he plays by himself late in the afternoon. He has three or four balls; one's Hogan, one's Palmer, one's Nicklaus, the other is Strange. Ninety-nine per cent of the time those dreams don't come true.
Curtis Strange to the press on winning the 1988 US Open.

*

Physically, yes, she's never going to be there. Mentally, she'll always be there. It's okay. We're all in this big group of people together in this world and there are no preferences dealt out when someone disappears from us like that.
Stuart Appleby at the 1998 US PGA championship on his wife Renay, who was killed in a road accident in London just after the Open championship that year.

*

I have come to Augusta with the best attitude I have ever had here. I'm not clowning around or joking as much. I don't feel like it. Besides, I don't want to lose my guest badges.

Lee Trevino before the 1978 US Masters.

Most of us learned the game as caddies. I started playing because I realised one day that I could hit the ball just as easy as I could hand a club to somebody.

American black professional **Charlie Sifford**, 1969.

Unless a miracle happens my golf days are limited; I may be forced to leave the game I love. There's not much I fear but I do fear leaving the game I love. I just thank God for the moment of glory He gave me.

US Open champion **Ken Venturi** after revealing in 1969 that he was suffering from a disease in his hands.
He later became a distinguished television commentator.

It wasn't a pretty 68 but it looked good on the scoreboard.

Justin Leonard at the 1997 US PGA championship.

I just hope to get off to a good start and be among them on Friday, then lay back in the bushes like a snake and bite them on the last nine holes.

Sam Snead at the 1974 US Open.

I gave away the US Open. The British Open was almost given to me. But had I won them all, I may have gotten out of the game. And I don't really want to quit. I'm still enjoying it.

Jack Nicklaus reflecting on how close he came to winning all four major titles in 1975 after taking the US Masters and the US PGA championships.

It's not that I don't enjoy playing. Heck, I don't think of golf as work. It's a game and it's lots of fun.

Johnny Miller on the reasons for taking time off during 1974, his best-ever season.

It's nice to go into the record book, but you can't buy anything with it.

Bernhard Langer after setting two scoring records in the 1991 Million Dollar Challenge. He eventually won the event.

Everybody wanted Arnie to win even though I live here. I don't really mind. Nobody in the whole world of golf has been more popular.

Part of **Guy Wolstenholme's** winning speech after beating Arnold Palmer in a play-off for the 1978 Victorian Open.

When in special training with the Spurs, if any opportunity arose for the players who fancied the game to have a round, they could avail themselves of the same. You get the fresh air, exercise and your mind distracted from the big match that lies ahead of you.

Tottenham Hotspur footballer **John Cameron** quoted in *Athletic World,* 1908.
But we had the Nigerian Open champion.

Gordon J Brand referring to his own achievement when told that the opposing Scottish team in the 1987 Dunhill Cup contained three Ryder Cup players.

𝕗

I know now how Lawrence of Arabia must have felt after spending most of his time under the ropes and in the sand.
Craig Parry on winning the 1987 New South Wales Open despite a wayward last round.

𝕗

That guy is putting at a bigger hole than I am. I don't know what got into him; I've never seen anything like that. Then, if you've got the guts to go to Vietnam, those putts don't seem too long.
Chi-Chi Rodriguez on playing partner Brian All in, a much-decorated war veteran, who won the 1973 Florida Citrus Open.

𝕗

That shot on eight just sort of landed on the green like a snowflake.
Sam Snead in the 1974 Quad Cities Open.

𝕗

I am by nature a hero-worshipper, as I guess most of us are, but in all the years of contact with the famous ones of sport, I have found only one that would stand up in every way as a gentleman as well as a celebrity, a fine decent human being as well as a newsprint personage and one who never once since I have known him has let me down in my estimate of him. That one is Robert Tyre Jones Jr, the golf player from Atlanta, Georgia.
Author **Paul Gallico** (*Farewell to Sport*, 1937).

𝕗

There is a 35-yard square of fairway about 250 yards out from the last tee at Lytham. I've been thinking about that piece of fairway for nearly a year because on July 12 at about 4.30 p.m. I may have to hit a shot under awful pressure. If I can't do that simple trick, I can't win the championship.

> **Peter Thomson** in the *Guardian* before the 1969 Open championship, won by Tony Jacklin.

The loneliest feeling of all is winning in golf. You're everyone's enemy, you've defeated all your friends and you're alone. People congratulate you but there's no real sharing.

> American professional **Jane Blalock** (Liz Kahn, *History of the Ladies Professional Golf Association*).

I wasn't born with this ability. I had to work bloody hard to become the player I am today.

> **Colin Montgomerie**.

That kid can play a little bit. I'll tell you one thing; he made me think a little more. He made me play golf to shoot a 69. I didn't want any amateur making me look bad.

> **Lee Trevino** on playing with college golfer Jim Simons in the 1971 US Open.

David choked too late.

> **Seve Ballesteros** referring to Welsh professional David Llewellyn who three-putted the last green but still halved his match with Ballesteros in the 1985 Dunhill Cup.

I asked God, please help Sheryl hang on a little longer because if I had got a phone call on Saturday night that she had gone into labour, I'd have been on a plane out of here. There are things more important than a golf tournament.

Mark Calcavecchia revealing how he was prepared to walk out of the 1989 Open championship – which he went on to win – to be with his expectant wife who gave birth a few weeks later.

This is one of those years that I'll be telling my grandchildren about but I worry that maybe I've peaked too soon, that I won't get any better, that I won't continue to improve.

Tom Watson after winning the 1977 US Masters and only a few weeks before capturing the Open championship in an epic duel with Jack Nicklaus at Turnberry.

I won't say that I'm going to win but I sure didn't come here to lose.

Carol Mann before the 1975 Dallas Open.

Let's face it, the days of touring caddies being drunks or winos are over. These kids out there are sharp. They're a credit to the tour. They make us look more professional.

Johnny Miller, 1974.

Don't ever call anyone Mister who you may one day have to play.

Ben Hogan to Dave Marr in 1960. Marr was then a new professional, but in 1965 he became the 1965 US PGA Champion.

Nicklaus, Casper, Lema and Player share several valuable traits with Palmer. They are at their best when it counts. The pressure of an important event does not harass them – it stimulates them.
                                    Herbert Warren Wind, 1966.

I was winning golf tournaments when John McEnroe was five years of age and I'll be winning tournaments, if I stay healthy, when I'm 55 and 60 years of age. Not many tennis players will be doing that.
              Gary Player's retort to an interviewer in 1984.

I thought I was at the end of the rope. I've always wanted to do much better but I've always fought my emotions. I'm my worst enemy out there when it comes to competing.
   George Burns on winning the 1985 Bank of Boston Classic.

For the past twelve months I've played better than anybody in the world – Player, Nicklaus, anybody. It's ridiculous to think I could keep up that pace.
                                        Johnny Miller, 1974.

I'm probably a better competitor than I am talented.
   Roger Maltbie after winning the 1975 Pleasant Valley Classic.

Tony is striking the ball now as good as I ever see him but he is no longer an optimist. He is a pessimist.
   Roberto de Vicenzo to the *Sunday Times* in 1978 on Tony
                                        Jacklin's decline.
A spectator remarked to me last October, 'I like to see you

fellows going for each other as hard as you can, it is such sport you know.' I failed to see the sport of the thing myself at that particular moment as I was busily and very earnestly engaged in 'going for' and doing my best to oust from the competition the 'other fellow'.

J H Taylor's reflections on winning the 1904 *News of the World* Match Play tournament.

People have always said: 'Jack, I wish I could play like you.' Well now they can.

Jack Nicklaus commenting on his declining form in 1994.

I was scared to death of that rough. I was very fortunate when I did miss a fairway. I never thought I'd be glad to see a fairway bunker.

John Schlee at the 1974 US PGA championship at Tanglewood.

This changes everything. Suddenly I'm a winner, a cut above the rest. I'm out of the also-rans.

Ian Roberts on winning the 1985 Tasmanian Open.

Though time all other griefs may cure,
All other hurts may mend,
The miseries of golf endure:
To them there is no end.

(*Nebraska Star,* 1930).

I'm not walking into the locker room expecting all of them to get down on their knees and bow for me. I'm just playing really well right now and I don't know how long it will last. I don't know if I'm for real.

Johnny Miller on the winning start to his 1975 season.

I'm a fighter, a perfectionist. I've kicked myself in the pants for 24 years to get where I am.

Deb Richard in 1987 on scoring her first tournament victory.

When you're choking and you got a lot of pressure on you, your mouth gets very dry and you start spitting cotton. I wasn't spitting cotton today.

Lee Trevino to the press during the 1984 US PGA championship, which he won.

He could fly to Australia tonight and change to the small ball and different clubs and still win. That's why I rate Gary Player one of the greatest.

Australian professional **Bruce Crampton,** 1971.

Golf is definitely a battle. It's a battle against yourself, a battle against your emotions, a battle against the golf course and a battle against all the other players.

Mark O'Meara on winning the 1991 Walt Disney Classic.

I never looked at the leader board all day. I had to play my own game. There was no point in looking, I can't alter anything out there. I did not want to put any extra pressure on myself by

thinking 'I'm winning the Open' if that happened.
Nick Faldo to David Davies (*Guardian*) on winning the 1987
Open championship.

There is nothing new to us. No situation or shot is ever new. We get more wise and less flustered. You'll never see an older man make an error of judgement.
Former British amateur champion and Walker Cup player **Joe Carr** on the value of experience.

It is today an accepted principle of golfing architecture that the tiger should be teased and trapped and tested, while the rabbit should be left in peace since he can make his own hell for himself.
Bernard Darwin.

Look at those spoiled bastards. They don't know the value of a dollar.
Veteran **Gene Sarazen** on players who refuse to search for their golf balls.

Sure, there'll be someone else along, 6 feet 4 inches, knocking it up to the hole, birdying his putts like crazy, who'll see off jack Nicklaus's records. It's the same all over in sport. No one is unbeatable for ever.
Jack Nicklaus after winning the 1978 Open championship.

I think it was Walter Hagen who said that anybody can win the Open once but it takes a great player to win twice.

Lee Trevino on winning his second US Open in 1971.

Great players learn they don't need to play their best golf to win. They only need to shoot the lowest score.

American sports writer **Rick Reilly**.

This is the sport I love, the competition I enjoy. I never feel that my world is falling down if I play badly. I know there will be another day, another week, another year.

Manuel Pinero after winning the 1982 European Open.

This going to the nineteenth is an odious business. It combines the excitement of a gaming table, a duel and a Roman amphitheatre, as Mr Malthus said of the Suicide Club.

Bernard Darwin on playing extra holes.

In those days when I woke up in the morning, I knew my first move would be to the bathroom. It was only nine feet from my bedroom but I could not get there on my feet. I had to crawl. At that point I thought that I would end my life in a wheelchair. I did not think I could ever play golf again.

Jose Maria Olazabal to *Guardian* golf writer David Davies on the physical problems that threatened his career.

He's going to need a veteran to explain why people start cheering after he misses a putt.

> Payne **Stewart** on Ryder Cup newcomer David Duval before the 1999 match.

Golf is a game you can still do in your fifties. I have never felt I can't still play.

> **Art Wall,** aged 51, winning the 1975 Greater Milwaukee Open.

If I could always putt like this, tournament golf would be a most enjoyable way to make a living.

> **Dan Sikes** in the 1968 Westchester Classic after eight single-putt greens.

He's a safe pick who won't start any controversy. He never says anything derogatory about anything.

> **Scott Hoch,** to *Golf Digest* magazine, on Ben Crenshaw's 1999 Ryder Cup captaincy. Later the American skipper wrote a controversial book in which he criticised the conduct of the European squad.

I'll be satisfied if he's just a great person. I don't give a shit about the golf.

> **Earl Woods,** quoted by Charles P Pierce in *GQ* magazine, 1997, on his son Tiger.

It doesn't matter how bad you are playing or how high you are shooting, you still have to be generous and pleasant.

Sergio Garcia at the 2001 Players championship.

Fear develops like this. Once you are ahead you start thinking 'Am I going to make these putts? Am I going to win these tournaments?' That makes it even harder to win.

Jack Nicklaus on tournament pressures.

You know deep down you are not playing well. Sometimes you think: 'When is this going to fall apart?' When it does, everybody says you choked. Yet you knew all along it could possibly happen.

US Open champion **Curtis Strange**.

Make no mistake these British golfers are getting better every year. They should never be underestimated and I predict that in the next ten years they'll win the Ryder Cup regularly both here and in Britain.

Lee Trevino at the 1971 Ryder Cup match.

Let me tell you something else. In my *destino,* there are many wins to come.

Seve Ballesteros after his first Open championship triumph in 1979.

I just don't think we should be classed alongside dogs and horses.
Greg Norman explaining to *Golf World* magazine in 1984 why he objects to betting on professionals at golf tournaments.

Heck, I'm like a duck. I wake up to a new world every day and just take what's coming if I can't alter it.
Lee Trevino on the eve of the 1971 Open championship on the pressures of winning his second major title of the year.

When God wants to play through, you'd better step aside.
Lee Trevino after being struck by lightning in the 1975 Western Open.

I am the last of the poor Woods. There will never be another poor Woods in this world. The Rockefellers did it. The Kennedys did it. Now we've done it.
Earl Woods on his son Tiger's multi-million dollar fortune.

A man like Oscar Obscurity will go up on the leader board listed as two under [par] after five holes. Denizens of the big top press facility will begin searching for information on Oscar. An older head will advise: 'Don't bother, old Oscar will be off the board in a couple of holes when he remembers where he is.' And it happens just as predicted.
American writer **Dick Taylor**.

He will be just like me at 71, still playing the game as hard as he can, still kidding himself that there is something left in the tank.

Arnold Palmer on Tiger Woods.

I created an image through my golf, through my being on a golf course. If things were going well I was alive like an electric light bulb shining in the middle of the fairway and everything was going to happen. You get an atmosphere and there's magic there. I know I created it.

Tony Jacklin to author Liz Kahn (*The Price of Success*).

It's tough at the top but tougher at the bottom.

Welsh professional **David Vaughan.**

Taking a blast in the heat of the moment is as much part of a caddie's responsibility as making sure he sees the correct line to the hole. That's why we're worth the money they pay us.

Peter Coleman, caddie to Bernhard Langer.

Don't be bloody silly.

Sir Michael Bonallack's initial response when asked to consider becoming Secretary of the Royal and Ancient Golf Club of St Andrews, a post he went on to hold for eighteen years.

I liked the course the way it used to be because it eliminated 90 per cent of the field, the players who did not have the game to handle it.

Jack Nicklaus on Royal Birkdale, 1971.

When I play good I have so much fun and so much pleasure that there's no money in the world that can buy that. I want to keep that for as long as I can.

Seve Ballesteros.

The game is just a mirror, that's all it is. Your weaknesses glare you in the face.

David Feherty talking to golf writer Lauren St John.

Maybe I should just be called the Golfer of the Week.
   Peter Thomson after producing a better score in a subsidiary event on the Old Course at St Andrews than the winner of the Alcan Golfer of the Year event did at the same time over the same course in 1967.

Look, 14 million people know I just got out of hospital and 14 million people don't think I can win the Open. I have everything to win and nothing to lose.

Lee Trevino before the 1972 US Open.

I am keeping my red-shafted three wood. That club will go six feet under with me. I will take it to my grave.
   Colin Montgomerie to sports writer Alan Fraser (*Daily Mail*).

And of course I shall appear in the PGA championship next year in my customary role as defending runner-up.
   Bruce Crampton in 1975 after finishing second to Jack Nicklaus for the fifth time in a major event.

Now that the big guy's out of the cage, everybody better run for cover.

Arnold Palmer after losing the 1962 US Open in a play-off to
Jack Nicklaus.

A job into which men drift, since no properly constituted parent would agree to his son starting his career in that way.

Bernard Darwin on golf writing.

I don't think I played better. I just missed more people.

US Vice President **Spiro Agnew** on his erratic play in the 1972
Bob Hope Desert Classic.

If there's nae wind, it's nae gowf.

St Andrews **caddie's** remark to Alistair Cooke on his first visit to
the Old Course.

It hurts to win. In my case my stomach tightens and stays like that until it's all over. There are lots of golfers around who in the same position suddenly blow up and put themselves out of the running. They won't admit it but deep down they almost wanted that blowup. It takes the pressure off them.

Ryder Cup skipper **Brian Huggett**.

I never wanted to be a millionaire. I just wanted to live like one.

Walter Hagen.

It's not your fault. It's my fault because I listen to you.
Seve Ballesteros to his caddie after taking the wrong club in the 1986 Open championship.

The fact that I didn't win an eighth Order of Merit title was probably what saved my marriage.
Colin Montgomerie, 2000.

Never worry. Never hurry. Always stop to smell the flowers along the way.
Walter Hagen.

The more I practise, the luckier I get.
Gary Player replying to suggestions that his success depended on luck.

We shall brush aside all doubts, handle all adversity and sweep to victory. If I go any further, I will break into song.
Nick Faldo to British writer Bill Blighton on Europe's 1995 Ryder Cup prospects.

It wasn't a good round. I was coming from out of the trees, out of the water, out of the traps and almost from out of bounds.
Homero Blancas en route to winning the 1972 Phoenix Open.

I've learned to be tough on the outside. But each time you win, you lose a little of your sensitivity. And that's a bad thing for a girl.
Catherine Lacoste after winning the 1967 US Women's Open championship as an amateur.

I want people to say: 'Did you ever see Nick Faldo play?'
Faldo on his place in history.

The luxuries of life are killing me.
American professional **Tom Shaw** after air conditioning in his hotel room stiffened his back muscles and cost him victory in the 1971 Andy Williams-San Diego Open.

I am playing smarter than I did twenty years ago but I get scared twice as fast. Putting jitters still get me; if I only three-putt twice in a round I feel like Houdini. I'm even money to walk four rounds without falling down dead.
Sam Snead, aged 60, in the 1972 Doral Eastern Open.

Winning at St Andrews sets even the champions apart. It lifts the truly great golfers from the rest. There are Opens. And then there are Opens at St Andrews. Therein lies the difference.
Former English amateur champion **Gerald Micklem** on the timeless challenge of the Old Course.

He was OK. He wasn't as great as maybe he thought he was.
Former US PGA champion and Ryder Cup skipper **Dave Marr** when asked to name his career epitaph.

I have never been misquoted, but I've often said I was.

Dave Marr.

The first time was difficult. The next time was hardest. The last time was easiest.

Enid Wilson on winning a hat-trick of British Women's Amateur championships.

Golf instruction books can be immensely valuable to the novice. What you do is balance it on top of your head and then swing the club as hard as you can. Once you have mastered the art of taking a full vicious swing without dislodging the book, you can play golf.

Peter Dobereiner in *Dobereiner on Golf,* 1996.

You can't trust anybody these days.

TV commentator **Peter Alliss** on witnessing American Walke Cup golfer Doug Clarke bless himself before attempting a bunker shot – and leaving the ball in the sand.

If profanity had an influence on the flight of the ball, the game would be played far better than it is.

Horace Hutchinson, 1886.

My, my, it looks like a couple of Shetland ponies have been mating in there.

Peter Alliss on television after American Richard Zokol took several attempts to escape from the Road Bunker at St Andrews during the 1986 Alfred Dunhill Cup.

During a tournament she never knits or goes to the movies. She feels the strain on her eyes while knitting or watching movies might leave her eyes less keen for golf the next day.

> ***Golf World*** magazine on Babe Zaharias, 1947.

Show up. Keep up. Shut up.

> Veteran caddie **Dave Musgrove's** rules of his trade.

Any pair of fools can three-putt but it needs real class to take four.

> **Bernard Darwin** on the unfortunate player in the Winchester-Harrow match who hit the ball in the wrong direction from twelve feet during his putting routine in the Halford Hewitt event.

He knows a lot about the rules but not much about being married.

> Architect **Pete Dye** after learning that rules expert John Laupheimer had pointed out to then wife Mary that she had unwittingly infringed the rules in the 1980 Women's International at Hilton Head.

If there is one tiny part of your game that is not quite right, the great course will find it out, no matter how hard you try to hide it.

> Five times Open champion **Peter Thomson** commenting on the Old Course at St Andrews.

No, I can't say it was fun. There was blood on every shot. But I do like the competition. I enjoy getting out there and mixing it up with the boys.

Sam Snead, aged 60, after taking 69 in the 1972 US Masters.

I feel like I'm just a little girl from Sweden that came over here to follow my dreams and hope to win a few golf tournaments. When I look at my biography in the LPGA book I get over-whelmed

Leading woman professional **Annika Sorenstam** 2005.

How I adore links golf where treacherous winds, hillocked fairways, blind holes and unreadable undulating greens give even the greatest professionals sleepless nights and daytime nightmares.

Ian Wooldridge *Daily Mail*, 2003 Open Championship at Royal St George's.

2

'A Legend in his Spare Time': The Making of a Hero

It is not enough simply to be a winner in tournament golf, because the achievement itself has never guaranteed that a player will be remembered for long. Rather it is the heroic image of the campaigner that holds sway, earning the respect and admiration of fans and rivals even in moments of failure.

In fact, being a winner is only part of the qualification. There have been many champions who slipped back into obscurity as quickly as they burst out of it and have long been forgotten. But the true stars live on. They set their own style both on and off the fairways. Their exploits add to the game's history and they leave the sport better than they found it.

In many ways they provide a metaphor for life. Bobby Jones demonstrated as much when he explained his attitude to his incurable illness as 'playing it as it lies' or the solemn-faced Ben Hogan proved it when bringing 'this course, this monster, to its knees' at Oakland Hills seemed to matter more than actually winning the 1951 US Open. That is the other thing about heroes. They live to their own high standards.

Me? An immortal? Hey, I like that. Like they used to say about Jack Nicklaus. A legend in his spare time.

> **Tom Watson** on being told he had joined the immortals J H Taylor, James Braid and Peter Thomson by winning a fifth Open championship (*Golf Journal,* 1983).

Hang your egos outside, let's put this effort into the team.

> Ryder Cup captain **Tony Jacklin's** order to his superstar players before the 1985 match which Europe went on to win (*Daily Mail,* 1993).

All of them should say a silent prayer of thanks to him whenever they stretch a cheque between their fingers. It was Walter who made professional golf what it is.

> **Gene Sarazen's** tribute to the flamboyant Walter Hagen, the game's first superstar.

The world never really saw what he was capable of. I reckon if he'd won the Masters in 1981 he might have won a bunch of majors.

> **Frank Nobilo** on the career of Greg Norman (*Golf World* magazine, 2001).

> Beneath the sod poor Tommy's laid,
> Now bunkered fast for good and all;
> A better golfer never played
> A further or a surer ball.

> The first verse of an **elegy** to Young Tom Morris (died 1875) published originally in *Chamber's Journal* and late in *Golfing* magazine, 1907.

Palmer usually walks to the first tee quite unlike any other pro on the circuit. He doesn't so much walk on to it as climb into it, almost as though it were a prize ring; and then he looks round at the gallery as though he is trying to count the house.

Charles Price on Arnold Palmer (*The World of Golf,* 1962).

I could never call him Arnie. I called him Mr Palmer. He has an aura. Everybody who calls out his name, he gives them something – a look or a smile. He's a special man.

David Duval, later to become 2001 Open champion, on Arnold Palmer (*Golf World* magazine, 1995).

Hey, you son of a bitch. You really can play this game.

Jack Nicklaus to Maurice Bembridge after beating him on the final green in the 1973 Ryder Cup match (Ryder Cup magazine, 1975).

He reappeared between the mounds beside Royal Birkdale's last green at the climax of the 1976 Open championship and played a most outrageously brave chip shot we all took to be an ill-conceived fluke. What we did not know then was that we had witnessed the embryonic flourish of a talent that was to dominate the game worldwide.

A **report** from the *Daily Mail* on how Seve Ballesteros first made an impact when he was runner-up to Johnny Miller in the championship he went on to win three years later.

Old Tom is perhaps the most remote point to which we can carry back our genealogical inquiries into the golfing style, so that we may virtually accept him as the common golfing ancestor who has stamped the features of his style most distinctly on his descendants. Thence players have gone out, inspiration has gone out to all the golfing world in these days of the modern 'boom' in golf, and the ultimate source of the inspiration, so far as we can trace it, is revealed to us in the person of Old Tom.

Horace Hutchinson's tribute to Old Tom Morris, 1899.

Woods has faced and played under threats to his life since he was a teenager. The cordons of security that have surrounded him on the PGA Tour have been off-putting to some but they will never be questioned again. Despite the obstacles, Woods has hewn to his mission to take golf to every corner of the world, becoming the game's Pied Piper in a way that early incarnations such as Gene Sarazen and Palmer never dreamed.

American columnist **Jaime Diaz** on the hidden dangers facing Tiger Woods (*Golf World* magazine, 2001).

There'll be beer and champagne and I'll have a bloody headache in the morning – and I don't care. Just so long as I'm alive.

Ian Woosnam explaining how he intended to celebrate his victory in the 2001 Cisco World Match Play championship (David Davies in the *Guardian*).

The galleries were applauding Nicklaus for breathing which slowed things up a bit. Still, the man is amazing.

Colin Montgomerie on playing behind Jack Nicklaus, then 59, in the 1998 US Masters.

There was punishment all the way. He was the boxer who had been knocked down but refused to go out. The champion in the making got his ball everywhere except on the fairway playing those last four holes. It was not good golf. But it was one hell of a fight.

Daily Mail columnist **J L Manning** on Tony Jacklin's third-round struggles en route to winning the 1969 Open.

You might as well praise me for not breaking into banks. There is only one way to play this game.

Bobby Jones on being praised for his honesty in calling a penalty stroke on himself for an infringement nobody else saw during the 1925 US Open.

You little son of a bitch, you're something else. That was nice going. I'm really proud of you and pleased for you.

Jack Nicklaus congratulating Tom Watson after he chipped in on the seventeenth hole at Pebble Beach to beat Nicklaus for the 1982 US Open.

I'm glad I brought this course, this monster, to its knees.

Ben Hogan on winning the 1951 US Open over the awesome Oakland Hills course.

I don't know what to say. I just want to give you a hug.

Nick Faldo's words to Greg Norman on Augusta's last green after making up a six-stroke deficit to beat him in the 1996 US Masters.

I'm doing the playin' and the caddie's chokin'.
  Lee Trevino's remark to the crowd before hitting his approach
    to force a play-off with Jack Nicklaus for the 1972 US Open.
                                           Trevino won the title.

Expressionlessly erect, alone in the throng beneath the afternoon
sun, the picture of Graham recalled a line from Carl Sandburg.
Having only the savvy God gave him, Lacking a gat, lacking
brass knucks.
  American writer **Edwin Pope** on David Graham striding to
  victory in the 1981 US Open (the official US Open magazine,
                                                          1984).

The moment the match ended, Thomson walked over and shook
Palmer's hand. It was obvious that what had begun as almost a
bloodletting had ended in something very near to a mutual
admiration society. 'Arnold isn't flogging at the ball the way he
used to,' Thomson said. 'I was beaten by a better man.'
  Gwyl Brown reporting the final of the 1967 World Match Play
      championship in which Arnold Palmer defeated Peter
                       Thomson (*Sports Illustrated* magazine).

If there is something to prove by all this, it is that your ordinary,
everyday woman with a husband and kid can excel.
  American professional **Judy Rankin** on winning six titles in
  1976 and becoming the first woman player to earn more than
        $100,000 in a season (*Golf Digest Annual, 1977*).

Fairways and greens, Cuz.

The note of advice Dave Marr found in his locker from fellow professional and cousin **Jackie Burke** before the final round of the 1965 US PGA championship which he went on to win (Ryder Cup magazine, 1975).

I'm so disappointed not to win. One day I shall win and I'll turn back my money to good causes.

Gary Player's pledge after narrowly missing the 1962 US Open title. True to his word, he gave away all his prize money to charity when he became champion in 1965.

It's been forty years. When you walk up the eighteenth and get an ovation like that, I guess that says it all. I think you all know pretty much how I feel. It's been forty years of work, fun and enjoyment. I haven't won all that much. I won a few tournaments. I won some majors. I suppose the most important thing is the game has been so good to me. I think that's all I have to say.

Arnold Palmer's emotional farewell to the US Open in 1994.

I will never forget the scenes at Turnberry when Nicklaus created pandemonium by sinking his big putt at the last and then called on the crowd to be quiet while Watson tried to hole his much shorter putt. There was a man calling on the crowd to be quiet and give the other fellow a chance to beat him.

Michael Williams of the *Daily Telegraph* on the 1977 duel between Jack Nicklaus and Tom Watson for the Open title (*The Golfer's Companion*, 1988).

His driving is far and sure; his iron or cleek approaches are beautifully straight and well pitched; and his putting on decent greens is most deadly. There may be some who can beat him on one of these points, but I know of no one who can surpass him on all three. Nothing seems to put him out; the most direful bunker – whether there by his own mistake or bad luck or by a foozle of his partner in a foursome – appears to have no terrors for him. Two points I cannot too strongly impress – he is perfectly respectful in manner and steady in conduct.

Letter from **Sir Hedworth Williamson** to the *Golfing Annual,* 1888, praising the virtues of Willie Park Junior who won the Open championship the previous year.

Willie Park Junior was perhaps the deadliest putter the game has ever known. He reckoned himself stone dead from two yards. He would practise eight hours a day at putting. He did much to elevate the status of the professional golfer.

A **tribute** in the *Golfer's Handbook,* 1975.

The only golfer I can compare him with is Arnold Palmer, whose similar blitzkrieg attitude to an immobile golf ball in the rough is to take about half a ton of flora and fauna with it in restoring it to where it should be. Ballesteros, however, does not share Palmer's social confidence, for he does not come from a nation in which accomplishment is the ultimate credential.

Ian Wooldridge on Seve Ballesteros's struggle for social acceptance in Spain (*Golf Illustrated magazine*).

I could take out of my life everything except my experiences at St Andrews and I'd still have a rich full life.

Bobby Jones on being made a Freeman of St Andrews in 1958.

He will be pointed out by the old to the young, as in earlier decades Thorpe and Ruth and Hagen and Louis and Grange and Cobb and Wills were to them, and they will always remember that they saw Jack Nicklaus play, in person.

Part of **Herbert Warren Wind's** tribute to Jack Nicklaus (the official US Open magazine 1978).

𝕗

Sometimes when a player makes it look as easy as she does, it's hard to appreciate how great she is.

American professional **Meg Mallon** on Australian Karrie Webb who won the 2000 US Women's Open (*Golf Journal,* 2000).

𝕗

The wind stood strong from the west; the flags strained at their masts and a great multitude was gathered about the first hole at Carnoustie. There was tension and expectancy abroad and a sense of history such as I have never known at the outset of any championship. On the tee, awaiting his call from the starter, stood the slight, grey figure of Hogan.

Pat Ward-Thomas on Ben Hogan's 1953 triumph (*Masters of Golf*).

𝕗

This stripling, bred to golf on the cow pastures of Massachusetts – for that is where he learned the game – has fairly and squarely beaten on his merits the greatest golfer who has ever lived, five times champion of Britain and once of America, and has at the same time beaten the longest driver and most powerful player who has ever hit a ball, who won the British Open last year. There was not the slightest fluke about it.

Daily Mail **report** on Francis Ouimet's 1913 play-off win over Harry Vardon and Ted Ray to become the first native-born American to win the US Open championship.

James Braid is the Kitchener of the golf course. He has much of the icy calm and resolution of the famous soldier. Had he not been possessed of quiet patience and power to plan he would not have retained the title of golf champion. Circumstances were against him. He had to start late on three days at Muirfield when the greens were worn by hundreds of feet and he had thus a disadvantage which was estimated at a stroke or two to the round – a really big handicap among expert players.

Edinburgh Evening News **report** on James Braid's 1906 Open championship win.

He is the most generous opponent that ever trod the links and in recent championships has been accused of being more generous than he ought to have been. And then he is one of the most modest men alive. He has never written any articles about his achievements, has never been interviewed and he is not available as an acquaintance to the general public who take a keen interest in him. When he has finished his game, he just shuts himself up to all but his friends.

Golf writer **Henry Leach** on John Ball after he won his sixth Amateur championship in 1907.

And ye say that man canna play gowff!

The legendary St Andrews professional **Andrew Kirkaldy's** withering retort to critics of John Ball after the Englishman scored that 1 907 victory.

He was a celebrity in the golfing world twenty years ago; today he has kept it up. And intertwined with these mighty achievements is his faithful work for two years in the South African War where his celebrated confrere Freddie Tait fell. Young golfers have much yet to learn from the successful but modest veteran.

Golfing magazine **tribute** to John Ball, who won his eighth – and last Amateur championship – at the age of 51 in 1912.

You moved your head. You moved your body. But how the hell did you move the hole to get in the way of the ball?

Walker Cup skipper **Joe Carr**'s jubilant question to Clive Clark after the Yorkshireman holed a putt of 35 feet across the last green to tie the 1965 match.

From humiliation to jubilation. From literal chump to deserving champ. David Duval made a journey across the sporting spectrum in exactly one year when yesterday he won the Open championship at Royal Lytham.

David Davies in the *Guardian,* 2001.

I am part of the pack. I can finally run with the big dogs again.

Jim Thorpe in 2000 on winning his first tournament after a fourteen-year drought. He won again the next week too.

Why did Melville allow saintly Billy Budd to be hanged from a yardarm? Why did Mozart have Don Giovanni refuse to relent over his decadence? These were the sorts of problems that Bobby Jones thought worth trying to solve, perhaps because they were insoluble.

Charles Price (*Bobby Jones and the Masters*).

When Royal St George's was waterlogged and too little, he thought, was being done about it, he put a suggestion in the book 'that the water in the bunker on the thirteenth be changed'.

Henry Longhurst on Lord Brabazon of Tara (*Only on Sundays,* 1964).

At the apex of his career, Hogan was about as convivial as a Trappist monk. He conquered golf with will power, forcing his slight physique to its utmost. Snead was the carefree hillbilly, everybody's pal, a kind of Will Rogers of the fairways with his homey wit and hayseed yarns. The only thing the two men had in common was a total commitment to golf.

American writer **Alfred Wright** on Ben Hogan and Sam Snead (*The Golfer's Bedside Book,* 1965).

There is now conclusive proof that for periods of the 1950s, the fate of the Western world was determined from a golf club in the United States. It was there above the professional shop at Augusta National that the American president, Dwight Eisenhower, the most powerful man in the world, set up his auxiliary cabinet room so that world affairs would not distract him from his abiding passion of golf.

Michael McDonnell in *The Complete Book of Golf,* 1984.

It's great to see. He's like every fifteen and sixteen year old kid. He just rears back and hits it as far as he can and if he can find it, he's okay.

Craig Stadler on watching John Daly burst through to win the 1991 US PGA championship.

When Seve gets his Porsche going not even San Pedro in heaven could stop him.

Jose Maria Olazabal giving playing partner Seve Ballesteros much of the credit for their 6 and 5 win in the 1989 Ryder Cup match.

He stands as probably the last graduate from the school of hard knocks and will certainly go down as one of its sharpest students.

> Author **Chris Plumridge** on Lee Trevino
> (*Golf Characters,* 1989).

Everybody should feel like this once in their life. If I felt any better it probably would be illegal.

> **Tony Johnstone** on winning the 1992 PGA
> championship.

Billy Joe Patton avers that Campbell is the only player who ever went to the first tee in the Masters and asked where the ball washer was.

> **Joe Dey** on American amateur golfer and former captain of the
> Royal and Ancient Golf Club, Bill Campbell (the official US
> Open magazine, 1988).

He was then, as he is now, a golfer with a lovely style, so easy and simple as the art that conceals art. To me, Bobby Sweeny has always represented the true weekend golfer. He seems to arrive at a tournament, after working assiduously at his business until the last moment, to get out of his car, to take a couple of practice swings and then to play first-class golf without apparent effort.

> **Eric Prain** on 1937 Amateur champion Robert Sweeny, who
> went on to reach the final of the 1954 US Amateu
> championship and was beaten by Arnold Palme (*The Oxford
> and Cambridge Golfing Society 1898–1948*).

I came here as a spectator six years ago. Today I played with Bernhard Langer. He's won the Masters! I was playing with guys I had seen on television and looked up to for years. I don't know what I'll do with the money. My family has never had money and I've never been around people with money.

Jarrod Moseley on winning the 1999 Heineken Classic.

Here he comes . . . the Queen Mother of golf. All he needs is a couple of corgis.

TV commentator **Peter Alliss** on 65-year-old veteran Gary Player as he walked on to Royal Lytham's last green during the 2001 Open championship.

Take my word for it. I'm no poof.

Former Ryder Cup golfer **Michael King** talking about his nickname 'Queenie'to Richard Dodd in *The Golfers,* 1982.

For innumerable years he was the head of his profession. It is due to him, more than any other man, that the profession has climbed so far above its old unsatisfactory condition. He is a natural speaker, a natural fighter, a natural leader who would have made his mark in any walk of life.

Bernard Darwin on five times Open champion J H Taylor, one of the founders of the Professional Golfers Association.

In Lusaka, the scene as Barnes rolled in the winning putt was charged with emotion. On to the green rushed the Head of State, Kenneth Kaunda, to proclaim: 'Well done, son!' and fling his arms around Barnes who responded: 'Thanks, Dad!'

Gordon Richardson's account of Brian Barnes winning the Zambian Open (*The Golfers,* 1982).

It looks like we are the average workers and he is the gifted one. He doesn't practise much. He doesn't need much practice. And he keeps hitting the ball straight down the fairway and straight on to the green and scoring well. What can you say?

Jose Maria Olazabal on Colin Montgomerie after the Scot won the 1999 Benson and Hedges International.

We've had a great game, Arnold. Let's call it a half.

Peter Alliss conceding a short putt to Arnold Palmer on the last green in the 1961 Ryder Cup match at Royal Lytham and St Annes.

It is important to put Jacklin, the sportsman, into historical perspective. He was of course a product of his times; one of the 'whiz kid' aristocracy of the 1960s who were extremely impatient for success and whose guiding doctrine was one of 'want it now' self-confidence.

It was a kind of mass break-out from self-doubt and inferiority that had trapped previous generations and there were many examples of this liberation – from the global success of the Beatles to soccer success in the World Cup and even the Wimbledon triumph of Ann Jones – all of them quite unimaginable peaks to a nation that had raised second-best to an art form.

Comment in the 1988 British Open Golf official annual.

Hold your head up Ken. You're a champion now.

Referee **Joe Dey Junior** to Ken Venturi as he staggered up the last fairway suffering from heat exhaustion on his way to winning the 1962 US Open championship.

I can only tell you there is no help. I can only get worse but you are not to keep thinking of it. You know that in golf we play the ball as it lies. Now we will not speak of this again, ever.

Bobby Jones's reply to golf writer Al Laney after he learned that the great golfer had been confined to a wheelchair with a crippling disease in the late 1940s.

Someone upstairs was pushing that baby in the hole the whole way. It was just like it was magical. Honest to goodness. I can't explain it and it certainly doesn't make any sense. The putter just moved and the ball just went on line.

Veteran **Dana Quigley** after holing a putt from 35 feet to win the 1998 Emerald Coast Classic.

He thrived on the head-to-head competition of match play. His attitude could be summed up like this: 'If my opponent throws his best golf at me, and if I am playing well, why, there are few things more enjoyable in life.' He could break an opponent's heart with his indecent recoveries and putting, but the quintessential thing about Patton was that if the day went against him, he remained spirited and cordial.

Herbert Warren Wind on American amateur Billy Joe Patton (Walker Cup programme, 1985).

I'm still totally convinced we have the twelve best players, today proved that. But put their guys together and they have magic at their fingertips.

US team member **Tom Lehman** paying tribute to the victorious European squad after the 1997 match at Valderrama.

I don't believe this is an appropriate time to play competitive golf. I feel strongly this is a time to pause, reflect and remember the victims of Tuesday's horrific attack.

Tiger Woods signalling his reluctance to play after the 2001 New York terrorist outrage. The Ryder Cup match was postponed for a year.

It is something to be the best in anything, of all the world, and Allan stood confessed the model player.

Dundee Advertiser on St Andrews legend Allan Robertson, 1859.

Maybe Cod gives some people something He doesn't give to the rest of us.

Miller Barber on Tom Watson.

The fine reputation he built up with Longhurst in the anchor position owed much, in his partner's estimation, to the effect his appearance had on opponents who had not seen him play before. He generally turned out in a deerstalker hat and an old teddy-bear coat secured around the waist by string which reduced him to something like a quarter swing.

He carried in a torn canvas bag, a motley collection of clubs, some steel-shafted, some hickory, a few with grips like a cricket bat. With them he would bring off shots that would have rejoiced the hearts of the ancients.

Author **Peter Ryde** on John Morrison who won Blues at Cambridge for soccer, golf and cricket, was recommended for the VC during the Second World War and occasionally played full-back for Sunderland (*The Halford Hewitt*).

It was a bit like watching Larry Adler playing the harmonica at the bottom of a Jubilee Line escalator.

Martin Johnson in the *Daily Telegraph* after witnessing the ageing Arnold Palmer take 84 in the 2001 Seniors British Open championship.

I feel incredibly relieved. The hounds would have been at me if I had lost.

Nick Faldo on winning the 1992 Irish Open in a play-off after squandering a four-stroke lead.

The memories came flooding back of all the hard times I have been through. There were times in the darkest days between April and September last year when I feared I might never play again. I even thought I would end my days in a wheelchair.

Jose Maria Oiazabal speaking after his comeback victory in the 1997 Turespana Masters following a crippling condition which threatened to force him out of golf. Two years later he won the US Masters for a second time.

I am the best in the village.

Costantino Rocca after seeing banners from local fans during the 1996 Italian Open proclaiming that he was the best golfer.

Maybe somebody channelled my body. Maybe Tiger was channelled in. I'll blame it on something extra-terrestrial.

Gary McCord on winning the 1999 Senior Classic at the fifth play-off hole.

I had to lean sideways to see the top of the flag.

Gary Player on his historic three-wood approach to the fourteenth green at Carnoustie on his way to winning the 1968 Open championship.

Everyone dreams of being a millionaire. If the taxman is not too harsh on me, I might have done it.

Ian Woosnam after winning the 1987 Million Dollar Challenge.

(Bob) Murphy is that combination that New York area sports fans can't resist – a cigar-smoking red-headed Irishman born in Brooklyn.

(Mark McCormack, *The World of Professional Golf,* 1969 edition).

Tiger Woods has become as pervasive as the weather in the lives of all other tournament professionals. His form governs the climate of their existence.

Sunday Times columnist **Hugh McIlvanney** during the 2001 Open championship.

When he competed for the Open title at Deal and St Andrews his temperament was more that of a holiday-maker than of a prospective champion.

Arthur Leonard Lee on Walter Hagen (*Guardian,* 1922).

Tell me, have you ever actually burst a ball?

Maurice Bembridge's question to big-hitting playing partner Jack Nicklaus in the 1968 Open championship.

Not recently.

Nicklaus's reply.

Cotton did more than just put money in the pockets of his fellow professionals by breaking down the social barriers that had kept them in their place. He demanded a revolutionary view of the sportsman's skill and insisted that such excellence was more than just a mere accident of birth. Hitherto, such talent held no more importance than the juggler's knack and as such could never be regarded as a proper vocation for grown men. Cotton was to change all that by observing an inflexible doctrine that supreme skill – be it from a surgeon, lawyer, engineer or sportsman – deserved full reward. It was in short the Gospel of Professionalism.

Golf Illustrated, 1986.

I am not going to quit just because I lost a golf tournament. I've lost a lot of golf tournaments and I've had disappointments before. I've had a lot of disappointments in my life and I hope to have a lot more. I hope to get close enough to be disappointed again.

Arnold Palmer on finishing third in the 1975 Hawaiian Open.

In 1982 I had my left hand on this trophy. In 1988 I had my right hand on the trophy. Now finally I have it in both hands.

Nick Price describing his two previous near-misses in the Open championship before winning in 1994.

I won a couple of Sheffield and District Alliance events last winter which was pretty good.

Mark Roe's response to the press when asked what other titles he had won besides the 1992 Lancome Trophy.

He has had his heart's desire, the results without the fuss. He regards fame much as the successful schoolboy regards the pompous prize-giver on the dais. He has golfed his way into an age which barely understands the qualities that made him great. His artistry, his avoidance of false intimacy, his contempt for the lurid, his deep but delicate humour, were unlikely to be appreciated in a world of see-me-drivers, provocative clothing, determined photographers and temporary heroes.

> **R C Robertson-Glasgow** on Amateur champion Roger Wethered (*The Oxford and Cambridge Golfing Society 1898–1948*).

I never stopped believing I could get in the winner's circle. I just kept trying to give myself pep talks and saying: 'Behind every adversity there's opportunity.'

> **Mike Reid** on winning the 1988 World Series of Golf.

What came as a shock and delight was the way he kicked down the doors, elbowed the mighty Jack Nicklaus, Hale Irwin and Tom Watson aside and plonked himself down in the seat of honour.

> **Peter Dobereiner** in the *Guardian* on Seve Ballesteros winning the 1979 Open championship.

It's my favourite colour. I thought I'd let you fellows see me in it before Sunday.

> **Lee Elder,** who became the first black golfer to play in the US Masters and turned up in an all-green outfit – the traditional colour of the exclusive Augusta National Club which had been criticised previously for keeping him and other black players out of the event.

He did what only a very great player can do; he raised the general conception of what was possible in his game and forced his nearest rivals to attain a higher standard by attempting that which they would otherwise have deemed impossible.

Bernard Darwin on Harry Vardon, 1937.

I guess I've shrunk a little in this weather. There are a lot of guys six feet under who would love to be playing today.

Gary Player after taking 79 in a storm during the 1987 Open championship.

Sure, everyone says I have great potential and they say I could be one of the future superstars, but that kind of stuff gets old after a while. You have to do it with your clubs. I don't want to be just a good player; I want to be a great player – maybe the greatest.

Tom Watson in 1975, a month before winning the Open championship, the first of an eventual tally of eight major titles.

When you're telling the story later on – and I know I'm going to be telling it a lot of times – it would be awful to say I shot 59 and then blew the tournament.

Al Geiberger on the pressures of winning the 1977 Memphis Classic after breaking 60 in an earlier round.

The win was worth the equivalent of giving fifteen hundred lessons so I suppose it has been a pretty good tournament.

Australian club professional **Geoff Parslow** referring to his prize money after winning the 1977 Victorian Open.

In the tradition of the team, he took whatever partner came along; sometimes it was Burdon Sanderson who had a passion for big-game hunting and who, it was rumoured, dashed off to deepest Africa as soon as the Hewitt was over, abandoning his clubs in the left-luggage office at Victoria Station until the next year.

Peter Ryde on 1938 Walker Cup captain John Beck (*The Hal
ford Hewitt*).

I'll be able to pay off my overdraft now and maybe buy a secondhand Ferrari.

Chris Moody after winning the 1988 European Masters.

For three holes I was really hurting. And when I have pain I get dizzy. I tried not to pass out because I don't think they'd have waited for me.

Ken Green on why he did not tell his playing partners about his physical problems as he won the 1988 Greater Milwaukee Open.

He had the character that every Amateur champion must possess which enabled him to say in the face of the impossible: 'I can cope'.

David Davies on Peter McEvoy.

What train?

Joyce Wethered when asked if a passing train disturbed her as she holed a winning putt in the 1920 English Ladies championship at Sheringham.

I knew I may never get another chance and I told myself that at least I must try 100 per cent otherwise I would not be able to forgive myself. I've had chances in the past and I didn't want to think when the time came to hang up my hat that I'd come close and not succeeded.

Nick Faldo on winning the 1987 Open championship.

He was just a kid and he turned up for the interview – I'll never forget it – in gold lame pants, gold cashmere sweater over a white polo neck and gold shoes. I thought, well, that's great – this kid really believes in himself.

Commentator **Ben Wright** on his first interview with a then unknown Tony Jacklin (Liz Kahn, *The Price of Success*).

I do not think that any useful service of comparison will be served by my giving a detailed account of the final game that I contested with Toogood the following day, as I am fully conscious from past experiences that my opponent, in the first eighteen holes, played 'streets' below his usual form which allowed me to obtain a lead of seven holes. This lead I found more than useful.

J H Taylor on winning the 1904 *News of the World* Match Play event.

What the hell do I say about myself? I fantastic player? I win fantastic play-off?

Angel Gallardo, who won the 1977 Spanish Open while also working as a golf writer for a Barcelona newspaper.

I was going to stay in there until it came out the way I wanted it to. I'm not saying God couldn't have got it out but He'd have had to throw it out.

Arnold Palmer after taking five attempts to play out of a bunker in the 1987 Open championship.

The sad, perhaps inevitable, paradox of Arnold Palmer is that future generations will take one look at the record books and wonder what all the fuss was about. So the compelling urge, here and now, is to warn future generations to distrust the fine print of the record book. It wasn't like that at all. Arnold Palmer was much more important than a handful of titles. His achievements can only be measured by what he gave and not what he acquired.

Golf Illustrated, 1985.

The world has not seen anything like what he's going to do for the sport. It's almost art.

Nike executive on Tiger Woods.

I didn't hit a golf ball for forty days but I was always optimistic. Still, when you lie in a hospital and wonder if you are going to play golf again for a year, it is bound to have a bearing on things.

Gary Player, winning the 1973 Southern Open after recovering from abdominal surgery.

Arnold's place in history will be as the man who took golf from a game for the few to a sport for the masses. He was the catalyst that made it happen.

Jack Nicklaus.

When I started, they said only rich people played the game. And I like to think I changed that so that now everyone can play golf.

Arnold Palmer, from his autobiography.

It has long been said in America that it was Arnold Palmer who put golf on the map, and it could be said that the late Sir Henry Cotton did the same in the United Kingdom and that Seve Ballesteros did the same for the continent of Europe. But what Tiger has done is to take it into the ghettos of America and into the kampongs and sprawling cities of Asia.
David and Patricia Davies (*Beyond the Fairways*).

Records only get broken. But a win is a win and nobody can take that away from you.
David Llewellyn after winning the 1988 Biarritz Open and scoring 60 to tie the European Tour record.

I don't think you would have missed that putt but in these circumstances, I would never give you the opportunity.
Jack Nicklaus after conceding Tony Jacklin's putt of two feet on the last green at Royal Birkdale to tie the entire 1969 Ryder Cup match.

Imagine him as he scrutinises a long difficult stroke, with arms quietly folded, an inscrutable quarter smile on his lips, for all the world like a gambler watching the wheel spin. And then the cigarette is tossed away, the club taken with abrupt decision, the glorious swing flashes and a long iron pierces the wind like an arrow.
Guardian golf writer **Pat Ward-Thomas** on Ben Hogan's 1953 Open win.

So now if he could avoid the masses of bunkers on the eighteenth he must surely be home. I saw the shot from just behind him and shall remember it to the end of my days. His swing never left him and this might have been on the practice ground. It might also have been fired from a rifle instead of a golf club – miles down the dead centre veering neither to right nor left.

Henry Longhurst on Tony Jacklin's final tee shot in the 1969 Open championship.

In 1977 I was tied for the lead in three major championships after 71 holes. And I lost all of them. What worries me is that I may be at my peak. And that means it can only get worse from now on.

Jack Nicklaus expressing his fears at the beginning of the 1978 season, a few months before he became Open champion at St Andrews for the second time.

Jack Nicklaus awoke on the morning of the final day of the Open championship at St Andrews, rose immediately from his hotel bed, quickly crossed the room, drew back the curtains and threw open the window. He stood for a moment, his eyes keen and his mind clear. He watched the tops of the trees arching in the wind. It was, he noticed, blowing from the west. For the three preceding days it had been from the east. 'Oh boy,' he said aloud, 'I like that.' He went immediately to the telephone and told the reception desk that he and his family would not be leaving that day after all. 'We'll be here another night,' he said.

Michael Williams on the second Open triumph of Jack Nicklaus at St Andrews in 1978 after three years without a major win (*World of Golf* 1979).

Instead of flinging his putter about and looking very angry, as some of our players have done, he has taken the hard knocks smilingly and earned great praise from older men who won championships because they, too, had the right temperament for a very trying game.

Report in the *Guardian* on Gene Sarazen's 1932 Open championship win.

No one ever mentions me or seems to know I'm around. I tied for second in the Masters but never saw my name in the papers. American professional

Bobby Mitchell after winning the 1972 Tournament of Champions.

I'm sorry Lee lost, he's such a great guy but I wouldn't let my wife beat me if I could help it.

Lee Trevino after beating Lee Elder in a play-off for the Greater Hartford Open, 1972.

He's going to change his clothes for the presentation. He knows it's all over.

South African **official** referring to Gary Player, who left the scorer's tent without waiting to see if John O'Leary could force a play-off in the 1972 Dunlop Masters.

They have one Tiger but we have twelve lions. Always remember, from out of the shadows heroes emerge.

European Ryder Cup team skipper **Sam Torrance** to his squad before the 2002 match against the United States which they won.

In all conscience I wouldn't have felt comfortable doing it.

Darren Clarke on refusing to take advantage of a lie in the rough that mysteriously had been improved overnight when rain stopped play in the 2006 Irish Open. He finished third.

3

'Where Can You Go to Have a Good Cry?' Losing

Defeat is the one humiliating experience that is shared by the greatest player and the humblest hacker. There is no escape. Gary Player used to console himself in vanquished moments by saying that even the best player in the world loses more times than he wins. But that doesn't make it any easier.

Then, of course, there are those truly savage defeats whose memory often cause the victim a succession of sleepless nights for years afterwards. Tony Lema was tormented by his failure in the 1965 World Match Play championship from a seemingly unbeatable position. Chip Beck called it 'the crucible of humiliation' when he endured a comprehensive defeat years later in the same event.

How people respond to defeat reveals much about their own character. Bobby Jones in his early years threw clubs until he acquired both competitive maturity and serenity. Walter Hagen could shrug off the most embarrassing flop and a few days after one such nightmare went on to win the Open championship with a superlative display.

The blinding truth about losing is that for all the hard luck, bad bounces, poor lies and other mitigating factors that may have come into play, the other guy played better on the day. It is that gruesome realisation that makes the journey home so hard to bear.

To tell you the truth, I thought they were a bunch of cry-babies and 1 told them that. I was on the course every day with water, fruit, candy bars and everything. That's all I can do for them. I can't play for them. The way some of them were playing I could have probably given them four a side. They got the socks beat off them.

US skipper **Lee Trevino** on his defeated 1985 Ryder Cup team.

Although we have lost we are going back to practise in the streets and on the beaches.

Lord Brabazon of Tara, President of the PGA, addressing teams and officials after the Americans won the 1955 Ryder Cup match in California.

It was like chasing a Ferrari in Chevrolets.

Tom Kite describing the futile attempt of the field to catch Seve Ballesteros during his runaway victory in the 1983 US Masters.

Arret! You mother! *Arret!*

American professional **Fred Marti's** anguished plea to his golf ball, which he hit over the green during the 1984 Canadian Open in French-speaking Montreal.

I kinda fell out of the sky. I felt like my parachute had a hole in it.

American golfer **Gil Morgan** on losing a seven-stroke lead in the 1992 US Open at Pebble Beach (the official US Open magazine, 1996).

That's the first sign you get – when it doesn't hurt any more. When missing the cut is not such a great disaster; it means you get home earlier and have the weekend off. Those are the signs that it has gone.

Ian Mosey on quitting tournament golf.

You do get the feeling sometimes that the rest of us are all out here playing for second place.

Fred Couples after Tiger Woods scored his sixth win in 1999.

I've got manure for brains. I feel like a rank amateur.

Craig Parry after last-minute errors cost him the 1999 Australian PGA championship.

I noticed my name going up on the leader board. I got so excited I started making bogeys. By the time the scoreboard guys reached the 'y' in my name they were already taking down the 'D'.

Ed Dougherty at the 1976 Westchester Classic.

As I looked at that second putt I was thinking about what I was going to do – throw the ball or club in the air and bow to the gallery. And try to be a humbler winner.

Doug Sanders recalling the moments before he missed the putt that would have made him 1970 Open champion at St Andrews. (Mark McCormack, *The World of Professional Golf*, 1991 edition).

You don't know how soul-destroying it is to walk on to a green and know you can't hole a putt from any distance.

Rodger Davis describing his putting woes before finishing second in the 1996 Australian PGA championship.

It never dawned on me that we would lose. We all played OK but I don't think anybody did their best out there for the team.

Mark Calcavecchia after the United States suffered a surprise defeat by the International team in the 1998 President's Cup.

It

People sympathised with me. Now I wasn't only the guy who always came from behind to win. I can also have my troubles. The tournament somehow allowed people to feel that much closer to me.

Arnold Palmer talking to Canadian writer Lome Rubenstein about his dramatic collapse in the 1966 US Open when he squandered a five-stroke lead over the last five holes and lost the title in a play-off.

It

Get away and let the big dog eat. In my dreams you always win, Jack.

Lee Trevino's warning as he realised Jack Nicklaus was about to win the 1980 US Open (sports columnist Kaye Kessler in the US Open magazine, 1984).

It

I started in a Rolls-Royce and ended up on a donkey.

Gordon Brand Junior after losing a six-stroke lead in the 1992 Balearic Open.

It

If you think I'm composed you are badly mistaken. I'm extremely embarrassed and I've never been so disappointed but I'll be there to tee off tomorrow.

Tom Weiskopf after taking 85 in the 1980 US Masters.

It

I'm shell-shocked. No, I'm sorry. I'm flabbergasted.
> **Nick Faldo** after scoring 81 in his title defence at the
> 1997 US Masters.

I kept seeing her ass all day, bending over to pick her ball out of
the hole.
> South African **Sally Little** on losing the 1982 Nabisco Dinah
> Shore event to Hoi I is Stacey.

There are so many train wrecks out there and I was just one of
many. Fair, unfair, that's golf. That's why we all play it.
> US tour professional **Scott Gump** on losing the 1999 Players
> championship by two strokes after hitting into water.

I'm sorry. I hope I wasn't in the way.
> **Lee Trevino** to playing partner Thomas Bjorn after scoring 80
> in the 2000 Open championship at St Andrews.

I'm tired of giving my best and not having it be good enough.
> **Jack Nicklaus** after losing his epic duel with Tom Watson for
> the 1977 Open championship.

A lot of could'ves, could'ves, could'ves.
> US Open champion **Tom Kite** describing how his last-round
> challenge failed in the 1994 US Masters championship.

I probably won't sleep tonight because I'll be thinking about every shot and what went on and what we did and what I could have done.

Nancy Lopez on losing the 1997 US Women's
Open to Alison Nicholas.

I think every good man is tested in the crucible of humiliation.

American professional **Chip Beck** after being beaten
9 and 8 by Seve Ballesteros in the 1989
World Match Play championship.

And no flowers by request.

Scoreboard carrier's remark to the Ganton
crowd after chalking up that Max Faulkner had
just lost by 8 and 7 to Dutch Harrison in the 1949
Ryder Cup match. Sports write Desmond Hackett in *The
Golfer's Year*, 1949.

I just want to say that I've never felt so bad for anyone in my life. You played too well not to win.

Jack Nicklaus to Mike Reid, who faded over the last two holes
to lose the 1989 US PGA championship.

Personally I have the highest respect for the winner, Mr Walter Travis – I could hardly fail to have, seeing that he gave me the soundest of beatings – but at the same time it is making no derogation from this high estimate to say that he was lucky to win. I do not wish this to be misconstrued. My meaning is that, however good a player Mr Travis may be (I have not the slightest hesitation in classing him as a very fine player), it implied a measure of good fortune that he should win the Amateur championship the first time of asking.

Horace Hutchinson on losing in the semi-final of the 1904 championship to the eventual American winner, Walter Travis.

Now that Arnold's become a member of the club, he's beginning to play like one.

Dave Marr after winning the 1965 US PGA championship at Laurel Valley and being told that Arnold Palmer, who had just become a member, had finished fourteen strokes behind him (Ryder Cup magazine, 1975).

Francis Broune, sone of John Broune, wabster in Banff, convicted by the Borrow or Justice Court of the Burgh of breaking into the buithe of Patrick Shane and stealing therefrom sume golff ballis; and the judges ordenit the said Francis to be presently tacken and careit to the Gallowe-hill of this burgh and hangit on the gallows thereof to death, whereof William Wat, dempster of the said assysis, gaive doome.

A seemingly minor felony in 1637 with dire consequences, outlined in *Golfing* magazine 1906.

After a nonchalant and, as I hoped, confident-looking swing, the greatness of the occasion took charge; a wild lunge at high speed, while permitting the toe of the club fractional contact with the ball, was barely sufficient to give a simple running catch to silly point. Actually the starter's box – from which the starter had wisely withdrawn – was stationed in this position and accepted the chance readily.

Tony Puckle's first tee shot for his team at Deal in 1931 (Peter Ryde, *The Halford Hewitt*).

I don't know how you do it.
  Irish champion **Billy O'Sullivan**'s crestfallen remark to essayist
Patrick Campbell, who fought back from being four down to
  win their fourth-round encounter in the 1949 Amateur
championship at Portmarnock.

Punch me if I go for the driver.
  Amateur champion **Michael Hoey** to his elder brother Edward,
who caddied for him round the narrow fairways of Royal
Lytham and St Annes during the 2001 Open championship.

Where the hell's Jane?
  Nick Faldo to the crowd after he clambered Tarzan-like up a
tree in a vain search for his golf ball during the 1992 US Open
championship.

I should be standing up, my arse hurts so much.
  Jose Maria Olazabal to the press after a comprehensive 8 and
7 defeat by Ian Woosnam in the 1992 World Match Play
championship.

My concentration was so poor yesterday I could hear a pin drop.
  Meg Mallon in the 1991 Mazda Japan Classic.
For me here this week the lights were on but nobody was home.
  David Feherty after missing the halfway cut in the 1992
Cannes Open.

It's hard to describe the feeling. One minute you're thinking about winning and the next you're numb with disappointment.
Mark Calcavecchia after losing the 1988 US Masters to Sandy Lyle (Mark McCormack, *The World of Professional Golf,* 1991 edition).

Oh boy. Where can you go around here to have a good cry? It's OK. I cry at supermarket openings.
Mike Reid after losing the 1989 US PGA title.

If I were Europe I'd make him captain for the next thirty years. If they don't want him, give him to us. That man is a winner.
American **Peter Jacobsen** on European Ryder Cup captain Tony Jacklin.

As I walked around the ball, even as I stood over it, my mind was full of nothing but feet, rows and rows of feet and shoes – brogues, moccasins, sneakers, boots, shoes, spikes, rubbers – the shoes of people in the front row of the grandstand which I could just see at the limit of my vision . . . all those boots and shoes kept popping idiotically in and out of my mind.
Peter Alliss, in his autobiography, recalling the fluffed chip shot in the 1953 Ryder Cup at Wentworth.

Let's go home and hide some Easter eggs.
Greg Norman to wife Laura after missing the halfway cut in the 1998 US Masters. (Mark McCormack, *The World of Professional Golf* 1999 edition).

It wasn't the end of the world. It just felt like it at the time.
>> **Mark Calcavecchia** on losing the last three holes of his 1991 Ryder Cup singles to Colin Montgomerie.

I saw the bear tracks on the green.
>> **Johnny Miller's** remark after Jack Nicklaus, playing ahead of him, holed a massive putt on Augusta National's sixteenth green to put the 1975 US Masters out of reach (*The Art Spander Collection*).

Hell, if you count all the cars my ex-wives are driving around in, I've probably got around thirty.
>> **John Daly** the former Open and US PGA champion.

You may have read my book *The Art of Negative Thinking*.
>> American professional **Rod Funseth** who shared the halfway lead in the 1977 US Masters but then faded from view.

I'm not feeling down. If I had played badly I might be. But when you are beaten by somebody, especially the way he played, you bow out gracefully. It was such a thrill to play to this standard of golf.
>> **Nick Price** on finishing runner-up to Seve Ballesteros in the 1988 Open championship.

I was humbled today. I blew it. But it's just a game, a game called golf. Sports are just sports. It's not life and death. Too many people in sports think the world owes them a living. It doesn't. We need to be put in our place. I was. I should have

won this. At one point the only way I could lose was to give it away and that's what I did.
Hubert Green on losing the 1986 Doral Eastern Open.

I tried to protect what wasn't mine. I didn't want to play defensively but knowing it and doing it are two different things.
Laura Baugh after losing a four-stroke lead and the LPGA Invitational title.

It seemed like every time I addressed the ball, somebody was moving or taking pictures.
Australian **Graham Marsh** in the 1972 Thailand Open.

Don't worry about it. The way we played this week I think I'll dig it up.
Losing US Ryder Cup captain **Jack Nicklaus** in 1987 after European skipper Tony Jacklin apologised for the way his victorious team danced on the last green at Muirfield Village.

They're not giving me hell in there, are they?
Greg Norman outside the press tent after losing the 1989 Open championship in a play-off.

I've got 94,000 dollars in the bank. Why should I stay around here for another 500 dollars?
Dave Hill on his decision to withdraw from the 1973 US Open because he was not playing well enough to make the 36-hole qualifying score.

I get too excited when I see my name on the leader board. I've been in contention a few times this year but lost my concentration every time.

Jamie Spence on finishing runner-up in the 1991 Lancome Trophy.

I shot 74 in the morning and that's not good enough to win a club tournament let alone an international match such as this. This is the second time he has beaten me in this type of golf and he deserved it. Believe me, I don't mind losing but I hate losing the way I did today.

Gary Player after losing the final of the 1973 Rothman's International Match Play championship to Peter Oosterhuis in South Africa.

Spare a thought, if you will, for Oxford undergraduate Michael McPhee who will spend the next eleven weeks three down with six to play because the match in which he played was halted by a blizzard and cannot be resumed until after the snow melts. What the heck, you may ask, was Master McPhee doing on a golf course in the first week of January when all sane and sensible men should have been at their firesides sipping whisky macs? He was not alone. There were a lot like him at the beginning of the week in Rye, the ancient Sussex port from which the sea has receded. They had gathered, as they do every year at this time, for the lunatic ritual of the President's Putter.

Golf World **report** of the 1985 Oxford and Cambridge Golf Society meeting. McPhee didn't win when play resumed.

I just wish he would get out on the Seniors Tour and get away from the rest of us other fellows.

Lanny Wadkins after losing the 1984 US PGA championship to 44-year-old Lee Trevino.

This putter won't be flying first class on the way home.
   Nick Faldo after missing four short putts in the final round of
                        the 1988 US PGA championship.

I can't understand how anyone can drive that badly and still win
an Open championship.
   Hale Irwin on finishing runner-up to Seve Ballesteros in the
                        1979 championship.

I've never seen her this pissed.
      Annika Sorenstam's husband **David** after she lost the
   Australian Ladies Masters in a play-off to arch-rival Karrie
                                                          Webb.

I think I can win. I've got nothing better to do this weekend.
   David Feherty at the 1994 Open championship. He didn't.

Her opponent's ball had landed into a bunker and lay in water
there; and she, not knowing that she could have lifted out with
a penalty of one stroke, played at least two strokes
unsuccessfully at it amongst the water and the other player, on
learning that she was not aware she could lift, very generously
offered to allow her to take it back and lift out. But that, of
course, the gentleman umpiring the match could not allow.
         Report from *Golfing* magazine on the 1908 Ladies
                        championship at St Andrews.

I have saved for fifteen years to come and play in the Open. It has been my dream. I would like to come back again and try but after this, I don't think they'll let me.

Japanese professional **Takashi Kobayashi** after scoring 90 and 102 in the 1977 Open championship.

I love the exposure. I just wish it was for something different.

New York professional **Bob Impagiia** to the press corps at the 1976 US Open after becoming the first player in the history of the championship to be penalised two strokes for slow play.

There are too many good golfers out there and they aren't likely to choke. Are they?

Maurice Bembridge after scoring a record-equalling 64 in the last round of the 1974 US Masters but deciding not to wait and see if he was involved in a play-off.

It is too much to ask a man to check his card for errors in arithmetic which his marker may inadvertently have made. It also points out a sorry weakness in the rules of the game that appoints a marker to keep score but doesn't make him responsible for its accuracy.

Peter Thomson after Guy Wolstenholme had been disqualified from the 1972 Victoria Open for a scorecard error.

It owes me four.

Greg Norman at the 1989 Open championship when asked whether he thought fate owed him at least one major title.

Cowboys don't cry.
  Texan professional **Art Russell** after scoring a best-of-the-day
65 in the last round of the 1983 German Open but finishing
down among the also-rans.

I'm not one of the great players but if nobody wants to win it,
then I'll be hanging around, ready.
  Australian **Mike Harwood** at the 1991 Open championship.
He finished in second place.

My putting book is selling well. I'm going to go back and read it.
Arnold Palmer after an indifferent display with the blade in the
1986 US PGA championship.

It doesn't hurt much any more. These days I can go a full five
minutes without thinking about it.
  Doug Sanders on the putt he missed to win the Open at St
Andrews 30 years earlier.

I lost my wife and family because I was away from home so
much. And the bills kept coming in. It's hard to keep your mind
on golf. I didn't have any heartaches in the Army. I knew when
I was going to get paid and how much. Maybe I should have
finished my twenty years.
                    US Open champion **Orville Moody**.

It is wrong to settle major championships by sudden death [playoff]. I don't want to take anything away from Larry Mize but I think it is more likely the real champion will win in an eighteen-hole play-off.

Seve Ballesteros after losing the 1987 US Masters at the first extra hole.

If it had been Nicklaus or Arnold Palmer, it might not have gone out of bounds.

Gene Littler on the manner in which the crowd parted to allow his tee shot to bounce through the green and out of bounds during the 1997 US PGA championship, which he later lost in a play-off to Lanny Wadkins.

Maybe I should have had a glimpse at the scoreboard when I was on eighteen.

Jesper Parnevik on wrongly thinking he needed a birdie to win the 1994 Open and dropping a stroke instead.

What a stupid I am.

Argentinian **Roberto de Vicenzo** after a scorecard error cost him a play-off for the 1968 US Masters.

I'd have been all over the place.

Milwaukee telephone operator **Walter Danecki,** who took 108 and 116 in the 1965 Open championship, explaining why he did not use the larger-sized American golf ball.

What the hell are you doing out there? You ought to find yourself a job.

> **Ben Hogan** to professional Gary McCord, who had not won a tournament in ten years.

We had a shot today but the fates looked the other way. There was a course to be played and we didn't make it.

> Australian captain **Greg Norman** on losing to Ireland in the 1988 Dunhill Cup.

From the Suggestion Book at Thorpe Hall Golf Club: August 1998. Would it be possible for the bar to stay open on a Saturday night after 9.30 p.m. which, to my bewilderment, was when it shut yesterday? I was also shocked that I was asked to leave at this early hour. Signed: A Concerned Member.

Response: Dear Concerned Member. I note the shock and bewilderment over the bar closing early and I will speak to the staff. However, in view that you reported this bar complaint in the Greens Suggestion Book I feel perhaps the bar had been open too long.

> ***The Suggestion Book*** compiled by Duncan Ferguson and John Wilson, 2001.

You could put any one of us on the European side and make it better. But the only Europeans who could help us are Laura Davies and Liselotte Neumann.

> American skipper **Beth Daniel's** boast before her team lost the Solheim Cup to Europe in 1992.

I figured I needed 66 today to have a chance. I shot 66 and didn't even come close.

Al Geiberger on finishing runner-up in the 1975 Greater Greensboro Open.

I said to myself halfway through the round: 'Beam me up Scotty.'
Guy McQuitty after following his first-round 95 with an 87 in the 1986 Open championship.

All I can say is that at least I was there for both of them.
Greg Norman after Larry Mize holed a massive chip shot to snatch the 1987 US Masters from him, then Bob Tway holed a bunker shot on the last hole to take the US PGA title.

My kids used to come up to me and say: 'Daddy, did you win?' Now they say: 'Daddy, did you make the cut?'
Tom Watson on his poor form in 1987.

There goes a hundred thousand dollars!
American golfer **Al Watrous's** remark as Bobby Jones played a miraculous recovery to beat him in the 1926 Open championship at Royal Lytham and St Annes.

I played well and I'm missing the cut by two shots. When that happens you know it's time to leave.
Jack Nicklaus playing in his last Open Championship, St Andrews 2005.

I'll wonder for the rest of my life what could have happened tomorrow.

Mark Roe on being disqualified before the final round of the 2003 Open Championship for signing a wrong card when only two strokes off the lead.

ſ

I didn't get any breaks. But that's like a manager claiming four goals were offside when you lose 6–0.

Colin Montgomerie on losing 6 and 5 to Paul Casey in the 2006 World Match Play Championship.

ſ

4
'All Mouth and No Trousers':
A Catalogue of Skirmishes

If sport really is a war substitute without the bullets, it still doesn't follow that people never get hurt. The injuries simply take different forms, both on and off the course, and golf is no exception to this dictum. Hidden behind its measured and seemingly controlled pace, there is a cauldron of emotions never far from the boil. How could it be otherwise in a competitive arena where the difference in technical skills among the very best is marginal and only strength of character, purpose and self-belief separate the winners from the losers?

Most of the time such forces are held in check and masked by a smile or a handshake at the end of the contest. But sometimes they escape so that the enmities and rivalries are there for all to see. In many cases they provide the motivation for command performances, pushing a campaigner to even greater heights in a determination to vanquish a particular rival. Not quite the unacceptable face of golf, but a scowl none the less.

He can intimidate people. I don't know how he does it. I would think it's confidence. I mean, we're all pretty confident, I think, and some people intimidate others more than others. He doesn't very often say 'Good shot'. He's just not as friendly and nice a guy as a lot of others are. He's not going to be a nice guy on the course or whatever you expect.

Bernhard Langer to the press before his match with Seve Ballesteros in the 1984 World Match Play championship.

I believe I am a gentleman on the course. When I'm playing match play or medal play – I don't talk, I concentrate. Maybe sometimes I will say a few words to my caddie but only to complain.

Seve Ballesteros after the 1984 encounter with Langer.

Like a pair of Trappist monks, Seve Ballesteros and Bernhard Langer went round separately and solemnly in the final.

Chris Rae, in the *Scotsman* newspaper, reporting the 1984 World Match Play final which Seve won.

Get out of my office.

The response of a Royal Lytham and St Annes **official** when Gary Player offered to buy eighteen rakes for the club before the 1958 Open championship because some of the bunkers were untended (*Daily Mail*).

She's an absolute prat and has really upset a lot of players. I hear she has called us all 'old hags'. As far as I am concerned she is all mouth and no trousers.

Laura Davies, quoted in the *Daily Mail*, 2001, on fellow professional Suzann Pettersen.

Now Frankie, my boy, follow that little fellow if you can.
Sam McCready's remark to Frank Stranahan after hitting a massive opening drive in the 1949 Amateur championship at Portmarnock. McCready eventually took the title.

If you are not going to ask me about my round then I am going back to my hotel.
Colin Montgomerie to waiting reporters at the 2001 Volvo Masters (*Golf Weekly*).

Ask anyone who has ever played golf. When you are three feet or less from the hole and near someone's line, you don't mark the ball with a quarter. You mark it with a non-reflective penny. The first page of the rules book talks about etiquette.
Defending champion **Tom Weiskopfs** criticism of his playing partner US Senior Amateur champion Jim Stahl Jnr, for marking his ball on the green with a silver coin instead of a copper one during the 1996 US Senior Open (*Golf World* magazine).

Right now I probably will never play golf again. I don't know how I can. I can't tell you how truly devastated I am; it's difficult to put into words. It's hard to understand why this happened.
Stahl's response (*Golf World* magazine, 1996).

I don't feel I've won a golf tournament out there but more a battle. I am very disappointed in the attitude of the crowd. There was absolutely no need to make a noise in the middle of my backswing or clap when I hit a bad shot. I just had to win after that but it is a pity that I have to go out on such a bad note. Certainly I will play in Britain again but not here. It was up to Lyle to do something but he did not. That's his decision. At times

I felt like saying something myself but I told myself to zip up my mouth.

Greg Norman on British crowds after he beat local hero Sandy Lyle in the final of the 1986 World Match Play championship at Wentworth.

I thought the crowds were reasonable. It was natural for them to be on my side. I'm the local boy. I'm British. There were a few idiots clapping at missed putts but it is only the sort of thing I would expect if I was playing Greg in Australia. In any case I had enough problems of my own to pay much attention to the crowds.

Sandy Lyle on the Norman outburst.

Personally I have not the slightest doubt that I was the first person to use this grip. I won my first medal in 1878 and I think it was two or three years later that I took to it. However, it was looked on as most foolish for a good young golfer to have done and also the stand [stance] I adopted caused much comment which I did not mind and felt it unlikely any golfer would copy. It must have been several years later when I first played with Harry Vardon and I am certain had he used it, I should have observed him at once.

Scottish golfer **J E Laidlay** in 1939, explaining how the overlapping grasp of a golf club, which became known worldwide as the Vardon Grip, was really his idea.

You have blackened his name and all of us Vardons want it put right. There are still a lot of us Vardons around so beware.

Extract from a **letter** sent to the *Daily Mail* following earlie suggestions that Harry Vardon did not invent the grip named after him but simply popularised it.

Let's stop playing each other and play the course.
Jack Nicklaus to Arnold Palmer when they were paired together in the 1967 US Open. Nicklaus won and Palmer finished runner-up.

I was playing with a man that I loathe playing with. There I was in a twosome with him, just me and him, for eighteen holes. There couldn't have been four words between us. He's getting old and his nerves are gone but I don't feel sorry for him because he shouldn't be out there.
Raymond Floyd in the 1969 US PGA championship on veteran former winner Jim Ferrier. Floyd, who won the title, was later ordered to apologise for his remarks.

I am sorry.
Peter Alliss to opponent Tony Lema after holing a spectacular putt from 40 feet in the 1963 Ryder Cup match in Atlanta. They eventually halved their match.

There is a story associated with a club on Long Island which shall be nameless. Knit shirts were introduced about the same time as shorts and this club decreed women could wear one or the other, but you couldn't wear both, because then you would be distracting at both ends.
Janet Seagle, curator of the USGA Golf House museum, 1978.

You can only take so much. I had 36 holes on Friday of that crowd rooting for Jacklin. I know Britain wants a champion. I want a British champion. I said so when I won the Open in July. But I'm sure nobody wants one at the expense of fair play.

Gary Player on crowd behaviour during the 1968 World Match Play championship.

I will be home reading the newspapers.

Seve Ballesteros explaining to the press why he had declined an invitation from US Tour Commissioner Deane Beman, with whom he had a long-running dispute, to play in the lucrative World Series of Golf in 1986.

It was the small unruly minority in the big gallery that besmirched the name of British sportsmanship. Just like their soccer fans. British golf galleries besmirched themselves last year when the Europeans defeated the United States in the Ryder Cup. Hal Sutton went back to the US devastated at the behaviour he had witnessed.

Greg Norman after he beat the home favourite Sandy Lyle for the 1986 World Match Play title, in the Australian *Courier-Mail*.

Get awa' oot o' there wi' yer bluidy magic lantern.

St Andrews professional **Andrew Kirkaldy** to an intrusive press photographer (Frank Moran in the *Golfer's Bedside Book*).

If you want the best then you've got to pay for them and that includes me.

> **Lee Trevino** to the press on the question of his appearance money in the 1973 Chrysler Classic in Australia.

Trevino spoiled an otherwise entertaining performance by an astonishing ill-mannered attack on the Australian PGA at the public prize-giving over the new by-law banning appearance money from next January. It is sad to think that our links will not echo with the sound of his dubious jokes again.

> **Peter Thomson** writing in the *Sydney Daily Telegraph* after Trevino had won the tournament.

It is cheating the public to play this way. It is cheating them to make them pay to see blokes shooting such high scores.

> **Lee Trevino** criticising the Royal Melbourne greens after the 1974 Chrysler Classic.

It is safe to say we have seen the last of him. That's the man I tried to tell you about last year but no one would listen.

> **Peter Thomson**.

To be frank, I really don't enjoy playing with Hubie. He talks too much on the course. He babbles on about nothing. He puts up a carefree facade but he's actually tense.

> **John Schlee** on fellow professional Hubert Green, 1974.

I talk about anything and everything and I mean everything.
Hubert Green.

Everyone thinks I am anti-Tony Jacklin and sees me as the villain who is trying to kill the goose that lays our golden eggs. They just don't understand that this decision brands us all as second-class pros.
Maurice Bembridge campaigning to ban appearance money in 1973.

But why are they picking on me? I'm just trying to make a living and I don't hurt anyone.
Black golfer **Charlie Sifford** after being targeted by racist hecklers in the 1969 Great Greensboro Open.

In 1961 you didn't get the best welcome to Greensboro and we regret it to this day.
Mayor **Keith Holliday,** at a special ceremony in 2001 in honour of Sifford, recalling one of two earlier incidents when the black golfer was heckled and issued with a death threat.

I believe David is looking for me. All I can say is I hope he doesn't miss me. It's a good thing we are playing as individuals this week and not as partners.
Graham Marsh at the 1985 Dunhill Cup after learning that Australian team mate David Graham resented his criticisms about accepting appearance money at an earlier event.

The American team is made up of eleven gentlemen and Paul Azinger.

> **Seve Ballesteros** revealing his Ryder Cup enmity
> to the press in 1991.

Eighty acres and a few cows. They ruined a good farm when they built this course.

> **Dave Hill** when asked to comment on what Hazeltine lacked
> as a venue for the 1970 US Open championship.

David Hill has been reprimanded and fined $150 for conduct unbecoming a professional golfer because of the manner of his criticism of the Hazeltine National Golf Course. In determining such matters, distinction is made between objective critical analysis of a golf course and the kind of criticism which tends to ridicule and demean the club. It is considered that Hill's criticism was of the second kind.

> Statement from Commissioner **Joe Dey Junio** after Hill's
> outburst.

I anticipated the fine but I have to say what I think.

> **Dave Hill's** response.

I think Tony wants to work harder. Everything is coming to him too easily at the moment. It is very tempting to play in one-day shows if you are getting a guarantee but he needs to set aside an hour every day to hit at least 100 practice balls.

> **Bob Charles** on Tony Jacklin, 1973.

I have no wish to become involved in a slanging match. Bob is entitled to his opinions and I'm not losing much sleep over them. I'm certainly not lazy.

Tony Jacklin's response.

Tony didn't name names but I took it personally. I'm as ambitious for success as anybody.

David Feherty responding to Tony Jacklin's criticism in 1987 that younger tournament professionals were too easy-going.

I don't drink except for an occasional glass of wine with dinner but I still felt Tony's comments were aimed at me. I have proved here that you can stay out late having a good time and still win tournaments.

Robert Lee on the same subject after winning the 1987 Portuguese Open.

As to my physical appearance, I am not a fashion model and have never pretended to be one. I am a professional golfer. But to be called a tank in print is very harsh. It isn't a nice way to wake up at 6.15 in the morning.

Laura Davies after she had been criticised by a journalist on the eve of the 1995 LPGA championship (*Golf World* magazine, 1997).

But those cats can't run this kid off. I'll be there – with necktie.

Lee Trevino after being informed that he would need jacket and tie to attend the official dinner of the 1968 World Match Play championship.

One day I'll beat you.
Ian Woosnam, then twelve years old, on losing the 1969 Hereford Boys championship to Sandy Lyle, who was the same age.

You'll have to grow a bit first, Woosie.
Lyle's reply, of which he was reminded years later when Woosnam beat him to become 1987 World Match Play champion at Wentworth.

We are in a heck of a battle for last place.
American professional **Tim Macy** to fellow tail-ender Harcourt Kemp in the 1971 US Open. Both missed the halfway cut.

Faxon is going through a divorce. Mentally I don't think he'll be with it. Mickelson isn't reliable on every hole and nobody is intimidated by Jeff Maggert.
Colin Montgomerie's crushing assessment of the 1997 US Ryder Cup squad.

I think he's the jerk of the world.
American professional **Fred Funk** after Colin Montgomerie's critical remarks about members of the 1997 US Ryder Cup squad.

Someone is afraid that Locke will pick up all the marbles. No other conclusion could be drawn even though personal popularity or lack of it undoubtedly enters into it.
Al Laney, in the *New York Times,* on the official decision in 1949 to ban Bobby Locke from the US professional circuit.

Harry, if that makes you feel good, then hit me again.

> **Christy O'Connor's** remark to Harry Weetman, who gave the Irishman a black eye during an argument outside the Stoke Poges clubhouse. (Weetman did hit him again and both men were fined by the PGA.)

He's spoiled and conceited and thinks that everything should go exactly the way he wants it to. He reminds me of a kid I used to play marbles with. When he couldn't win, he'd pick up his marbles and go home.

> **Dave Hill,** in his autobiography, on fellow professional Tom Weiskopf.

Some of us aren't very happy about it. We were all told to be in Washington to get on a plane. If one can do it, why can't we all do it?

> **Lee Trevino** on the decision by Jack Nicklaus not to travel with the US Ryder Cup squad to the 1973 match at Muirfield.

So far as I was concerned Huggett was totally and utterly out of line. I went and took him to the other side of the fairway and told him he was captain until the next evening and this wasn't Crystal Palace football team – it was twelve different individuals. If he had taken me aside it would have been different but you can't say what he did in front of all those people.

I got back to my room and about half an hour later Huggett phoned me to say he was sorry I had been dropped from the team the next day. I said that was all right, there was no need to apologise and I put down the telephone. It was a personal thing, that's all.

> **Tony Jacklin** on his very public clash with Ryder Cup skipper Brian Huggett, who accused him of not supporting his team-mates during the 1977 match.

I thought it was absolutely ludicrous dropping Tony from the Ryder Cup team on the last day. He won the Open over that course.

Peter Oosterhuis on Huggett's decision to omit the former Open champion from the last-day singles at Royal Lytham and St Annes in 1977.

Seve is so detrimental to his game right now. He can't shut his mouth up because he keeps chastising other players for what they have done. I don't understand the guy. I really don't.

Greg Norman to *Sports Illustrated* magazine after both he and Ballesteros lost a play-off for the 1987 US Masters to Larry Mize.

This is my driver, man. If he goes, I go too. I can drive out the same way I drove in.

Lee Trevino to an Augusta National official who claimed the golfer's black chauffeur did not have the correct parking label.

It's hard to have a great champion with bad technique.

Nick Faldo on Paul Azinger, who won the 1993 US PGA championship.

I would hate to have won two world championships – the British Open and the Masters – knowing I had used illegally-grooved clubs.

Gary Player's reference to Tom Watson's unwitting use of clubs that did not conform to the rules, in his autobiography *To Be the Best*.

It would degrade the championship if I were to get involved in a debate with the little man.

>   **Tom Watson** after Gary Player's accusations on the
>   controversial golf clubs.

f

If you're going to sit in the team room, you have to be motivated and be prepared to say some pretty tough things, such as what you feel about your opponents. The thought that somebody might be thinking that the sentiments expressed would be great for their next book would be just too dangerous.

>   **Nick Faldo,** following Mark James's team-room revelations
>   after the 1999 Ryder Cup in his book *Into the Bear Pit*.

f

To say I plagiarised his methodology is baloney. Let's face it. There's only so much stuff in the golf swing. We are not reinventing the wheel here.

>   Golf teacher **David Leadbetter,** quoted in *Golf Digest*
>   magazine, on suggestions he copied ideas from Mac O'Grady.

f

I finally found someone more neurotic than me.

>   Golf guru **Mac O'Grady** explaining the reason he stopped
>   coaching Seve Ballesteros.

f

If he wants to fix traps, he shouldn't do it at my expense.

>   **Johnny Miller** accusing Gary Player of gamesmanship in the
>   1973 World Match Play championship after alleging that the
>   South African took four minutes to rake a bunker while the
>   American was waiting to play his next stroke.

f

If you want to say something to me, say it after the round when I can do something about it.
> **Greg Norman** to heckling fan in the 1986 US Open championship.

Tour officials became so desperate for appeal, that quasi-pornography got the nod. Is our organisation so unaware of the real glamour and attraction staring it in the face that it must resort to such trash?
> American golfer **Jane Blalock,** in the *Miami Herald,* 1981, on fellow professional Jan Stephenson's pin-up pose on a bed.

He stated that he has no respect for me as a man or as a captain. These are hard cruel words but to be quite frank, they fly over my head like barbed arrows.
> **Dai Rees** in his autobiography on Harry Weetman's attack after being dropped from the winning 1957 Ryder Cup team.

I thought we were all agreed – and Ken was party to these discussions – that the Ryder Cup wouldn't be open to the guy with the biggest chequebook. I didn't think we were prostituting it to that extent.
> PGA Executive Director **Sandy Jones** on his disagreement with European Tour counterpart Ken Schofield over whether the 2009 Ryder Cup match would be played in Wales (Lauren St John in the *Sunday Times* magazine, 2001).

As far as I am concerned, my feud with the press is a thing of the past and I aim to be more co-operative in the future.
> **J C Snead** after winning the 1987 Westchester Classic.

There was a lot of back-biting about foreign players. The Dave Hills, the Mike Hills, the Bob Goalbys, the Gardner Dickinsons – all thought foreign players should never be allowed in. I had something to prove. I always will have. That will stay with me till the day I die. They are no better than we are. No better at all. More privileged maybe, because they were born in a country that is more wealthy and has better facilities, but they are no better.

Tony Jacklin on the animosity he encountered on the US Tour (Ryder Cup magazine, 1987).

I decided to seek the views of a few other people, including some of the players and everybody's reaction was the same: bin it.

Mark James, in his account of the 1999 Ryder Cup, on what happened to Nick Faldo's good luck message (*Into the Bear Pit*).

I'm a fragging American and no one treats me like that.

American golfer **Muffin Spencer-Devlin** as she walked out of a banquet at Woburn Abbey in 1990 after being barred from sitting at the top table.

Tom Lehman calls himself a man of God, but his behaviour has been disgusting today.

Sam Torrance on the American's antics at the 1999 Ryder Cup.

There was over-exuberance, no question about it. It wasn't a very good thing but what's done is done. Europe had a great party at Valderrama and we had to watch and now it's their turn.

Tom Lehman after the 1999 Ryder Cup victory.

I felt embarrassed for golf. It went beyond the decency you associate with proper golf. I love the Ryder Cup and I don't want to see it degenerate into a mob demonstration every time we play.

Sir Michael Bonallack after the 1999 Ryder Cup match.

ƒ

So what if he has the most perfect bowel movement on tour?

Dave Hill on Gary Player's constant boasts about his fitness.

ƒ

I enjoyed the golf Peter Thomson played this week. I've been on tour for nine years and this was the first time I've had the pleasure of seeing him win a tournament.

Mason Rudolph at St Andrews, 1967.

ƒ

If I'm not playing in tomorrow's four balls, I'll really have something to scream about. I'm sick at being dropped.

Open champion **Sandy Lyle** after being omitted by skipper Tony Jacklin from the afternoon series on the opening day of the 1985 Ryder Cup.

ƒ

He told me the British Open was the finest tournament in the world and anybody who's exempt [ie, a player who can walk straight in to a championship] should be required to play. I said: 'OK, Brad, if that's the way you feel, fine. We don't need to talk about it any more. I'm sorry you feel that way and if you're not going to apologise for raking me over the coals, then fine.'

Scott Hoch, to *Golf Digest* magazine, after Brad Faxon criticised him for declining to play in the Open championship.

ƒ

I have to admit I was playing with an extra bit of determination today. Gay has said some nasty things about me in the past but I think Gay Brewer is a very great player.

> **Gary Player** after beating the American in the 1967 World Match Play championship.

I said sorry and I was still saying sorry all the way up the next hole. He wouldn't talk to me.

> **Colin Montgomerie's** light-hearted account of how his partner Ian Woosnam reacted after the Scot hit his approach into a bush during the 1995 Perrier Foursomes tournament in Paris.

I guess every story needs a villain and I'm glad he's found one in me. I hope he feels good about making money out of taking shots at other people's character and integrity. I think he ought to be proud that he's dragging the Ryder Cup through the muck.

> **Tom Lehman** responding to criticisms by Mark James, in his book, following the 1999 match.

I always like to win. But I guess you can say we Americans take particular pleasure in beating Peter.

> **Arnold Palmer** referring to Peter Thomson before the 1967 World Match Play championship final. Palmer won.

I blame the press mostly but I also think Tiger could have come out and said right away it was no big deal. I never joke with Tiger about race. I've never got that close to him. When a white player makes a joke about my colour, I take it for what it is – a joke.

> Fiji professional **Vijay Singh** commenting in *Golf Digest* magazine on the furore that followed Fuzzy Zoeller's alleged racist remarks about Tiger Woods.

If you are looking for me to shed a tear, it's not going to happen.
Phil Mickelson on learning arch-rival Tiger Woods had scored
75 in the USPGA Championship 2005.

I know what Laura is all about. As a spectator it's fun to watch.
I try not to watch too much. She plays with her heart. i like to say
I play with my brain.
World Number One **Annika Sorenstam** on Laura Davies.

It doesn't mean we're not good. It just means she's exceptional.
She's toying with us, like a mouse and a cat.
Laura Davies, 2005, on Sorsenstam's supremacy.

It's not going to cause us any grief in the morning because he's
going to be cheering instead of playing.
US Ryder Cup captain **Hal Sutton** on dropping Phil Mickelson
from the team after the American star switched to a new set of
clubs then made a crucial error to lose his foursomes match.

5

'You're Choking, You White-haired Bastard': The Golf Fan

From the very beginning, the spectator has had a passionate involvement with the game of golf. It matters who wins and who loses and not just how good the performance may have been.

The small boys who cried when their hero John Ball was losing the 1906 British Amateur championship on his home course at Hoylake, illustrate the point. The placard held in the rough with the message 'Hit it Here, Fats', directed at Jack Nicklaus as he prepared to topple national hero Arnold Palmer in the early 1960s, continues that theme.

Astute players never respond; they seem to favour instead a kind of theatrical belief that an invisible curtain exists between performer and audience and must never be lifted in case the illusion is broken. Those who do respond or retaliate find themselves fighting a losing battle, no matter how crudely and unfairly some fans seek to influence the outcome of a contest.

You're choking, you white-haired bastard!
Drunken **fan** in the crowd at the 1986 US Open to Greg Norman.

Hit it Here, Fats.
Placard being held in the rough by an Arnold Palmer supporter watching Jack Nicklaus.

Why don't you start blaming yourself instead of the greens, you mug.

Irate **fan** (who later apologised) to Gary Player after the South African complained about his approach shot bouncing through a green in the 1968 Australian Open.

When Ball was coming to grief on that fatal Thursday, mournful wails of 'What are you doing, Johnny?' were frequently heard in the crowd. And when Laidlay was beating Ball, a Northern writer declared that 'small boys holding on to the rope wept audibly'.

Golfing magazine **report** of the 1906 Amateur championship when local hero John Ball lost in the third round.

Get on with it!

Irate **fan** to Nick Faldo who refused to play his approach to the last green in the 1988 Dunhill Cup at St Andrews, claiming that fog obstructed his view of the flag. Spectators in the grandstand also gave him a slow handclap but he refused to play on until the next day.

SEE THIS ONE NICK?

The massive **banner** St Andrews University students hung from their windows at Hamilton Hall the next morning as Faldo returned to play his delayed shot – and lost.

I hope you don't choke like last year.

Drunken **spectator**'s shout as Peter Senior played his last tee shot in the 1995 Australian Masters.
(He didn't and won the title).

Hey Woosnam! This isn't some links course. You're at Augusta now.

> **Spectator** at the fourteenth tee while Ian Woosnam waited to play his shot in the 1991 US Masters. The spirited Welshman went on to win.

Have a good day and don't choke.

> **Spectator** to Fred Couples as he walked to the practice ground for the final round of the 1992 Los Angeles Open (which he won).

Pay attention to what's going on. Jesus.

> Open champion **David Duval** to a member of his gallery during the 2001 US PGA championship (Will Buckley in the *Observer*).

But what they did to Hal was embarrassing. That's the kind of thing that's over the top, the kind of thing that's got to stop here. It's only a small percentage but it's enough to hurt what is otherwise a great event. This is too good an event and too good a golf course to be tarnished by a few loudmouths. I'm a little concerned that some of our guys might not come back to play here in the future.

> **Tom Lehman** admonishing fans who booed Hal Sutton but cheered local heroes John Daly and Phil Mickelson in the 2000 Phoenix Open.

But today the gallery several times violated the true ethics of the sport by cheering wildly whenever Ouimet gained a point. Both Ray and Vardon were playing shots either just before or after Ouimet and it was plainly evident that these outbreaks annoyed them. Approaching the seventeenth hole Ray deliberately stopped in the midst of a swing and refused to play until the cheering ceased.

New York Tribune **report** of the 1913 US Open play-off in which twenty-year-old local amateur Francis Ouimet defeated Harry Vardon and Ted Ray, then the best golfers in the world.

I will admit that occasionally there was sufficient noise to jar anyone accustomed only to the restraint and reverent silence of a British gathering, but there was never anything which, by the wildest stretch of imagination, could be said to be offensive or intentionally unsportsmanlike. I can personally testify that the American crowds are extremely fair to the British visitor.

Harold Hilton commenting on the same incident in *Golf Illustrated* magazine.

Perhaps we were too busy celebrating our home-grown championships to care about this little international contest. But that has all changed. We learned how much the Ryder Cup means once we had to fight for it. We learned by seeing the British, Germans, Welsh, Irish, Scots and Spaniards flock to our shores to cheer their team on. We learned from them how to act towards the tournament. And we learned from them how to care about winning it.

American sports writer **Ken Burger** summing up the 1991 Ryder Cup match in which the US team scored a dramatic last-green victory over Europe (*Charleston News and Courier*).

I finish second behind Sandra Post. When the tournament is over, a woman comes over to me – walks right up to me and says: 'What's wrong with you?' What's wrong with me? I wanted to deck her right there.

American LPGA golfer **Pat Bradley**.

Gene, they don't want to see you play. They just want to see if you are still alive.

Augusta National chairman **Hord Hardin** to Gene Sarazen, then in his nineties, who claimed he was getting too old to hit the ceremonial opening stroke of the US Masters championship in front of thousands of fans (*Golf World* magazine, 1995).

I've always been intense. I enjoy my job but it's a job. It's like Doug said when someone in the gallery told me to smile: This is not the Ice Capades. You don't fall on a double axel and get up and smile and everything's okay.'

Dottie Mochrie explaining her husband's outspoken exchange with a fan while she was winning the 1994 Tournament of Champions.

Do remember, Finch-Hatton, that you are playing for your side and not for yourself.

Irate **supporter** to the Oxford captain who seemed to be conceding too many of his Cambridge opponent's missable putts in the University match.

And do remember that you are playing for neither.

The reply by **Denys Finch-Hatton,** whose exploits were later featured by Karen Blixen in the book *Out of Africa* and who was killed flying his own plane in Kenya (*The Oxford and Cambridge Golfing Society 1898–1948*).

It's all right, Mister, the hole hasn't moved. I'm keeping my eye on it.

An impatient fan's remark to Frank Jowle who seemed to be taking too long studying a putt in the 1949 *Yorkshire Evening News* tournament (Desmond Hackett in *The Golfer's Year*).

I never thought I'd live to see golf played so well.

Gene Sarazen after Greg Norman won the 1993 Open championship at Royal St George's (*Daily Mail*).

Losing the Ryder Cup did not bother me as much as the behaviour of the galleries. All that cheering when we missed shots. I've never known anything like it before and especially not from a British crowd. You expect so much from them.

US Ryder Cup player **Peter Jacobsen** after the 1985 defeat by Europe.

The crowd was again large and, almost to a man, devoutly praying for the success of Mr Low. The latter's good shots were applauded to the echo but those played by Mr Hilton were watched in oppressive silence, his mistakes being hailed with every sign of jubilation. He ignored the expressions of partisanship, summoned up all his pluck, resourcefulness and cheerful philosophy and achieved a brilliant triumph.

Golfing magazine **account** of Harold Hilton's one-hole victory over local hero John Low in the 1901 Amateur championship at St Andrews.

And now we shan't be long.

> The voluble opinion of St Andrews **fans** when local heroine
> Dorothy Campbell was four up after six holes in the
> semi-finals of the 1908 British Ladies championship.
> But the match went to the 22nd hole and she lost
> (*Golfing* magazine, 1908).

In the middle of all this a man carrying a ham sandwich and a cardboard glass of stout came running over the hill, his face suffused in excitement. 'He's up to his doodlers in the pot bunker. Ye've got him cold!'

> Part of author **Patrick Campbell's** account of his epic last-hole
> victory over Billy O'Sullivan in the 1949 Amateur
> championship at Portmarnock.

In my eagerness to see Hagen come through I thought how wonderful it would be if I knew some strange magic words that would cause Walter's opponent to fluff a bunker lie or roll a short putt eight feet past the hole. And so when matters became tense and the Hague's [sic] nearest opponent was about to make a shot, the success of which would put Walter deeper in the hole, I made up words of magical gibberish in the sort of despairing, infantile hope that they might be the ones necessary, the words of power that would summon Beelzebub to joggle the fellow's elbow at the critical moment These charms I mumbled to myself, well out of earshot of the contestants. This was strictly between me and Old Nick.

> Author **Paul Gallico** recalling his days as a sports writer
> watching Walter Hagen (*Confessions of a Story-teller*).

Get that guy's autograph and I'll find out who he is later.
Spectator to young son at the 2001 Memorial Tournament.
Why do you want to stop it?
Sam Snead's crushing reply to a spectator at the 1965 Open
championship who asked him how he managed to put stop on
a three-iron shot.

I'll sign autographs for thirty minutes. I want time for myself but
I know it's something I've got to do. The easiest thing would be
to say 'get lost' but I've got to accept it or be a jerk. You can't go
halfway; you've got to go one way or the other.
Defending champion **Johnny Miller** at the 1973 US Open.

Don't bother me, kid.
Lee Trevino to a young autograph hunter at the same event.

Rubbish!
Heckler in the crowd to Tony Jacklin who missed a short putt
in the 1974 Double Diamond International.
The Open champion then won five of the next six holes.

As he scaled the bank the crowd stormed up after him and lined
the edge of the green, barely restraining themselves. He holed
his short one and the next instant there was no green visible,
only a dark seething mass in the midst of which was Bobby,
hoisted on fervent shoulders and holding his putter Calamity
Jane at arm's length over his head lest she be crushed to death.
Bernard Darwin in *The Times* on Bobby Jones's victory in the
1927 Open championship at St Andrews in front of 12,000
spectators.

Such crowds appear in their most uncontrollable form at St Andrews, North Berwick and Hoylake; and as the railways companies run cheap popular trains on the occasion of the Open championship or an important professional match, one can readily conjecture how impossible it is for the stewards of any club to regulate the vagaries of such a promiscuous army of sightseers.

Editorial on unruly fans in *Golfing* magazine, 1906.

There is now in golf an unruly element who boo, jeer and hiss at crucial moments as they deliberately try to antagonise players. We've all seen this sort of thing in other sports in Britain and it's now happening in golf. They were at me right from the start of my match with Sandy. I don't know whether they had a few bob on Lyle but they did their best to upset me and sometimes they succeeded. There must have been a bus load of them out there and they all seemed to be called Jimmy.

Howard Clark, after losing to Sandy Lyle in the 1986 World Match Play championship. Later Greg Norman complained about crowd behaviour at the same event.

More bonhomie was to follow at the 225-yard, par-three eighth, where Montgomerie's dark contemplation about a tee shot falling a good twenty yards short of the putting surface was interrupted by a shout of: 'Good shot, Monty.' The Scot pulled his tee peg from the ground and – this time getting the yardage exactly right – bounced it neatly off the top of his tormentor's head.

Martin Johnson in the *Daily Telegraph* describing how Colin Montgomerie dealt with a heckler in the 2001 US Open at Tulsa.

About fucking time.

Tiger Woods commenting on a marshal's attempt to control the crowd as he prepared to play a stroke in the 2001 US PGA championship (Will Buckley in the *Observer*).

𝕱

The other sad truth about golf spectatorship is that for today's pros it all comes down to the putting, and that the difference between a putt that drops and one that rims the cup, though teleologically enormous, is intellectually negligible.

John Updike on the US Masters (*Golf* magazine, 1980).

𝕱

Towards the end he had a gallery of fully 10,000 people, who stampeded like a herd of crazy buffaloes after each shot, and the only way one saw him play the last hole was from a bedroom window of a house overlooking the course. At least nine thousand of the ten thousand people could have seen little of the golf, though they persisted in blocking the view of those whose duty it was to record the happenings.

Guardian **reporter** on crowd behaviour during Sir Henry Cotton's 1937 Open championship triumph.

𝕱

You can forget it, Hoss. There's no way he can make it. He don't make them kind any more.

A **spectator** overheard during the 1968 US Masters as Arnold Palmer stood over a six-foot putt (Mark McCormack, *The World of Professional Golf* 1969 edition). He missed.

𝕱

Does not a caddy in truth take charge of our lives and control all our thoughts and actions while we are in his august company? He it is who comforts us in our time of sorrow, encourages us in moments of doubt, inspires us to that little added effort which, when crowned with rare success, brings a joy nothing else can offer. It is he who with majestic gravity and indisputable authority hands to us the club that he thinks most fitted to our meagre power, as though it were not a rude mattock but indeed a royal sceptre. It is he who counsels us in time of crisis, urging that we should 'run her up' or loft her' or 'take a line a wee bit to the left with a shade of slice'. Does he not enjoin us with magisterial right not to raise our head? Are we not most properly rebuked when our left knee sags or our right elbow soars; or our body is too rigid while our eye goes roaming?

An extract from a letter to *The Times* by the eminent surgeon **Sir Berkley Moynihan** in February 1929.

There weren't very many of them, just a couple or so, but this kind of behaviour is totally uncalled for. Anyway it was counter-productive because it made me mad and all the more determined.

Hale Irwin after fans cheered his errors against Tony Jacklin in the 1974 World Match Play championship.

It was a header Pele would have been proud of.

Vijay Singh after his ball hit a spectator on the head and bounced back into the fairway en route to his victory in the 1990 El Bosque Open.

I was naturally unhappy at what happened to the lady but I still feel I should have won.

Ian Woosnam after his ball hit a woman spectator and bounced out of bounds in the 1990 Cannes Open. She was taken to hospital.

Any time I went out to dinner or for a couple of drinks with friends, people would come over and tap me on the shoulder and say 'Hey, man, what's your problem?' I'd just tell them the other guys weren't letting me win. Then during a tournament I'd miss a couple of short putts and the yellin' would start again. What did they think anyway? That was I was lippin' out these putts on purpose? If I had known what the hell I was doing wrong, I sure would have corrected it.

Lee Trevino on his run of poor form before winning the 1974 New Orleans Open.

The golfer is essentially a hero-worshipper; and not only is he a hero-worshipper but he has faith in the methods of the heroes, a faith that is touching. He has at the same time a sublime confidence, although hitherto latent, in his own abilities for heroic achievement; he has not a doubt that, by adopting the methods of his heroes, he will join the demigods on the Olympian heights.

Horace Hutchinson, 1900.

I've never to this day doubted that such luck could happen but having Gene's ball jump back through a fence and be found teed up could have resulted only from the hand of the good Lord or one of those red-sweatered caddies roaming the course.

Walter Hagen voicing his suspicions about Gene Sarazen's supporters after his opponent hit out of bounds during the 1923 US PGA championship.

All Lancashire was there to watch. I bought a coach ticket just to get over there and see Von Nida slaughtered. During the entire match Cotton acted as though Von Nida wasn't there. He didn't even look at him. When Von Nida had to play a shot, Cotton was on his shooting stick, his back to Von Nida peering down the fairway.

Their only conversation came once when the golf balls were on different sides of the fairway but about the same length. Von Nida asked if it was his shot. Cotton, already seated on his shooting stick, had demonstrated that it most certainly was but acknowledged the query with a nod of his head.

When the match ended the whole gallery swarmed on to the green to get near Henry and pat his back. The first one to reach him was his wife. She kissed him. That said it for us all.

Golf writer **Jack Statter**'s account of the encounter between Henry Cotton and Norman Von Nida in a post-war PGA Match Play championship.

Considering that St Andrews is a place where Mr Hilton has not always had fair play and where on more than one occasion he has been treated in very unsportsmanlike manner by the 'gallery', it is indeed refreshing to receive from the Auld Grey Toon the following appreciation of the great Hoylake player's golf.

Comment on a reader's letter supporting Harold Hilton in *Golfing* magazine, 1907.

Miss it again.

Heckler's remark to Jack Nicklaus when he missed a short putt in the 1967 US Open and faced a difficult return.

As a spectacle, something to see, and a sensation, something to feel, I have known nothing in golf comparable to the progress of Tolley round a great golf course on a great occasion. Some golfers bring up the rear of their attendant procession, like a shepherd behind the silly sheep; some become engulfed, whether by accident or design, in the middle of the wave or maybe the bodyguard; but Tolley was nearly always and easily, to be seen like a Captain or prefect of war at the head of an obedient and marvelling legion.

But more often than could be known, the sight belied the truth and inside the seen battle was being waged another, secret and bitter, against all the forces of stretched nerve and sensitive temperament. So, in a sense, some of his highest triumphs were won twice over.

R C Robertson-Glasgow on Cyril Tolley (*The Oxford and Cambridge Golfing Society 1898-1948*).

It is statute and ordained that in na place of the Realme there be used Fute-ball, Golf or uther sik unproffitable sportis contrary to the commoun good of the Realme and defense thereof.
The third Parliament of **King James IV,** 1491.

All his subjects be very glad, Master Almoner, I thank God, to be busy with the golf for they take it for pastime.

Henry VIM's first wife **Catherine of Aragon** in a letter to Cardinal Wolsey, 1513.

The Army appeared as though out of a dream, parting the heavy mist that rose from Bay Hill's fairways. There were about 60 of them, pastel-clad soldiers, following the man whose golf game and aura had inspired minions and whose indomitable spirit had refused to bend. Until now.

American sports writer **Larry Dorman** on Arnold Palmer's failure to qualify for the 1985 US Open (*Miami Herald*).

How much money did you make last year?

Hubert Green's retort to a heckler in the crowd during the 1974 US Open.

They yelled and hollered and here I am playing like a hot dog. They sounded more like baseball fans to me. Either from the old Dodger days or perhaps the Mets.

Bob Murphy on New York fans during the 1968 Westchester Classic.

Remember Winged Foot!

A **heckler** shouting at Tom Watson during the 1975 US Open and referring to the American's collapse in the last round of the previous championship.

The reason I love golf tournaments is that the spectators are motivated by a benign and sportsmanly impulse; they simply want to see every player get the damn ball in the damn hole.

Lynne Truss for *The Times* at the 2006 Open Championship.

Short of carrying him down the fairways like an ancient Scottish king, it's hard to see what more the West Coast clan can do to help Colin Montgomerie win this Open.

Columnist **Paul Hayward**, *Daily Telegraph* 2004.

6

'You Will Always Be a Hooker, Princess': And Other Gaffes

In the world of thoughts best left unsaid, the tongue is always bitten a millisecond too late, after the damage is done. Perhaps we expect too much of sportsmen whose primary obligation is to demonstrate their supreme physical skills, not to exhibit the art of diplomacy.

However, sportsmen are heroic figures and earn both adulation and attention from an adoring public who hang on their every word. It is therefore a duty to engage brain before opening mouth. When the sequence goes wrong the results can be both embarrassing and devastating.

The repercussions following Fuzzy Zoeller's attempted jocular remarks about Tiger Woods, for example, were considered racist and cost Zoeller a multi-million-dollar contract with a coast-to-coast department store. But perhaps the greatest punishment for the gaffe-makers is that they end up looking rather sheepish and rather stupid. And they know it before the last word has left their mouths.

Hello World. There are still courses in the United States I cannot play because of the colour of my skin. Are you ready for me?

The controversial **Tiger Woods** advert for Nike in the *Wall Street Journal* announcing he was turning professional.

Tell him not to serve fried chicken next year. Got it? Or collared greens or whatever the hell they serve.

Fuzzy Zoeller's infamous remark about a popular black American diet he advised Tiger Woods not to serve to his fellow champions at the 1998 US Masters.

You may be a princess but if you hold the club like that you will always be a hooker.

Golf teacher **John Jacobs's,** unintentional *double entendre to* his pupil Princess Lilian of Belgium whose golf grip, he decided, was too strong (*Golf in a Nutshell with* Peter Dobereiner, 1995).

It would be ridiculous for me to say I'm going to win but I'll be surprised and disappointed if I don't.

Johnny Miller before the 1974 US Masters.

Done, through, washed up.

American journalist **Tom McCollister's** verdict in the *Atlanta Constitution* newspaper on Jack Nicklaus – a week before he won the 1986 US Masters championship.

When athletes in other sports lost whatever edge made them excel, they often retired to a lifetime of golf. What then is a Nicklaus to do?

> **Mike Downey** in the *Los Angeles Times* during that same US Masters. Nicklaus went on to win at the age of 46.

They're going to kick the crap out of the other guys. In the past, Europe had guys like Nick Faldo and Bernhard Langer who could really get after it. Now they've got Darren Clarke going down the fairway smoking a cigar.

> **Steve Elkington** on American prospects of victory in the 2001 Ryder Cup (which was subsequently postponed because of the terrorist attacks in New York and Washington).

I wouldn't mind if I was the next superstar. A lot of demands on your time then but I think I can put up with that.

> **Steve Strieker** after winning the 1996 Western Open.

Who is that? And how does he get a handicap low enough to play in this?

> Scottish golfer **Gordon Cosh** before being informed that he was watching the unorthodox swing of Michael Bonallack, the defending Amateur champion.

A hidden impishness suddenly surfaced. Clampett began hitting tee shots from his knees, plumb-bobbing in bunkers and putting between his legs. At the twelfth hole the USGA withdrew the invitation. Clampett was going.

> American writer **Marino Parascenzo's** account of Bobby Clampett being asked to leave the course because of his antics while playing as a marker in the 1979 US Open.

While it's not as if I did anything wrong, the rules are the rules and I have to live by them. The irony is that because of my training as an accountant I am meticulous about checking my card. In fact I'm always the last to leave the scorer's hut. Having said that, I'm glad the problem came to light when it did. I would have hated to find out in six months' time and know I hadn't won fair and square.

Padraig Harrington on being disqualified while leading the 2000 Benson and Hedges International Open because he had not signed his scorecard.

The par here at Sunningdale is 70 and anything under that will mean a score in the sixties.

BBC TV sports presenter **Steve Rider**
(*The Sporting Word,* 1994).

You couldn't really find two more completely different personalities than these two men, Tom Watson and Brian Barnes; one is the complete golf professional and the other the complete professional golfer.

BBC TV commentator **Peter Alliss**
(*Private Eye's Colemanballs,* 1984).

Well, if I can help you, I will. Don't worry about it.

Arnold Palmer's words of encouragement to playing partner Billy Casper, who trailed him by five strokes with five holes to play in the 1966 US Open and confessed he was worried about holding on to second place. Palmer collapsed dramatically and Casper won the title in a play-off.

If we can't beat Paraguay we might as well go home.
Scottish captain **Colin Montgomerie** in the 1993 Alfred Dunhill
Cup. They couldn't, so they did.

Chris, the boys are hitting the ball longer now because they are
getting more distance.
Byron Nelson in an interview with ABC TV sports announcer
Chris Schenkel (*Golf Anecdotes,* 1995).

Just the sort of chap we're looking for, agreed the selection
committee when they looked at the letter of application for the
job as golf professional. This chap Saunders was not only
extremely intelligent, well-educated with a degree in
psychology, but was also an accomplished golfer and fully-
trained in the craft of club making and repair. Get him along for
an interview. Saunders didn't get the job. The committee was
staggered to find that Saunders was a WOMAN. Good Lord!
The early tribulations of Vivien Saunders
from *The Complete Book of Golf.*

I don't believe in jinxes. You control your own ability and what
other people do is beyond your control.
Greg Norman before crashing out of the
1990 US Masters after two rounds.

What's there to be nervous about? There's nobody out here to
make me nervous. Why shouldn't an amateur win? There's just
more pros around here than us, that's all.
Lanny Wadkins, then a college golfer in the 1971 US Open
(won by Lee Trevino).

Yeah, I know what you mean. I've had a hard time too. I was up all night and then I had to do the TV.

Nick Faldo, according to Scott Hoch, after the American said he had not slept much after losing the 1989 US Masters play-off to the Englishman (*Golf Digest* magazine).

Frankly, he never really enjoyed playing in Britain where visiting, he said, was like 'camping out'.

Renton Laidlaw on Sam Snead (*Golfing Heroes,* 1987).

Gosh, it's gone quiet here, hasn't it?

Ken Brown's remark to the crowd just before missing a putt to lose the 1986 European Open.

Things have come to a pretty pass when a mere porter, who may know nothing about the game, can ask such prices. Whether he will do so much longer remains to be seen because the 'pram' or automatic caddie is cutting into his profits. He will have to come down in his demands or be counted with the dodo and the brontosaurus. In fact, if after a few years, some copy of this book remains on which eating time has not made a meal, the reader may wonder what sort of creature this caddie was and if indeed he ever really existed.

Bernard Darwin writing angrily in 1954 after being charged 30 shillings by a caddie to carry his clubs.

I've never played it.

Sandy Lyle's response in 1991 when asked what he thought of Tiger Woods.

My foot got in the way.
> **John Daly** explaining how his putter became bent in the 1991 Johnnie Walker World championship.

Don't ask me why I did it. I didn't do it on purpose. It just happened. I was probably focused too much on what I was trying to do.
> **Bernhard Langer** after mistakenly picking up his marker on a green before replacing the ball during the Holden International, thus incurring a penalty.

He had only the simplest of approaches to play but alas! up came his head and the ball, feebly struck, trickled into a bunker before his nose.
> A phrase frequently used by golf writers to denote sudden and unexpected disaster and originally coined by *Daily Telegraph* correspondent **George Greenwood.**

I would like to thank my parents – especially my father and mother.
> Part of **Greg Norman**'s winning speech at the 1983 World Match Play championship.

There you can see Vicente Fernandez. He's limping because one leg is shorter than the rest.
> Commentator **Roddy Carr** to television viewers at the Irish Open.

This is a tough mother.
   Tony Lema after his first practice round at Royal Birkdale for
                              the 1965 Open championship.

I would like to thank the press from the heart of my bottom.
   Part of **Nick Faldo**'s winning speech after his 1992 Open
                              championship triumph at Muirfield.

It's the worst three-putt in the history of golf.
   Television pundit **Johnny Miller** after South African Retief
   Goosen, needing two putts from twelve feet to win the 2001
   US Open outright, took three (but won the play-off for the title
                              the next day).

The doctor said I would be out for three or four weeks. It was my
fault but fortunately it was a clean break.
   Jose Maria Olazabal, reigning 1999 US Masters champion, on
   being forced to withdraw from the US Open with a broken
   bone in his hand after punching the hotel room wall in
                              frustration after a poor first round.

I beat everyone else except Tiger and this was my best Open
finish.
   Colin Montgomerie on being runner-up to Woods in the 2005
                              championship at St Andrews.

They cater to the foreign players and that stinks. They fail to realise it's our tour, our Masters. To most of the foreign guys, it's just the US Masters. To them it could be the British Masters or the Scandinavian Masters or the Malayan Masters. They don't care.

US professional **Billy Andrade** on the Augusta National club policy of inviting overseas players.

7

'No Sex After Wednesday':
Aspects of Life on Tour

Every occupation has its own ethos which is understood and
accepted by its members and this holds true for competitive
golfers, despite their nomadic way of life and the constantly
changing background against which they perform.
But the common experience they share – the pitfalls, the glories,
the setbacks and the miseries – also gives them a refreshing,
sometimes bleak, honesty. They can reveal their innermost
thoughts and emotions in the certain knowledge that such
confessions will be understood by their peers.

Whether it is Open champion John Daly describing the
newfound joy of winning a tournament while sober, or even an
enthusiast like Prince Andrew revealing how golf helped to stop
him getting angry with himself, the message remains the same:
confession is not only good for the soul but is illuminating for
those who are listening too.

What now, I remember thinking, thunderbolts striking me?
There I am at St Andrews, playing with the King and I knock it
out of bounds at the first. That was tough.
Ian Baker-Finch on the low point of his slump while paired with
Arnold Palmer in the 1995 Open championship.

It's hard to watch what he is going through. I know it is harder for him than us but, shit, it's still hard to watch.
US PGA champion **Wayne Grady** on the Baker-Finch decline.

I started drinking four years after I started playing golf. And I started playing golf when I was four.
Open champion **John Daly** on his alcoholism.

This is the first tournament I have won on the PGA Tour in a sober manner. I'm still shaking. Thank God it's over. Nothing could mean more than winning sober. To win again is a great feeling. But the best feeling is that I know I can win a golf tournament sober. **John Daly** on winning the 1994 Bell South Classic.

Every time he wins the Victorian Open, I get pregnant. Both our boys were born nine months after celebrating his Victorian Open victories of 1976 and 1978. I might just pack a suitcase and leave for the city if he wins tomorrow.
Robin Wolstenholme referring to husband Guy before the final round of the 1980 event. He won.

I've always had three rules for playing well on tour: no push-ups, no swimming and no sex after Wednesday.
Sam Snead (*Golf Digest Annual,* 1977).

That was the turning point. If I had held off that big strong dude at Oakmont I might have done it another five years. But he's got too much confidence.

Arnold Palmer on losing the 1962 US Open in a play-off to Jack Nicklaus which signalled the dawn of the Nicklaus Era Will Grimsley in the *International* magazine, 1987).

🏌

Everyone wants to win the Open but I have never had any great desire for it – it was never paramount in my thinking. I wouldn't have liked all the ballyhoo that goes with winning the Open but then if I had won it, there wouldn't have been any fuss because I wouldn't have allowed it.

Neil Coles talking to Robert Green (*PGA European Tour Yearbook,* 1988).

🏌

I'm so happy to be on the Tour, a little speck in the history of American sports.

Mac O'Grady on finally qualifying for the US circuit in 1982, ten years after turning professional.

🏌

While I played very well in winning the championship of America, I do not believe I should have been the logical winner. Dame Fortune treated me most kindly and enabled me to win.

Part of **Francis Ouimet's** letter to *Golf Monthly* after the amateur defeated Harry Vardon and Ted Ray in a play-off for the 1913 US Open.

🏌

She's been tickling my toes at night. It clears my head.

Sandy Lyle explaining to press during the 1988 US Masters – which he won – how his physiotherapist girlfriend Jolande (later to become his wife) cured his head cold.

I'll tell you what my life's like with Sandy – my wages must be

the best on tour, must be, and when I stay at his house at Wentworth he brings me tea in the morning. That can't be bad, can it?'
Dave Musgrove, who caddied for Sandy Lyle when he won the 1985 Open (*Sunday Times*).

Sometimes I wish there was no tomorrow.
Nick Faldo after scoring 83 in the 1999 Players championship.

I can tell you now that I'll know exactly when I want to retire; but when I reach that time I may not know.
Jack Nicklaus, 1977.

Before Muirfield I couldn't believe anyone was better than me. After, I knew I wasn't the best any longer.
Tony Jacklin to John Hopkins in the *Sunday Times* after losing the 1972 Open championship to Lee Trevino.

I am yesterday's man – or I will be tomorrow.
Walker Cup captain **Peter McEvoy** facing the prospect of relinquishing the job after leading the Great Britain and Ireland team to its first successful trophy defence in the history of the match (David Davies in the *Guardian*, 2001).

It's age. I'm not the only one to be struggling. Most players lose something. Look at Seve. He still has his putting. It's his long game that's gone.
Ian Woosnam talking to John Hopkins on the vagaries of playing form (*The Times*, 2001).

I can't swim.

> **Pat Hurst** explaining why she would not make the winner's customary plunge into the lake at the 1998 Dinah Shore tournament. She waded in instead.

I began to realise I would never be a great tournament player. I didn't have the temperament. I lacked the guts or the nerve – call it what you like. Whenever I had the chance to win I would invariably lose.

> **John Jacobs** who became one of the most respected teachers in the game as well as the architect of the multi-million pound European Tour, quoted by Dudley Doust in the *Sunday Times,* 1972.

As I get older I must be becoming a better teacher. This must be true because more of my pupils have started hitting the ball out of my sight. Or could it be my eyes are fading?

> **Harvey Penick's** *Little Red Book,* with Bud Shrake, 1993.

I remember hearing Hogan say, 'Nobody shoots 64 on this course.' Then I went round the corner of the lockers and got Lema's autograph for a friend of mine back home. I guess it's like Andy Warhol said, that everyone will be famous someday for fifteen minutes. I still have the cap I wore. I still have the bag I used and I still have the clubs. I put them in the attic and never used them again.

> Rives **McBee,** then an unknown professional, who stunned the superstars by setting the course record at the Olympic Club which swept him to a short-lived lead in the 1966 US Open (Pat Sullivan in the official US Open magazine, 1987).

I only play three matches and I hit three fairways the whole week. I clean all the rough and all the branches on the golf course. I'm sure that all the members of Oak Hill – they're not going to lose any golf balls any more.

Seve Ballesteros describing his erratic play during the 1995 Ryder Cup match.

I used to get very upset at myself and then I thought, 'What's the point of shouting and screaming at myself?' So over the years I have become a much calmer person as a result of playing golf, I suspect.

Prince Andrew, the Duke of York, in conversation with John Hopkins (*The Times,* 2001).

If golf was would-haves, could-haves and should-haves, I would have won everything by now.

Amy Alcott on losing the 1994 LPGA Classic.

I sold every silver trophy I had to raise some money for the family. I got very little for them and every penny had gone by the next day because I went to the races and lost the lot. We Irish are great gamblers when we've no money.

Joe Carr (*Golfing Heroes,* 1987).

We have a gym at home gathering dust. Just goes to show after all that hard work I've done in the gym this winter, my right arm is definitely stronger.

Darren Clarke's wry remark about his preference for a tipple after beating Tiger Woods in the 2000 Andersen Consulting Match Play championship.

The tearing up of a card is generally regarded as a rather discreditable business, showing at once vanity and pusillanimity in the tearer; and I must say that I did feel something more of a man when I have gone on to the bitter end and handed in the horrid thing.

Bernard Darwin in *Mostly Golf,* edited by Peter Ryde.

I kept getting tears in my eyes. I had to say to myself: 'Hey, you've got some golf left to play.'

Jack Nicklaus recalling the last three holes of his 1986 comeback victory in the US Masters at the age of 46.

I wanted to accept this trophy with dignity. But I guess that's just not my style.

Amy Alcott after jumping into a lake with her caddie after winning the 1991 Dinah Shore event.

When I saw who was watching me I made up my mind that the shot would be my best in the tournament. So I addressed the ball very carefully with my brassie and topped it all along the ground. I never felt so silly in my life.

Walter Hagen's reaction when he realised the Prince of Wales was watching him as he won the 1928 Open championship (R Endersby Howard in the *Daily Mail*).

My days as a winner are numbered. I don't hit it as close to the flags as I used to. I don't putt as well as I used to. Hell, when you get old you don't do anything like you used to. Age is gonna get you and I'm not going to fight it. When I can't break 74, I'm gone.

Lee Trevino after winning the 1980 Tournament Players championship.

I now realise that I should have worked harder. I would have won a lot more. I only wish I had thought of this ten years ago.
Brian Barnes in the 1980 Martini International.

I wish I could see the light at the end of the tunnel but somebody turned the light off.
Lee Westwood commenting on his slump in form during 2001
(*Golf Weekly*).

The most exquisitely satisfying act in the world of golf is that of throwing a club. The full backswing, the delayed wrist action, the flowing follow-through, followed by that unique whirring sound, reminiscent only of a passing flock of starlings, is without parallel in sport.

Henry Longhurst.

I never could hit that fairway.
Walker Cup golfer **'Laddie' Lucas** after crash-landing his Spitfire during the Battle of Britain beside the ninth fairway at Prince's Club in Kent where his father was the secretary.

I was sweating up. I could feel my legs trembling like I'd been hit by a perfect left hook and the palms of my hands were moist. I tell you something, I don't think I ever felt more nervous than I did that day before any of my fights, whether they were championship fights, or stepping into the ring with AM.
Heavyweight boxer **Henry Cooper** in conversation with Ron Wills, recalling his first appearance in a pro-am event with Australian Kel Nagle (*The Golfers*, 1982).

In my first Ryder Cup match I played with Tommy Horton against Nicklaus and Watson a couple of months after Tumberry in 1977 and we held them to 5 and 4. We weren't intimidated but we had an inkling they might be slightly better than us.

Mark James (*Golf Weekly,* 1995).

Usually I'm rubbish at this time of the year.

Peter Senior on winning the 1992 Benson and Hedges International Open.

The key to British links golf is the word frustration. You can hit the perfect shot and all of a sudden it will bounce straight right or, for no apparent reason, jump beyond the hole. If I played over here four straight weeks I'd be a raving lunatic.

Tom Watson to the *Sunday Times,* 1977.

I wouldn't have thought it would take more than 300 rounds of golf until I won again after winning in Qatar but I only have myself to blame for getting in my own way.

Andrew Coltart after capturing the 2001 Great North Open.

The fact was that Hagen, Jones and I all had weaknesses in the sand although Haig compensated by chipping from traps most of the time.

Gene Sarazen on the problems that led him to invent the sand wedge, now part of every set of clubs (the official US Open magazine, 1979).

I've had a lot of good years here. I can take a bad one.
Jack Nicklaus, six times US Masters champion, on missing the
halfway cut in the 1994 event.

Now I know what Olazabal means when he says it's pretty
nerve-wracking off the tee when you don't know whether you're
going to hit it straight, right or left.
Jesper Parnevik on winning the 1999 Greater Greensboro
Classic.

In my early career, I lived by the putter. Today I died by the
putter.
Tom Watson on squandering a winning chance in the 1994
Pebble Beach Pro-Am.

I don't really care what people think about my lifestyle. I'm a
bachelor and if it makes me a playboy to be seen with a different
girl every now and then so be it. I can't see me finishing eighteen
holes and hurrying back to the motel to practise putting on the
rug.
Raymond Floyd during the 1973 US Open.

It's a lovely feeling to have whacked Monty. He's a good friend
but he's the last man you want breathing down your neck in a
tight situation. When he gets the bit between his teeth he's hard
to beat.
Frank Nobilo on beating Colin Montgomerie for the 1996 TPC
of Europe title.

I ought to be allowed to work up to the old warrior. There should be a Private Bogey against whom I could compete. After I made a little progress I should be allowed to pit myself against Corporal Bogey and so work through the military graduations until I can meet the redoubtable Colonel with some chance of success.

H G Wells, quoted in *Golfing* magazine, 1907, on the difficulties of playing to par, then popularly known as Colonel Bogey.

I enjoy watching first class golf; but I have long ceased to study the methods of first-class male golfers. After the age of 50, it is more profitable to watch the best women golfers.

Lord Bill Deedes (*The Grown Ups Annual,* 1990).

I'm a very good golfer and I've achieved a lot more than I ever thought I would. People around me put more emphasis on winning a major than I do. You don't hear me say I'm gearing up for the Masters. I can't tell you my game is going to be right on the second week of April every year.

Mark O'Meara in 1998 before winning the US Masters.

My brother and I have a pawnbroking business back home. I suppose I could have pawned my clubs. Trouble is, the way I'd been playing they wouldn't have fetched much.

Australian professional **Peter Senior** on winning the 1990 European Open.

When you are on your own with no one to talk to and you can't get home, it's terrible. The worst week was the Masters.

Ian Woosnam in 1988 on life on the US Tour.

The faraway bull in the field looks very small. But when it comes close you think 'My God'.

Jose Maria Olazabaf after agreeing to speak at the golf writers' annual dinner in St Andrews, 2000.

This speech is a bit like my tee shot. I don't know where it's going.

Jose Maria Olazabal on accepting an award at the PGA European Tour annual dinner.

When you're young, you think it's inevitable that you're going to win sooner or later but when you're old the inevitable is over with.

Lee Trevino after winning the US PGA championship at the age of 44.

I must be in danger of believing all the publicity about how good I am supposed to be and winning should be easy for me.

Peter Oosterhuis at the 1973 Penfold-Bournemouth tournament.

I never see them at family reunions.

US Amateur champion **Chris Patton** when asked by a reporter whether he was related to General George Patton or Walker Cup hero Billy Joe Patton.

When I get on a hole I don't like I just pretend it is a hole I do like and all my worries disappear.

British champion **Marley Spearman** on her tactical approach to competitive golf (*World Sports* magazine, 1962).

My goal has always been to win here and at times I thought I played well enough to win but someone always seemed to sneak past me.

Ken Brown after winning the 1987 Southern Open.

A couple of years ago I was always thinking I had to birdie to make money. It began to get better for me once I learned to dis-associate the money. Thinking about money will consume you.

US Open champion **Lee Janzen** after winning the 1992 Northern Telecom Open.

I said to myself, 'This is getting silly. Don't stop'.

Christy O'Connor Junior after scoring seven successive birdies in a course record 64 during the 1985 Open championship at Royal St George's.

I have a condition where my heart races. It does not seem to have anything to do with excitement. It doesn't worry me and usually stops when I bend down to mark my ball on the green.

David Howell after winning the 1998 PGA championship in Australia.

I reserved my worst round of the year for today.

Colin Montgomerie reflecting on a 76 in the 1992 Open championship.

More thinking. More smart play. More headache.

Se Ri Pak from South Korea explaining her tactics in winning the 1998 US Women's Open.

I think I overestimated my abilities and underestimated my intestinal fortitude.

American professional **Jim Colbert** on the reasons he had not won until the 1974 American Golf Classic.

Every time her ball is seen heading for a gorse bush our heartfelt prayers go with it, and though attainment will swiftly prove disenchanting, it is a great moment when at last she waves us on and we stampede courteously past. It is at that precise moment that we are most likely to hit our own ball into a gorse bush, for it is a law of nature that everybody plays a hole badly when going through. To be there and then repassed is one of the bitterest humiliations golf can bring.

Bernard Darwin on being held up by a woman golfer (*Country Life* magazine).

That's more money than my bank manager has ever seen in my account.

Wayne Grady, then a 21-year-old unknown, scoring his first tournament win in the 1978 Westlake Classic.

I think Bobby Jones held up his hand from somewhere and said: 'That's enough, boy.'

Nick Price after failing to set a new course record for Augusta National during the 1986 US Masters.

It's not the arrow. It's the Indian who's to blame.

Jose Maria Olazabal complaining about his putting in the 1989 French Open.

Of course I surprised myself and everybody in the field too. It surprised my wife too.

Jack Nicklaus after scoring 63 in the 1991 Doral Open.

When you don't play golf at all and you're afraid you're going to miss the ball, it's terrible. These hands are 97 years old. All the meat has gone. They're all skin and bones.

Gene Sarazen at the 1999 US Masters on his fears about hitting the traditional opening shot. He died two months later (Mark McCormack, *The World of Professional Golf,* 2000 edition).

Whenever the major championships come along I sit down while everybody else stands up.

Hubert Green to Michael Williams of the *Daily Telegraph* before winning the 1977 US Open.

It seems the harder I try, the worse I get.

Betsy King, 1994.

I looked down the list of competitors there and I was the only person I'd never heard of.

British Amateur champion **Peter McEvoy** after competing in the 1978 World Series.

That may not be the most stupid shot I've ever hit, but it's in the top two.

Jeff Sluman after hooking his ball into trees during the 1992 World Match Play championship.

I felt much better after I did that. I know it isn't nice for the fans to see but you just have to release your frustrations.

Payne Stewart after slamming his wedge into the ground because of a bad shot in the 1990 US PGA championship.

I had it for eighteen months. Signing 3,000 autographs a day. I was starting to resent people wanting things from me rather than feeling honoured by it.

Nick Price after winning the 1994 Open championship and US PGA titles (Mark McCormack, *The World of Professional Golf,* 1995 edition).

I wanted the crock of gold so my conscience made me write down 'professional'. But I don't charge if I give a lesson.

Milwaukee postal worker **Walter Danecki** who scored 105 and 113 in the qualifying rounds of the 1965 Open championship, explaining how he fooled authorities with his entry form.

Just the thought of finally coming in and winning made me want to sit down and bawl.

Judy Clark on scoring her first tournament victory in the 1985 Boston Five Classic.

I'm trying to get my name on trophies. By the time I'm dead, all the money will be gone but the trophies will still be there.

Fuzzy Zoeller on finishing runner-up five times in 1994.

I've been playing two tournaments each week, one against Woosie and one against everyone else.

Colin Montgomerie on his battle with Ian Woosnam to top the 1996 Order of Merit table.

All my players are seasoned campaigners. They have won tournaments and probably millions of dollars. But they feel like rookies when it comes to the Ryder Cup – even those who have played before.

US captain **Raymond Floyd** at the 1989 match (Ryder Cup magazine).

I was choking from the first tee. It must have looked as though I couldn't get back to the barn quick enough, but I got there just in time. It's not my idea of championship golf to finish double-bogey, bogey, but it's two shots better than the next guy. That's all that counts.

Hale Irwin on winning the 1979 US Open.

I want to apologise to Arnold for having to watch me go through the jitters out there on the putting greens. I'm sorry. I really am.

Ben Hogan after being paired with Arnold Palmer in the 1966 US Masters.

Instead of not enough insulin, my body makes too much. So now I watch what I eat and I carry fruit on the course. Now, if I have a bad day, I can say I ran out of apples.

American professional **Dan Sikes**, 1973.

I had joy and sorrow today. Joy because I won an important tournament. And sorrow because I've beaten my friend and idol.
Eduardo Romero after beating Seve Ballesteros in a play-off for the 1991 Spanish Open.

The rough is so tough on me. Thank God for fairways.
Fred Funk at the 1992 US PGA championship.

Now that really chapped me off. My wife was madder than me. She said: 'Honey, I recognise you every time I see you and the children recognise you half the time.'
Lou Graham, the surprise 1975 US Open champion, commenting on a newspaper report that he was difficult to recognise.

I didn't think I should get away with it among so many fine young players.
Henry Cotton on winning the Open championship in 1948 at the age of 41.

It looks like the only way I'll ever beat this guy is if he's taken ill.
Colin Montgomerie after losing the 1990 Lancome Trophy to Jose Maria Olazabal, who in their early days had also beaten him for the British and European amateur championships.

I can never forget my sadness. It's just that some days you feel better than others. I had to make a choice and I don't really think it was difficult for me to come back. I mean this is a golf course and golf is what I do. So here I am ploughing on. Lytham is a sentimental journey for me and will always be my course. Probably by the end of it, I'll be sorry I entered. But I hope not.

Tony Jacklin, a few weeks after his first wife died suddenly in 1988, talking of his return to Royal Lytham and St Annes where he won the 1969 Open title.

When I got four or five ahead I thought, 'Boy, you'd better not stuff up now or you'll really cop it.'

Ian Baker-Finch on his runaway 1991 Open championship win.

I'm applying myself, working hard and enjoy golf more. I never liked playing before. And when you don't enjoy your job it's difficult to do well.

Raymond Floyd, 1975.

On Tour you are an individual. You play only for yourself and if you lose it doesn't bother anybody else. Now, all of a sudden, you are representing the United States of America. When I stand out there and they raise the flag and play the national anthem, I get goose bumps.

Raymond Floyd on the pressures of Ryder Cup team golf (Ryder Cup magazine, 1995).

In Switzerland I was reading one of my own instruction books and realised I was too open at address. How easy it is to forget the fundamentals of this game.

Seve **Ballesteros** to the press at the 1989 European Masters.

Must have been when I went from nappies to shorts.
>> **Nick Faldo** during the 1990 US PGA championship when
>> asked the last time he had scored 80.

I played one fellow on one leg and shot 38 for nine holes. I played another on my knees and shot 41. And I played one guy in 95 degree heat wearing a rain suit, I guess he thought it would take too much out of me but I beat him by five holes.
>> **Lee Elder** on his early days as a golf gambler.

Ever since 1986 when I hit my second shot into the water at the fifteenth at Augusta, my confidence has been a little bit down. From where I was I would have been a winner eight times out of ten. Then the next year I missed a short putt in the play-off and I started to wonder if my time was, well, you know.
>> **Seve Ballesteros** to David Davies (*Guardian*) after
>> winning the 1988 Open Championship.

I wore slacks on the practice tee Tuesday and everybody looked at the name on my bag to see who I was.
>> **Payne Stewart** at the 1985 US Masters underlining how
>> much his colourful plus-twos had become his trademark.

We've been friends and rivals since junior golf days but before today I was always the one doing the congratulating.
>> **Lori Garbacz** on defeating Nancy Lopez in the
>> 1989 Tucson Open.

So he waited outside with the clubs under the window of our fourth-floor room and I went upstairs and packed our meagre belongings. Then I leaned out the window and dropped them to Charley. Then I nonchalantly walked downstairs and past the old lady behind the counter.

Jimmy Demaret, later to become US Open and
Masters champion, on the early hardships when he and
his caddie slipped out of a hotel because they could
not afford to pay the bill. Two years later he sent
them a cheque for the outstanding amount
(*My Partner Ben Hogan*).

My best golf year in 1973 was the worst with my wife and family. I said, to hell with that; if that's what it takes to be the greatest golfer in the world, I don't want it.

Tom Weiskopf (Liz Kahn, *The Price of Success*).

I can't believe it. I don't know when it will hit me. Maybe I'll find a place and go and cry.

Mike Hulbert on his first tournament win in 1986.

I guess I was just trying too hard to win. Then I'd do something wrong, make a couple of bogeys, knock myself out of it and give up. I've seen other guys out here that win. They seem to just let it happen. That's what I'm gonna try.

Mac McLendon before winning the 1972
Southern Open.

Jones said blandly, 'I don't see any necessity for trees on a golf course.' He chuckled as we looked down at the rows of mammoth pines that define the cathedral aisle of the tenth. 'I

never had these in mind,' he said, 'they just happened.'
Alistair Cooke on Bobby Jones at Augusta (*Golf* magazine, 1980).

One of my attributes is that when I get ahead, I seldom fold. The trouble is I don't get in the lead often enough.
Dave Stockton after winning the 1976 US PGA championship.

I'm not gonna sit here and lie and say I went to bed last night thinking I could shoot 65 and get back in the tournament. What I was thinking about last night was going home. I made a plane reservation for 2.50 this afternoon that I'm very pleased to have to cancel.
Curtis Strange who followed his opening 80 with a second-round 65 in the 1985 US Masters.

I wasn't thinking. My mind was doing things it shouldn't have been. It should've been strictly on that putt, nothing else. Then it was the biggest surprise in the world when it didn't go in. I'd been saying to myself, This is what it all comes down to – all the hardship and heartache – all comes to this moment.' Then it crashed down on me.
Scott Hoch on missing a putt to lose the 1989 US Masters play-off.

I showed up but my golf game didn't.
Beth Daniel on losing the 1989 Corning Classic.

I'm past the stage of saying this is a learning experience. When the touch had to be there I didn't have it.

Fred Couples on finishing runner-up in the 1990 US PGA championship.

I'm putting so good, I feel like a time bomb about to go off.

Johnny Miller after winning the first three US events of the 1974 season.

It was my turn to run into a buzz-saw.

Patty Sheehan on losing the 1990 du Maurier Classic to newcomer Cathy Johnson.

Golf is the only thing I know, but I can't hit the ball a hundred yards. I can't break 90. I would like to teach but I don't know anything about the game any more.

Jack Fleck, who beat Ben Hogan in a play-off for the 1955 US Open, on making an unsuccessful comeback in the 1977 event.

Drinking on planes is normal really. There are normally about five or six of them who sit together. Wayne's been doing it for fifteen years and only now someone has complained.

Australian Open champion Wayne Riley's wife **Louise** after he had been accused of unseemly behaviour on a flight.

I don't go much for those in-depth interviews that want to know the colour of your curtains and how many times you make love to your wife.

Tom Watson to the *Daily Mail,* 1982.

I'm no good at defending titles. I missed the cut here, at the Players championship and nearly missed at last year's British Open. I just played rubbish golf. The only good job I've done this week is make a perfect fool of myself.

Sandy Lyle after missing the halfway cut in his 1989 defence of the US Masters.

At least I'm still alive.

Colin Montgomerie's reputed remark to a colleague after being officially ticked off for his behaviour (*Golf Digest* magazine, 1994).

That 45 is the highest nine holes I've ever played. I don't even remember shooting that much when I was eight years old.

Lee Trevino during the 1973 Byron Nelson Classic.

When you stand on that first tee for your country, suddenly you worry whether you'll get a good drive away. You hope you don't top it.

Billy Casper, US Open and Masters champion, on the personal pressure of Ryder Cup golf.

Mars is in conjunction with my natal moon.
> **John Schlee** explaining why he scored 67 in the 1973 US Open third round at Oakmont.

I feel like a villain. They don't come any finer than Gene Littler. I almost wished that someone else was out there. He's someone I like and look up to. At this point in his career it would have meant an awful lot to him.
> **Lanny Wadkins** on beating Gene Littler in a play-off for the 1977 US PGA championship after Littler had recovered from cancer.

There's no way known that I'll ever be a tournament player again. That's hard enough with two arms.
> **Jack Newton** following the freak aeroplane accident in which he lost his right arm and eye.

I was 149th in the money winnings last year and 179th this year. That's plummeting.
> **Morris Hatalsky** before winning the 1990 Bank of Boston Classic.

I am staggered and bewildered. This sort of thing has never happened to me before.
> Australian newcomer **John Davis** on winning the 1974 Victorian Open.

I hate getting old and wrinkled and not having a nice body but the good thing about not being the glamour girl any more is that I don't have to worry about that part of my life.

Former US Open Women's champion **Jan Stephenson** (Liz Kahn, *The History of the Ladies Professional Golf Association*).

🏌

It is like if I smash you very hard in the face four times a day, you do not like it very much. But if I smash you only once in the day, you say 'Shit, this feels good'. The pain I now have is heaven compared to what it was.

Jose Maria Olazabal explaining to *Guardian* writer David Davies how he copes with pain.

🏌

Could anyone make me believe that six days of just golf, 36 holes a day, would have stripped eighteen pounds off me, as that six days at Oakmont did in 1919?

Bobby Jones and O B Keeler (*Down the Fairway*).

🏌

No matter how hard the press beats me up, I deserve it. They won't be any harder on me than I am on myself.

US Open champion **Curtis Strange** after losing the last two holes of a crucial Ryder Cup singles in 1995 to Nick Faldo.

🏌

Sport is something I've grown up with. I've lived through my dad's tantrums off the course when he's had a terrible round. That has given me an insight when I'm interviewing players.

Television sports presenter **Kirsty Gallacher,** daughter of Ryder Cup skipper Bernard, in *Night and Day* magazine.

🏌

The more I hit it, the hotter I got. I moved it three feet. I just lost my cool.

> **Lee Trevino** on how he took an eight in the 1985 Open championship at Royal St George's, Kent.

The fatal night, with my mind still made up, called clearly for a bottle of this powerful nectar with which to slide peacefully away and I attacked it with maudlin vigour, but alas, or rather hooray, I must have exceeded the stated dose and the Glenmorangie got the better of me before I got round to taking the pills.

> **Henry Longhurst,** in the *Sunday Times,* on his failed suicide attempt after being diagnosed with a tumour.

There was an emptiness after I won the Open. I'd worked so hard that I couldn't imagine why I didn't feel more over-whelmed. Later I realised it is the doing that is the achievement, not the winning. The fun of doing spurs you on.

> **Carol Mann** to author Liz Kahn after capturing the 1965 US Women's Open.

For the past month I have not been able to sleep and my golf has gone to pot. Just thinking about the Ryder Cup team has cost me a lot of money because I've been playing a different kind of golf. The way I like to play this game is to visualise the ideal shot and then give it a rip. If it comes off, then it's just beautiful. But for weeks I've been poking the ball around, trying to keep out of trouble and that's not my style. The silly part of it is that I cannot force myself to play the way I want to.

> **Christy O'Connor Junior** on the pressures of trying to qualify for the 1975 Ryder Cup squad.

When am I going to fall apart?

> **Noel Henke's** constant question to himself during the final round of the 1990 BC Open. He didn't. And won by three strokes.

ϯ

That has eliminated some hurt for not winning the British Open. I've proved to myself I'm not a choker.

> **Ian Baker-Finch** after winning the 1984 New South Wales Open.

ϯ

Everyone misses them, not just me.

> **Seve Ballesteros** explaining why he liked the narrow Royal Lytham and St Annes fairways where he won the 1979 and 1988 Open championships.

ϯ

A typical day. Six to eight brandies before going out to hit a few balls on the range. I'd then come back into the bar and have ten to twelve pints before going home. In the evening I'd open one of those three-litre boxes of wine and that would be gone by the time I went to bed. Mind you, the wife would probably have had the last glass of it.

> **Brian Barnes** on his daily routine before he gave up alcohol.

ϯ

It took a gambling story to get me on the front page of the *Daily Telegraph* when they had earlier hardly acknowledged the fact that I had won my second major of the year.

> **Laura Davies** after reports of her £500,000 gambling losses over a ten-year period.

ϯ

Back in South Africa I used to think I was the greatest. It took me some time to accept the fact that, in America, i am just a terribly tiny fish in a very large pond.

Professional **Sally Little** (Mark McCormack, *The World of Professional Golf,* 1977 edition).

I remained heart-broken for the rest of the day. To see your enemy top into a hazard at the eighteenth and then to fluff it in after him . . . well, well, I will say no more.

Bernard Darwin on losing a crucial match in the 1947 Halford Hewitt event.

What I believe I said to you was that I have probably marked my ball incorrectly, that I cannot deny ever having replaced the ball in something like the spot I originally marked it. I also said it was not an intentional act.

American professional **Jane Blalock** to LPGA officials in 1972, (Liz Kahn, *The History of the Ladies Professional Golf Association*).

I've got all the talent in the world but I'm not using it. The next ten years are my prime years. I'm going to work.

Tom Weiskopf before winning the 1973 Open championship.

I know if I was in the gallery I would have been cheering someone else. I would have been a little tired of seeing the same guy win again.

Johnny Miller in 1976 after capturing the Tucson Open for the third successive year.

I didn't bring a coat or anything. I'm not into dinners, man. You can't get a coat and tie in this fat boy.

> **John Daly** on his reasons for missing the former Open Champions' dinner at St Andrews 2005.

I feel like I'm running and everybody is chasing me. How fast can I run? Sooner or later I'm going to get tired and the guys are going to catch me.

> **Vijay Singh** on topping the World Rankings in 2005.

He's not here anymore. It's not like I can pick up the phone and say 'Pops, what do you think about my putting stroke?' Those days aren't here anymore.

> **Tiger Woods** at the 2006 Open Championship on the death of his father Earl.

As long as they don't test for wine, I think I'm all right.

> American professional **Cristie Kerr** on being told drug testing would be introduced on the US Women's Tour in 2008.

8

'I'm Not God You Know': Explanations of Failure

There is always an obvious explanation for failure in golf – provided no blame is attached to the one who has failed. That, after all, would be too much to bear: acceptance of one's own fallibility leads only to more self-doubt on future occasions.

Thus Ted Ray could blame his putts that fell short of the hole in the afternoon on the fact that the grass on the greens had grown somewhat since he had played them in the morning. O B Keeler, the chronicler of Bobby Jones, had harsh words for nearby robins after he took four putts. And Greg Norman swears he was distracted by a worm which popped its head out of the ground as he was about to play.

All plausible causes for poor performance, of course, but also evidence of a self-serving logic that provides the player with credible reasons why the simplest things sometimes go awry, even when there is no obvious obstacle to success in the way.

I was short on putts in the afternoon. This was due, I believe, to the fact that the grass on the greens grew somewhat since the play in the morning. The longer grass held back my ball so that I was short a foot or more on a simple eight-foot putt.

British captain **Ted Ray** explaining his defeat at the first Ryder Cup on American soil in 1927.

I was trying to discover what liberties I could take with the rough.

Jack Nicklaus explaining why his tee shots kept missing fairways during a practice round for the 1979 Open championship at Royal Lytham and St Annes.

I know the gallery want me to lose. They are delighted when I'm beaten. For this reason I don't like playing in South African tournaments.

Gary Player to *Golf International* magazine, 1972.

We had one player drop out, one transferred and one ran off with Nick Faldo.

Coach **Rick La Rose** explaining the depleted ranks of the Arizona University women's golf team.

A big worm popped its head out of the ground beside the ball and I was so surprised I took my eye off the ball.

Greg Norman after topping his tee shot in the 1982 European Open.

I can't shoot 66 every time. I'm not God you know.
    Seve Ballesteros after taking a final-round 75 to win the 1991
                                                    British Masters.

It simply seems to require more skill than I have at the moment.
    Ben Hogan explaining why his tee shots persistently failed to
    stay on the short twelfth green at Augusta during the US
                                                            Masters.

Why did you pick today to set a course record? What the hell do
you think you are doing, man? I'm tired.
    Sam Snead to Tommy Aaron who scored a last round 64 to
    force, then win, a play-off in the 1969 Canadian Open.

Holy cow, how can a man putt with robins stomping around.
    O B Keeler to Ed Danforth after taking four putts at the
    East Lake club in Atlanta (Sidney L Mathew, *Life and
                                        Times of Bobby Jones*).

You under-clubbed me. Do that again and I fire you. Get out.
    Seve Ballesteros to his caddie during the 1986 US Open.

My mind was always keen to play but unfortunately my body
was saying 'no' today.
    Colin Montgomerie on losing to Brad Faxon in the
    1997 World Match Play championship.

I figured the cameras were still rolling and my father was watching at home so I figured I had better not say anything. But I wanted to.

Scott Hoch on being distracted by a television technician while playing a crucial tee shot at Augusta National's sixteenth hole in the 1989 US Masters. The ball landed in a pond.

Boys are the golfer's perfect alibi. They snivel, hiccup, fidget, wander off looking for larks' nests, rattle the clubs or, as at one critical moment at Deal, drop the flagstick with a resounding thump. You can always blame that 'wretched boy'. And how gratifying once again to be shouting: 'Stand still there!' in one's best barrack-square voice and not be answered back.

Henry Longhurst on the boy caddies at Deal (Peter Ryde, *The Halford Hewitt*).

They've won hundreds of tournaments and millions of dollars. Possibly they are helping each other out too much. They got where they are on their own.

US Ryder Cup skipper **Raymond Floyd's** explanation why his team performed poorly in the fourball series of the 1989 match.

Fortunately I haven't been pushed into the 'best player never to win a major' category yet. I suppose it's because I'm only 26 years old and I suppose it's because I haven't come close to winning one yet.

Lee Westwood at the 1999 US PGA championship.

The thing about this game is that when you think you have it, it jumps up and bites you. But if you keep giving me a chance one of these days I'll learn how to finish it off. I just keep knocking. Maybe I'm going to ring the doorbell next time.

> **Payne Stewart** after losing the 1985 Byron Nelson
> Classic with a six on the last hole.

It's my grandmother.

> **Seve Ballesteros's** quip to Jeff Sluman after his ball bounced
> back on to the fairway after hitting a leader board being held
> by an elderly woman in the 1992 World Match Play
> championship.

I hit a perfect tee shot and then I went to the John. I never got my mind back on what I was doing.

> **Jack Nicklaus** explaining how he took a triple bogey
> seven in the 1978 US Open after paying a quick visit to a
> portable toilet (*Dunhill Golf Yearbook,* 1979).

The Far Eastern countries have improved dramatically over the last ten years. They can compete as well as anyone and proved that today.

> Scottish skipper **Colin Montgomerie** after his team's surprise
> defeat by China in the 1998 Alfred Dunhill Cup.

There was no point in carrying on with the golf I was producing. It wasn't fair to my partner or the spectators who had come to watch.

> Defending champion **Michael King** explaining why he
> walked out of the 1980 Tournament Players championship
> when he was thirteen over par.

A balaclava, a Japanese hand-warmer that went out, sheepskin gloves, umbrella, many layers of clothing and a minute boy caddie, all aids to keeping warm and dry, just made the first holes tolerable. My partner's caddie had already turned back, ostensibly to change his shoes, but understandably had not shown up again. At least my boy came clean. A piping voiced inquired: 'Can I go home, sir? I'm very cold.' I hadn't the heart to refuse but it meant one of my hands was now exposed on the metal trolley handle.

England cricketer **Ted Dexter** describing in the *Observer* the arctic conditions in which the 1966 Halford Hewitt tournament for public schools was played.

As we all sat waiting for warmth to re-penetrate we had just one consolation. Our golfing experience had been enriched in a way that Nicklaus would never know. Of course, he never went to a public school.

Ted Dexter's postscript to that 1966 match, again in the *Observer.*

I felt like punching that caddie on the nose. But I just told him, 'Look, don't you ever say anything to me when I'm ready to swing.'

J C Snead after hitting a poor tee shot that cost him a bogey six when his caddie offered him some last-minute advice about wind direction in the 1978 US Open.

I'm a mental basket case. I have the mind of a twelve-year-old, a total waste of space. Disgusting, absolutely disgusting. It's disheartening. I've got the yips on my putts and the yips on my chips. I was just trying to hit the thing at the pin, an eight iron, for crying out loud, from the middle of the fairway and I hit a 125-yard duck hook.

Mark Calcavecchia after a last-hole disaster in the 1991 Southwestern Bell Colonial event.

I had a letter from this bloke in Scotland the other day. 'Don't worry,' he wrote, 'it's not your fault. It's the ball's.' He went on for ten pages explaining that no two golf balls had the same centre of gravity and that's why my putts veer away.

Tony Jacklin detailing his putting problems to *Sunday Times* writer Dudley Doust.

What do you think about throwing some grass up, seeing it blow in one direction, then suddenly change direction before it hits the ground?

Arnold Palmer on his problems of club selection during the 1971 US Masters.

I thought with a start like that I might as well give it both barrels. I was thinking about shooting 60. Wait a minute, I didn't play well.

Hubert Green, who was five under par after the first five holes in the 1973 Greater Hartford Open and eventually scored 63.

You can describe my round as having moments of ecstasy and stark raving terror. I looked like I knew what I was doing at times and at other times I looked like a twenty handicap player.

Arnold Palmer 1968 US PGA championship.

It caught me right on the downswing and it was very disappointing. It makes me angry but there's no point in complaining.

Australian **Craig Parry** explaining how a camera flash from a spectator put him off his bunker shot in the 1998 Ford Open championship.

Everything was bad. And I feel sorry for all the people who were expecting to come and see me play. I gave everything in the Masters and I gave everything I had left here.
Seve Ballesteros after missing the halfway cut in the 1988 Cannes Open.

It seems as though every time I've shot a good round and had a chance to win, someone beats me.
Jack Nicklaus on losing the 1984 Doral-Eastern Open to Tom Kite.

I felt tired and when I feel tired I neither walk in the same way nor see the lines when I am on the greens. I have to rely on the eyes of my caddie and that is not the same thing at all.
Bernhard Langer at the 1985 World Match Play
championship.

I allowed myself to be led astray by Ian Woosnam. Woosie is a great lad and very helpful with his golf tips though I don't remember too much of the putting lesson he gave me at 3.30 a.m. He'd stopped all this wine by the glass nonsense. We upgraded to wine by the bottle, a trick he had learned from Ian Botham.
England cricketer **Darren Gough,** from his autobiography *Dazzler,* on being drunk when he played against South Africa in a Test match.

I have been hurt this year, playing as badly as I have. That's the awful thing about it, being champion and playing poorly. I know what it's all about, but I haven't been able to work on my game as I should. I've been over-committed and sidetracked by business and social demands and everything else that goes with being a champion.

Tony Jacklin before the 1971 defence of his US Open title.

I think that shot was the first time I let my ego get the better of me. My style of play is to win and win as soon as I can. I wanted to try and hit a high shot but I hit the ball too high and too hard. I didn't get enough weight transferred in my swing and I left the clubface open.

Greg Norman on why his approach missed the last green and cost him a chance of the 1986 US Masters.

I'm searching for the perfect swing. I'm searching for something that's not there. I tried twenty different things today and nobody else out there would have done that. This game is too tough. If I'd have known, I'd have taken up tennis or something. I have a chance. But if you're a betting guy don't bet on me.

Johnny Miller during the 1978 US PGA Championship.

I'm the kind of player who makes eye contact with fans during a round and with this hat I don't get distracted. It helps me with my concentration.

Gary Hallberg explaining to the press why he wore a stetson in the 1984 US PGA championship.

Before I won the Open, Christine and I had no problems at all but the publicity after that was colossal. Everybody wanted a bit of me.

Sandy Lyle on the failure of his first marriage.

I am a golf professional and didn't want to damage my hands.
South African **Bobby Locke's** explanation to the court in 1978 on why he fired his gun in a dispute with a painter and decorator.

I was going to go for broke. That's how I ended up – broke.
John Mahaffey after taking too many risks and failing to win the 1984 Houston Open.

I played my game, sir. I played my game.
J H Taylor on losing heavily in a challenge match to Harry Vardon.

Today was moving day. Move into contention or move out. I stayed where I was.
Payne Stewart in the 1987 Open championship.

About the time you think you have something going, you get a reason to be humble. I got a lot of humility out there today.
Billy Casper after taking 40 strokes for nine holes to lose the 1969 US Masters.

I had to find out if I misread it or mis-hit it. I read it right. When the pressure was on I just didn't hit it straight.
Hubert Green after retrying a last green putt that cost him the chance to force a play-off for the 1978 US Masters.

We just didn't get it done. I can't tell you how many times we were inside of them, laying one shot less, and walked off the green with a half. If they're going to make a twenty-footer and we're going to miss an eight-footer, what can you do?

US skipper **Tom Kite** on the failure of his Ryder Cup stars, Tiger Woods, Davis Love III, Justin Leonard and others in the 1997 match.

I felt that if I holed a putt, it would have been an accident.

Tony Jacklin after putting lapses cost him the 1968 Dunlop Masters.

I wasn't in a really good frame of mind when the Masters came around. I was really messed up.

Tom Weiskopf in 1979 after his home burned down and he was diagnosed with a stomach ulcer.

Sometimes I have got so wrapped up in what I am doing that I don't realise how slow I have been. I would have preferred not to have been slow. But maybe it just took me longer to do something.

Jack Nicklaus on claims that he was a major slow-play offender.

My most common mistake at St Andrews is turning up.

Mark James.

The trip took us longer than usual because of the traffic. It took about twenty minutes. I arrived three or four minutes late. I was

very hot when I heard the decision and that's the reason I left quickly. I didn't want to say anything there I would be sorry for.
Seve Ballesteros after being disqualified from the 1980 US Open for turning up late on the tee.

It was like a game of 'gotchas'. I stood over the ball and thought: 'Who's going to grab me next?' I can't play that way. I'm not looking forward to going out tomorrow.
Gary Player after anti-apartheid demonstrators threatened him during the 1969 US PGA championship in Dayton, Ohio.

The hell with demonstrators. This big cop bothered me. He looks at one hole and says he doesn't like the look of the crowd on the left of the green. Could I knock the ball over to the right-hand side?
Jack Nicklaus during the same episode.

After a good deal of deliberation he putted straight on the hole but the ball remained some inches short. Everyone was surprised that he did not give the putt a chance but it afterwards transpired he was under the impression that he had two to tie and, in consequence, was not taking any unnecessary risks.
Eyewitness account of **James Braid** playing the last hole of the 1904 Open championship; he lost by a stroke.

I scored well enough to win but J D ran the tables on the greens. He made a hundred and fifty feet of putts. But I can't complain. I did the same thing the first three days.
Tom Watson on losing the 1978 US PGA championship to John Mahaffey.

My cold is much worse. I didn't sleep at all last night. I feel weak and I can't see properly.

Seve Bailesteros during the 1979 European Open.

I came very, very close to pulling out. You'll never know how bad I felt. I could hardly breathe.

Seve Bailesteros after the 1983 European Open.

If you take out the 8 I had on the seventeenth then I'm right back in this tournament.

Graeme McDowell at the 2006 Open Championship in St Andrews.

It's not that I wasn't stroking the ball well. It was just not going in.

Vijay Singh on putting problems at the 2005 Open Championship

9

'A Good Obituary Doesn't Excite Me': Personal Judgements

There is never any hesitancy on the part of players, particularly senior and established ones, in giving their verdict on the qualities of their rivals. It is part of the camaraderie that exists between them and extends at times even to the offer of help and advice when play has gone awry and a fresh eye is needed to sort out the problem.

Moreover, they display a generous enthusiasm which celebrates the achievements of others, even at the cost of personal success. Jack Nicklaus, the acknowledged King of Augusta with six US Masters titles, steps aside gracefully full of praise for the new hero, Tiger Woods. Eric Brown recognises the abrasive confidence that he knows will make Tony Jacklin a champion. There is a clear-eyed judgement in both cases which not only identifies a special talent but values it.

This perception runs through all aspects of the sport and its characters. American writer Dan Jenkins referred to the nobility Arnold Palmer brought to losing and the unmixed joy he brought to trying. Ben Hogan perceived that everybody studied greens before they putted but only Bobby Locke knew what he was looking for! Such observations help to define the nature of the game and the character of those who play it.

Golf is the most rugged, individualist sport there is. Of all athletes, golfers may most properly be able to have said 'I did it my way'. There are no team-mates to cover mistakes, no referees to monitor the games. There is a pact between sport and man.

American columnist **Jim Murray** (Ryder Cup magazine, 1987).

Some men who played golf after Jones hit the ball farther, some maybe straighten Certainly, many had scored lower. A lot of them won way more tournaments and one of them, Jack Nicklaus, more championships. But nobody ever played golf like Bobby Jones. And nobody ever would.

Charles Price (*Bobby Jones and the Masters*).

It's a shame Bob Jones isn't here. He could have saved the words he used for me in 1963 for this young man because he is certainly playing a game with which we're not familiar.

Jack Nicklaus on the victorious Tiger Woods at the 1997 US Masters.

I thought when I met him for the first time he was a big-headed so-and-so. For a long time after that I had no reason to change my opinion. He has all the shots. Guts. Dedication. And he's cocky. He has a chance of winning any tournament he plays in this year, including the Open championship.

Eric Brown commenting on Tony Jacklin in *Golf Monthly*, 1967. Two years later Jacklin was Open champion.

To hold that a golf player was negligent merely because the ball did not travel in a straight line, as intended by him, would be imposing upon him a greater duty of care than the creator endowed him with facilities to carry out.

Verdict by the Missouri Court of Appeal, 1937.

He makes more bad shots in a single season than Harry Vardon did during the whole period, 1890-1914, in the course of which he won six Open championships. But he beats more immaculate golfers because 'three of those and one of them' counts four and he knows it.
  A C Croome on Walter Hagen in *American Golfer* magazine, 1926.

Did you ever see a worse shot?
  Bobby Jones's remark to playing partner Harry Vardon after the eighteen-year-old American topped a simple pitch shot into a bunker during the 1920 Open championship.

No.
                                                                Vardon's reply.

If you want to be a great player you must be able to get up and down. I've watched Tom Watson hit seven greens and shoot 70 in the British Open. I think that's the art of playing golf well.
  Hal Sutton in 2000 after winning the Greater Greensboro Chrysler Classic.

To be a complete golfer, you have to win the Open, you just have to.
  Tom Watson after winning the 1982 US Open.

Every great player's game is based on a thorough appreciation of his limitations. He plays to his strengths, which is another way of saying the same thing.
John Jacobs (*Golf in a Nutshell,* with Peter Dobereiner, 1995).

The undulations in the cranium of Peter Alliss, according to a phrenologist who examined them before seven million television viewers on the BBC's *Tonight* programme, suggested three features about him: he has the intellectual resources of a scientist; he lacks sustained concentration; and he would make an average golfer.

World Sports magazine, 1963.

Believe me, man, I don't play golf for pleasure. Hey, did you ever see a dentist in his office on his day off? No way. And you want me to remember holes? Ha! Let me ask you – do you remember the girl or girls you were dating back in 1966? No you don't. Well, I forget golf courses.

Lee Trevino talking to American writer Kaye Kessler in the official US Open magazine, 1987.

The history of Scottish golf is written chiefly in terms of a wine merchant's catalogue. There are long lists in the Club records of magnums of claret lost or won on the links.

Horace Hutchinson (*Golfing* magazine, 1898).

I don't know him but I've seen him smile and that's quite enough to put me off wanting to know anything about him.

David Feherty on Phil Mickelson.

I don't believe this hungry sportsman theory. If you've really got the will to do something, it doesn't matter what advantages or disadvantages you've got. This is obvious from looking at any golf tournament. Everybody hits the ball pretty much to the same standard. Yet some people win and some lose. It's that will to do it – to really fight to do it – that brings results.

Neil Coles (*World Sports* magazine, 1962).

The yips are that ghastly time when, with the first movement of the putter, the golfer blacks out, loses sight of the ball and hasn't the remotest idea of what to do with the putter or, occasionally, that he is holding a putter at all.

Tommy Armour.

But the bitter, inescapable truth remains. Once you've had 'em, you've got 'em.

Henry Longhurst also on the putting yips (*Golf Digest* magazine, 1973).

Is he just a firework, a rocket that went up into the sky and then that was the end of it? Well, there's no question that for a brief period Jacklin was a sensational golfer.
Sir Henry Cotton to Liz Kahn (*The Price of Success,* 1979).

He's raised the bar to a level only he can reach.

Tom Watson after Tiger Woods scored his Open victory at St Andrews in 2000.

Doug has been described as looking like the aftermath of a direct hit on a pizza factory.

Former US PGA champion **Dave Marr** on the flamboyant sartorial style of Doug Sanders (*Golf Digest* magazine, 1983).

I'm ready to let it go. I'm not sorry I didn't quit earlier but I'm ready to let it go for a very good reason. I really don't think I can compete any more. The US Open is a complete examination of a golfer. The competition, what it does to you inside, how hard it is to work at it, how hard it is to make it happen when the conditions aren't your conditions – in all of that you have to persevere and work at it. I enjoy that. I enjoy the punishment. I suppose I must be a masochist of some kind but I enjoy that. Hard and fast were my favourite conditions. That's when I excelled. Now I can't make those conditions work.

Jack Nicklaus in 2000 after scoring 82 in his last US Open.

A player whose stroke is affected by the simultaneous explosion of a bomb or by machine gun fire, may play another ball from the same place. Penalty: one stroke.

One of the 1939-45 wartime **rules** devised by the secretary of St Mellons Golf and Country Club.

European courses require more imagination and that's why our tour has more character. There are a hell of a variety of courses and weather and there's no use complaining about the greens one week because they'll probably be worse the next week.

Nick Faldo comparing the US and European tournament circuits (*Golf Illustrated* magazine, 1991).

He is the most immeasurable of all golf champions. But this is not entirely true because of all that he has won, or because of that mysterious fury with which he has managed to rally himself. It is partly because of the nobility he has brought to losing. And more than anything, it is true because of the pure, unmixed joy he has brought to trying.

Dan Jenkins on Arnold Palmer (*The Dogged Victims of Inexorable Fate*).

To be sure, the Old Course lacks that element most sought after in a modern golf course – fairness. The absence of clear definition of targets, inconsiderable kicks, the unlevel stances, the concealed bunkers, the vast and sometimes steeply sloping greens see to that. But a degree of patience often yields some solace.

Raymond Jacobs (*The Golfer's Companion*).

It's the great original; it's positive, rewarding, inspiring and exciting.

Open champion **Peter Thomson,** also on the Old Course (*The Golfer's Companion*).

Jones's personal charm and his modesty in triumph are assets which make him an invaluable travelling advertisement of the finer and rarer qualities of the American race.

News Chronicle **editorial** on the announcement in 1930 that Bobby Jones had retired from top-class golf at the age of 28.

He is the complete embodiment of the grand old golfing spirit, the decline of which is often deplored. He is so staunch a conservative that he has scarcely even tried steel shafts. Hickory is good enough for him.

The *Daily Mail* on Bobby Jones in 1930.

I don't know what image is. I suppose it's some sort of chemistry or style. Some people have it, some don't. Palmer was interesting because he was aggressive, free-wheeling, a hitter. So is Ballesteros. He'll try to hit over any lake on the golf course because the public comes to see him do it. He's a marketable guy because of it.

Hale Irwin at the 1980 US Open.

I'm not concerned about getting in the record books. A good obituary doesn't exactly excite me.

American professional **Joanne Carner** (*Golf Digest* magazine, 1983).

♠

I told an interviewer that Jerry was the best golfer I had ever seen – from the shoulders down. Trouble was he didn't have much of a golfing brain. I supplied it for him that day. He did most of the work.

Lee Trevino recalling his winning partnership with Jerry Pate in the 1981 Ryder Cup match (*Daily Mail,* 1993).

♠

No one else quite so adequately expressed how far women's golf had come since those far-off days when women swung at the ball as though they were beating off purse snatchers with an umbrella.

Charles Price on American golfer Glenna Collett Vare (*The World of Golf,* 1962).

♠

If today's popular papers had existed in the year 1567, it is not too difficult to imagine just how much they would have made of the fact that Mary, Queen of Scots was spotted playing golf in the grounds of Seton House only days after her husband Lord Darnley had been murdered. Her Highness had by all accounts first learned the game while at school in France but her golfing career was dramatically cut short when 'she failed to maintain the basic relationship between head and shoulders which golfers from time immemorial have deemed essential'.

Lewine Mair (*The World of Golf,* 1982).

♠

I saw a Darren Clarke today I hadn't seen before. I knew he was capable but he did to Tiger Woods what Tiger Woods has been doing to other people. He kicked his butt and looked him in the eye as he was doing it.

Butch Harmon, coach to both Woods and Clarke, after the Ulsterman beat the American for the 2000 Andersen Consulting Match Play title.

Darren flat outplayed me. He hit the ball beautifully and made a lot of putts. I was trying to find my golf swing. I did a lot of it with smoke and mirrors today, with a lot of hands and timing it well.

Tiger Woods on his defeat.

He won a US Open and two PGA championships. But he never got his due. You don't win three majors if you can't play.

Dave Stockton in 2000 on fellow professional Larry Nelson, who was passed over as a US Ryder Cup captain.

As for Abe Mitchell, he was an awful putter. Never gave him a thing. Not even a short one. I wouldn't give Harry Vardon a putt for the same reason. A great player from tee to green but when he got there it was bad.

Aubrey Boomer (*Daily Mail,* 1989).

There developed in my right forearm a nerve which puzzled a good many medical friends and subjected me to indescribable mental torture. Whenever I prepared to play a short putt (it was only close to the hole that I had any trouble so that the affliction must have been born largely of imagination and environment), I would wait for the nerve in the right arm to jump. The instant I felt it was about to jump, I would make a dash at the ball in a

desperate effort to be in first with the shot and what happened as
a consequence of this haste may readily be imagined.

Harry Vardon writing on his putting problems (reprinted in the
Golf journal, 1979).

Bunkers serve two purposes. They are for framing a green – to
give it definition and to give the player an idea of the distance he
has in hitting the green. And for beauty. They are not for trapping
people.

Ben Hogan talking to American writer Nick Seitz (*Golf Digest*
magazine).

Even ten years ago, the thought of one European putting a green
coat on another would have been dismissed totally. Currently
Europe's best players are better than America's best. That's just
the way things are at this moment. Supremacy is cyclical.

David Davies, golf writer for the *Guardian,* quoted in the
Augusta magazine, 1990.

Years from now when the money is spent, I'll think about this win
and the memories will be my real winnings, my real happiness.

Curtis Strange after winning the 1980 Westchester Classic.

Certainly the element of luck enters too much in this
championship competition. The idea of the tournament is to
select a golfer who is manifestly better than others or at least as
good as they are. It goes without saying that this tournament
does nothing of the kind and therefore, from the championship
point of view, it is a nonsense.

Henry Leach commenting in the *Observer* on the vagaries of
match play in the 1908 Amateur championship.

The first thing to be said about my captaincy is that I am not hellbent on starting a third world war, unlike some previous British captains who have approached the match as though they were leading the Light Brigade into the valley of death. There was the fiery Scot Eric Brown who ordered his men not to help their American opponents search for their balls in the rough. He rescinded the order when faced with a mutiny over the idea of such unsporting conduct.

Tony Jacklin, European team captain, quoted in the Ryder Cup magazine, 1983.

In match play you always have to expect the worst.

Colin Montgomerie after withstanding a counterattack from Mark O'Meara to win the 1999 World Match Play championship.

Miss Leitch brought power into women's golf; Miss Wethered brought power combined with perfection of style and a hitherto unknown degree of accuracy.

Daily Telegraph writer and former champion **Enid Wilson** on the comparative skills of Cecil Leitch and Joyce Wethered.

Fourteen is where the back nine begins.

Royal Lytham and St Annes club professional **Eddie Birchenough,** quoted by Ken Jones (*Independent on Sunday*) at the 2001 Open championship.

As a test of nerve, skill and temper, it seems to me to require a deal of beating, while its health-promoting tendencies are indisputable. Football and cricket have charms for those who participate in them; but to play the former a man must be young while the latter has hours of inaction which, even to the player, are weariness to the flesh.

Novelist **Carlton Dawe** on the virtues of golf (*Golfing* magazine, 1907 edition).

I think foursomes is a goofy game, frankly. It's a bloody British invention for old ladies at golf clubs. They love it. I said before we started I am not a fan of foursomes. I think it's outdated, history, gone. The sooner we get rid of it, the better.

International skipper **Peter Thomson** talking about the format before the 2000 President's Cup match with the United States (Mark McCormack, *The World of Professional Golf,* 2001 edition).

When I inquired at one Melbourne club if they had women members I was told: 'No, why do you ask?' I mentioned that I had seen women on the course and indeed there were two of them right now putting on the eighteenth green outside the bar window. 'Oh, they're not women members,' I was informed brusquely. 'They are associates.'

Peter Dobereiner (*Observer,* 1984).

As I said before, it would be idle to shut one's eyes to the fact that there is a certain amount of wagering in connection with the game, and it undoubtedly has the object of giving an added interest to many whose golfing ability is not equal to the task of taking a prominent part in the competition itself.

Irish Golfer magazine, 1902.

It is extremely unlikely that the disasters that occur to every beginner are in the least degree the fault of the clubs and the player will only get himself into a quandary if he allows himself to think so.

James Braid (*Golf Guide and How to Play Golf,* 1906).

No one in the world could have holed that putt. Jack Nicklaus wouldn't have holed it nor would Tony Jacklin. And I certainly wouldn't have holed it.

Seve Ballesteros after Bernhard Langer missed a last-green putt to lose the 1991 Ryder Cup to the Americans at Kiawa Island.

Never count the Americans out until the last putt. They're never finished. I've seen it happen too often.

Henry Longhurst at the 1965 Walker Cup match when the Great Britain and Ireland side needed only one point from seven matches to score an historic win. The Americans duly counterattacked to tie the match.

God measures men by what they are,
Not what in wealth possess,
This vibrant message chimes afar,
The voice of Inverness.

The **inscription** on the long-case clock which still stands in the Inverness Club in Toledo and was presented at the 1920 US Open championship by professional golfers, led by Walter Hagen, to mark the first time professionals were allowed into a clubhouse at a championship in the United States.

The European Tour is a sociable circuit – a friendly affair in which even fierce rivals dine together in the evening, go out for a drink and generally leave their golf back at the tournament.

They are also an adaptable lot – one week coping with the lushness of La Manga in Spain followed perhaps instantly by the fast-running bleakness of Turnberry. That breeds a personal strength and confidence that relishes a new challenge every week and is not taken aback by dramatic change.

PGA magazine comment on the attitude which helped European professionals to score their first Ryder Cup victory on American soil in 1987.

It marks an epoch in the history of the sex and, without unduly straining a point, it may be said that golf has been a factor of no small importance in the mental and physical development of the modern girl.

Edwardian writer **Blanche Hulton**.

This unexpected consistency by Faulkner showed that for once in his mercurial career he had the head, hands, and heart of a great player. Perhaps his victory will make him into a more reliable competitor in future.

The *Guardian* on Max Faulkner's 1951 Open championship triumph.

He's a freak of nature, worlds apart from us in every way.

Michael Campbell on Tiger Woods.

A woman, that's the only thing I can think of that could rattle him. And I don't even think that will rattle him.

US professional **Greg Kraft** on how Tiger Woods's dominance might end (*Columbus Dispatch*).

I don't like it yet. But 1 don't dislike it. And I thought I'd like it less than I do.

Mark Calcavecchia's opinion of the Old Course at St Andrews after his first practice round for the 1989 Dunhill Cup.

But of all animals I have found sheep, especially Scottish sheep, the most benevolent between tee and green. Perhaps their natural covering, which absorbs and nullifies the most severe and unexpected blows, makes for an even temper as well as temperature. But in their disposition also there is something uncommonly reassuring.

R C Robertson-Glasgow (the *Observer*).

Don't worry, John. There are five courses out there. You're bound to hit one of them.

David Feherty to John Daly at the Dunhill Cup at St Andrews.

Indeed on the links he is an artist; self-reliant and, as you might say, self-supporting; more tightly strung as to temperament than his genial and healthy aspect might convey to the casual eye; fitly framed for strong battle, but not impervious to the access of sometimes unreasonable mistrust in his own skill; an artist in the execution of strokes, especially the spoon shot and the pitch-and-run obediently halting at the correct station; a past master – almost totally 'past' in a world of sullen standardisation – at the selection of those hickory clubs which restore to the mind's fond eye the picture of the professional in his shop parting from some fruits of his craft as reluctantly as a lover from his loved.

R C Robertson-Glasgow on 1938 Walker Cup captain John Beck (*The Oxford and Cambridge Golfing Society 1898-1948*).

I guess my year is intimidating to some of the pros which is why they don't play well when I'm up there. They feel I can walk on water. I don't think I'm that good but maybe I'm better than I think. Either that, or the rest of the pros are all playing crummy.

Johnny Miller on winning eight titles in 1974.

Norman, for his age and experience, is without doubt the best-looking golfer I have seen in Australia, at 21. I have been wrong about 21-year-olds before so I'll say nothing until he reveals more.

Peter Thomson on Greg Norman, 1976.

Greg's the big shark and I'm a little fish. But I'm a bigger fish now than I was yesterday.

Australian **Steve Elkington's** verdict on fellow countryman Greg Norman, after winning the 1991 Players championship.

I don't see how you can say Tom Watson is the favourite in the Masters until Jack Nicklaus retires. He will always be king at Augusta.

Jerry Pate in 1980.

It's just what we need. Peter fills the ten-year gap after people like myself, Lyle, Ballesteros and Langer. I hope this victory will inspire the other young players.

Nick Faldo after losing the 1988 Benson and Hedges to twenty-year-old Peter Baker in a play-off.

Julius can hit his tee shots down those turnpike tunnels and not hit either side. I'm telling you, of all the guys up there on that leader board he scares me more than anybody. When he putts you can't tell by looking whether he's just practising or that it's fifty grand if he sinks it.

Lee Trevino on former champion Julius Boros in the 1973 US Open.

🏌

I did not come all the way to London to say I was quitting. I will still compete in the majors and though I am not the force I once was I will take them very seriously and might even win one.

Jack Nicklaus at the 1986 World Match Play championship.

🏌

Only Ian Woosnam's sacked caddie packs in more clubs.

Soccer writer **Joe Lovejoy** (*Sunday Times)* on the number of managerial jobs held by Graeme Souness. A reference to the fact that Woosnam was penalised at the 2001 Open championship for having more than the permitted fourteen clubs in his bag.

🏌

She's just a great player and she's going to get better. She has the game to dominate the tour in future. Once she gains experience we're all going to be in trouble.

Nancy Lopez in 1988 on Laura Davies.

🏌

He's the type who comes in the locker room and asks how you are and wants a real answer.

Tom Weiskopf on fellow professional Joe Inman (Mark McCormack, *The World of Professional Golf,* 1977 edition).

🏌

If Seve had won, too much would have been expected of him. He is only nineteen and I don't think he or anybody else of that age could handle it. His time will come.

Johnny Miller after Seve Ballesteros finished runner-up to him in the 1976 Open championship.

I love the golf course. You can exercise all the colours of your talents.

Mac O'Grady on Shinnecock Hills, the venue for the 1986 US Open.

I don't visualise us having the Pizza Hut Masters.

Hord Hardin, Chairman of Augusta National, answering a press question in 1988 on possible corporate sponsorship for the US Masters.

It was the most unspectacular round I've ever seen. Down the middle, on the green, in the hole.

Playing partner **Tommy Aaron** on Deane Beman's 62 in the 1969 Bob Hope Classic.

At the end of my career nobody will remember how many Ryder Cups I played in, just how many tournaments I won.

US Open champion **Lee Janzen** after being omitted from the 1995 US team.

Men trifle with their business and their politics but never trifle with their games. It brings truth home to them. They cannot pretend they have won when they have lost nor that they had a magnificent drive when they foozled it. The Englishman is at his best on the links and at his worst in the Cabinet.

George Bernard Shaw, reprinted in *The Sporting Word,* 1994.

In no other sport must the spectator move.

John Updike on watching a golf tournament (Golf magazine, 1980).

Everyone examines greens, but only he knows what he's looking for.

Ben Hogan on South African Bobby Locke's putting prowess.

A good course is one which tests every club in the bag, from the driver to the chip shots from long grass around the greens and with tough pin placements. A tough course makes a golfer think and we should all be made to think if we are to confirm that we are in the top bracket of players.

Jack Nicklaus after winning the 1976 Australian Open.

He's sneaky. He's out there just plodding along with that fast awkward swing of his and you're not paying any attention and then – zap! – all of a sudden he runs off four birdies in a row and you're wondering what happened.

John Mahaffey on Gene Littler winning the 1975 Memphis Classic.

What the world thought was that, in her, Scotland had found a most worthy young champion with length, control, and all the long dull list of virtues.

Eleanor Helme on Mrs Andrew Holm's win in the 1930 Ladies
Championship.

🏌

'It's a good game,' Laidlaw said quietly. 'But I suspect all professional sportsmen. Grown men devoting their lives to a game. They're capitalism's temple prostitutes.'

An extract from **William McIlvanney's** novel *Laidlaw* (1977)
featuring his unorthodox detective hero.

🏌

He was a cocky, brash little young man who had the audacity to think he was already a good player. I tolerated him because I thought he might develop into the greatest player I had ever coached.

Teaching professional **Conrad Rehling** to Ron Wills after Jerry
Pate won the 1976 US Open (*World of Golf,* 1977).

🏌

I don't think Daniel Boone could play from there.

Seve Ballesteros to the press after taking a penalty drop from
undergrowth during the 1988 Open championship.

🏌

No, it is match play, man against man, that is the true essence of golf. Beside it, stroke play, as a famous champion of earlier days contemptuously put it, is 'no better than rifle shooting'.

Henry Longhurst in *Golf Digest Annual,* 1977.

🏌

It is not that he drives unusually far, or that he approaches and putts miraculously well, but that he is so unvaryingly good at driving, approaching and putting alike. This is what wins him his championships.

Horace Hutchinson on amateur Harold Hilton, who won the Open in 1892 and 1897.

Once again Hagen has shown that concentration counts, and that a man who refuses to smoke during a round has the advantage over his rivals who cannot keep their pipes or cigarettes for other times.

Arthur Leonard Lee in the *Guardian* on Walter Hagen's 1924 Open championship win.

I watched a lot of great shots out there, I'm only sorry I wasn't hitting them.

US Masters champion **George Archer** after losing the 1972 City of Auckland Open.

He's too dumb to notice the greens were very tough today. I love Bobby. But he gets a little foggy at times.

John Schlee on Bobby Nichols winning the 1974 Canadian Open.

I read where one writer said that since I'd been married the only thing I'd added to my game was my name.

American professional **Kathy Guadagnino,** nee Baker, in 1988 after three years without a win.

The bad thing about golf today is the search for perfection in the turf. They have lost the origins of the game as a cross-country adventure. The fairways are too good, the greens too pure and the bunkers too easy.

Peter Thomson five times Open champion, talking to *The Times* golf writer John Hopkins.

If there is any consolation in his subsequent defeat by Jimmy Carter then it must be that his abilities as an eighteen-handi-capper will not hereafter receive such international attention.

Verdict on President **Gerald Ford**, who took 94 strokes at the Congressional Club in a pro-am before the 1976 US PGA championship.

Sandy goes along in a world of unconscious competence.

Peter Alliss on Sandy Lyle's laid-back approach to golf.

The golfing girl of today should indeed be grateful that she need not play golf in a sailor hat, a high stiff collar, a voluminous skirt and petticoats, a motor veil or a wide skirt with leather binding. In the winter we had our skirts bound with leather so that the mud we collected could easily be sponged off; but oh! the weight of the petticoats, the skirt with its collection of mud and the unhealthiness of the whole thing.

Mabel Stringer recalling women's golf at the beginning of the twentieth century (*Golfing Reminiscences*, 1924).

The two best players I've ever seen at ignoring their own mistakes – and I'm talkin' about some really ugly shots in big pressure spots – are Nicklaus and Watson. They refuse to be embarrassed. In fact everybody on tour knows that Nicklaus probably hits more unbelievably terrible, almost amateurish shots than any great player who ever lived.

Ben Crenshaw to author Tom Boswell (*Strokes of Genius,* 1987).

You go out and play your game. Sometimes it comes out as 68 and sometimes as 74. That's not fatalism, that's golf.

Peter Oosterhuis.

I get pissed off. I simply do not understand someone who hits a ball that lands behind a tree and can look at it and say 'Well, that's golf.

Simon Hobday.

He's an excellent coach even if he is a cross between Sid Vicious and Old Father Time.

Chris Moody on Ulster professional David Jones, who helped improve his putting style.

I played crap. He played crap. He just out-crapped me.

Australian professional **Wayne Grady** on being beaten in extra holes by Greg Norman in the 1990 World Match Play championship.

He decided money wasn't that important. He just wanted to concentrate on playing golf. He became very good . . . but he fell short of being a superstar.

Mark McCormack on US Masters champion Ben Crenshaw.

Sometimes the guy has no filter between his heart, his brain and his mouth but his opinions aren't detrimental to the game.
TV pundit **Johnny Miller** on Colin Montgomerie.

He's done everything for the Open here. But for Palmer in 1960, who knows where we'd be? Probably down in a shed on the beach.
Nick Faldo's tribute to Arnold Palmer as the American legend played his last Open in 1995. (Mark McCormack, *The World of Professional Golf*, 1996 edition).

Watch only the very best players. See what they do that makes them different. Then pinch it. But never try to make yourself a direct copy of any other man. You have your own talent. You are your own man.
Henry Cotton presenting his 1970 Rookie of the Year award to Stuart Brown.

A tenacious little sod. All I had to do was my part because for sure he would do his.
Tony Jacklin on his 1975 Ryder Cup partner Brian Huggett.

A reserve of nerve, gameness and sheer cold determination.
O B **Keeler's** verdict on Walter Hagen.

Player, golf's Little Big Man, is of course a phenomenon. He rants about his religion, his dedication and the searing nature of difficulties he has mastered. But there is no doubt about his place in the deity of the game.
Sports writer **James Lawton** on Gary Player.

Tiger is a great guy, probably the most professional sportsman in the world, but the intensity of his life is just ridiculous. That was really brought home to me when he explained why he loved scuba diving so much. He said it was because the fish didn't recognise him.

Lee Westwood, quoted in the *Mail on Sunday*.

If we were in charge, we would have far more match play. That is real golf. I love match play.

Seve Ballesteros.

He was treated like a horse. Put him in every race no matter how good he was.

David Leadbetter on English newcomer Justin Rose, who missed 21 successive halfway cuts in tournaments when he turned professional.

He plays like a beautifully proportioned field gun, automatic with perfect range.

Daily Telegraph golf writer **Leonard Crawley** on Jack Nicklaus.

Not so obviously gifted but with a concentration that is almost audible and remarkable powers of application.

Leonard Crawley on Gary Player.

It seemed afterwards that the only fair thing for us to do was to form the team of British-born players residing in Britain. I am quite sure that all interest would go out of the competition if this were not so.

An extract from a letter from **Samuel Ryder** to *Golf Illustrated* in 1931 on the controversy over overseas-based professionals being barred from the Ryder Cup.

I have no doubt that Jones and Hagen would have matched all today's players if they had modern equipment. Henry Cotton also.

Sir Donald Bradman.

Another thing is his course management is different. I would have loved to have smashed a driver down that first hole but, no. Three wood, keep it on the left hand side, draw it in here, hold it up here, fade it in here. I think sometimes Faldo is trying to do too much with the ball instead of actually standing up and hitting it.

Colin Montgomerie on playing with Nick Faldo in the Ryder Cup (*Golf Digest* magazine, 1997).

She played with a sureness and a confidence that this was the right club and I can hit this shot. That is hard to do.

TV pundit **Dave Marr** on American woman professional Mickey Wright.

It's not a good read.

> American prodigy **Michelle Wie** at the 2006 Women's British Open when asked if she was going to study the Rules of Golf more closely after a second inadvertent infringement in her first season as a professional.

The primary cause was getting divorced. Okay?

> **Colin Montgomerie** in 2004 on dropping to 81st position on the World Rankings following the break up of his marriage.

10

'We Certainly Aren't Cheating':
The Stress of Conflict

In the heat of the moment when emotions run high, there is only one opportunity to do what is right. Or rather, what is thought to be right, however misunderstood that action subsequently may be. A controversial incident between two players can sour their relationship for the remainder of their careers; other times an apology and a handshake settle the matter amicably with perhaps just a couple of drinks thrown in for good measure.

Curiously enough, it is the narrow interpretation of the rules of golf and a disregard for the spirit of the game that seems to cause most trouble. Nick Faldo was absolutely correct that playing partner Sandy Lyle had infringed the rules by attaching tape to his putter during play in the Kenya Open. But the controversy arose because he waited until the end of the round to report it and did not warn the Scot that he thought something was wrong. Similarly, Arnold Palmer and partner were well within their rights to claim a hole in the 1971 Ryder Cup match because the American caddie provided for Bernard Gallacher asked Arnie what club he had used. But Bernard was not even aware of the exchange and Arnie lost a Scottish admirer as a result.

Traditionally, the manner in which the game is conducted matters as much as, if not more, than the standard achieved. Thus, the Great Britain and Ireland Walker Cup squad in 1953 refused to claim a point from their American opponents for carrying too many clubs because 'we don't want a point that way'. In fact, they lost. But the spirit and integrity of the game had been upheld and that, to them, mattered more than the outcome.

I know I am going to come out of this looking like a sneak.

Nick Faldo on reporting playing partner Sandy Lyle for adding tape to his putter to minimise the glare of the sun during the 1980 Kenya Open. Lyle had unwittingly broken the rules by altering the playing characteristics of the club during play, which brought about his disqualification.

🏌

What upsets me is that it was done behind my back.

Sandy Lyle on the fact that Faldo notified Kenya Open officials at the ninth hole but did not inform Lyle that he considered there had been a breach of the rules.

🏌

Here comes Arnie now, driving to the first tee and breaking eight rules before he tees off.

Trey Holland, United States Golf Association president, on the implications of Arnold Palmer's endorsement of an illegal golf club.

🏌

OK, you can fault me for the fact that this club cannot be used in competition and shouldn't be. But to say it is cheating for a guy to go out and hit a club that lets him enjoy the game a bit more, I think is carrying it a bit too far.

Arnold Palmer's response to the criticism.

🏌

Put in your book I'll never play that course again. I can't play there. They can invite me all they want to but I'm not going to play there any more.

Lee Trevino in the US Masters at Augusta National in 1969. He did return.

🏌

He's going to play whether you play or not.

Theodore Havemeyer, President of the United States Golf Association, to a group of competitors who threatened to boycott the 1896 US Open because a black caddie, John Shippen, was included in the field. Shippen finished fourth.

It has been determined that Mr King cursed PGA Tournament Players Division official Pete Sesso, grabbed Mr Sesso's throat in a threatening manner and choked Mr Sesso.

Statement from TPD Commissioner **Joe Dey** after American professional Jim King was suspended for a year following a slow play dispute in the 1973 USI Classic.

I asked him to get out of the way. I never touched him.

King's reply.

This is by far my worst experience in golf. Our whole team is disgusted. We all ask ourselves, 'Is this how badly they want to win the Cup?' I thought it was an embarrassment. The more I think about it, the madder I get.

Annika Sorenstam after her American opponents recalled the chip shot she holed in the 2000 Solheim Cup match, claiming she had played out of turn.

I gave you the benefit of the doubt at the last hole. Now I know it wasn't an accident so don't start this gamesmanship stuff with me because you are dealing with the wrong guy.

Harry Bannerman to opponent Gardner Dickinson in the1971 Ryder Cup match after the Scottish professional noticed his American rival had twice noisily ripped off his Velcro golf glove as he was about to putt (*Daily Mail,* 1993). Bannerman won the match.

It is only fair to call upon those who are in haste to throw off the St Andrews rules on the grounds of localness, not to measure their merits as a code by the eternal fitness of things but by something which, like the Bembridge rules [the Royal Isle of Wight Golf Club no longer in existence], has, as Captain Eaton their able compiler says, 'been compiled with the object of framing a set of rules for the game of golf which shall suit all greens alike'.

Sir Walter Simpson advancing the claim for widespread adoption of the English club's rules of the game because the St Andrews rules applied too strictly to local Scottish conditions (*The Golfing Annual,* 1888).

As long as the hazards of various greens differ so much, it is impossible to have uniform rules. The whins at Wimbledon, the narrow course and rabbit holes at Hoylake, the roads at Blackheath, the station master's cottage at St Andrews etc. are nearly all different hazards and it seems absurd to me to class them all under one penalty. What I think would meet the most pronounced want, is to have fixed rules for fundamental principles leaving each club to fix their own local rules. How absurd it would be for Hoylake to have the St Andrews rule as to a ball on clothes laid out for drying.

Anonymous **letter** to *The Golfing Annual,* also in 1888, which intriguingly outlined the rules philosophy that was eventually adopted worldwide.

Finally Mr Lamb complains that St Andrews has one rule for match play and another for medal play. This must be so. They are entirely different games, played in different ways with different ends in view. The old game is the match game; the medal game is an innovation of more recent years; and it would be impossible to make rules for both games the same without spoiling either the one or the other.

B Hall Blyth's letter to *The Golfing Annual,* 1888, on another aspect of the rules controversy.

The spirit rather than the letter of the law was all-important.
> **Bobby Selway,** Chairman of the championship committee,
> explaining why they took no action against Bobby Locke who
> had innocently putted from the wrong position – a clear breach
> of the rules – on the final green at St Andrews in winning the
> 1957 Open championship. They decided he had earned no
> material advantage.

T

We don't want to win a point that way.
> Walker Cup captain **Tony Duncan** protesting that
> American rivals should not be disqualified for having
> too many clubs in their bag during the 1953 match.
> They were reinstated and went on to win the point.

T

But are you allowed to play this watering hole before the
eighteenth? There should be a two-pint penalty.
> The remark by a **member** of Moortown Golf Club before
> Nigel Denham opened a window and played a successful
> recovery shot after his golf ball bounced into the clubhouse
> during the 1974 English amateur championship. Denham had
> been obliged to remove his golf shoes before entering the
> clubhouse and the Royal and Ancient law makers at
> St Andrews later decreed that his score should not
> have stood because, by opening the window,
> he had improved his line of play.

T

I am not an ambassador of apartheid. Anyone who says that is
just starting propaganda. I try to be an ambassador of goodwill
and love. I am a sportsman not a politician at all. I do not believe
in apartheid in sports and I have done many things trying to
show that.
> **Gary Player** on television after protests during the 1979
> French Open.

This is my land. I am South African. And I must say now, and clearly, that I am of the South Africa of Verwoerd and apartheid.
Gary Player (*Grand Slam Golf,* 1966).

We were told it [apartheid] offered a separate but equal way of life to all Africans of whatever creed or colour.. .The sad irony was that the way of life was certainly separate but far from equal.
Gary Player (*To be the Best,* 1991).

As far as I'm concerned, I finished second and received first-place money. We all know who really won the tournament.
Jack Kay on winning the 1994 Asian Masters after Nick Faldo was disqualified for an earlier rules infringement when he was six strokes ahead.

I don't mind losing a tournament when it's my fault but when it's not my fault, it sucks.
Sophie Gustafson after officials imposed a one-hole penalty which cost her the match in the 2001 WPGA International Match Play championship because her caddie rode briefly on a buggy in contravention of tournament rules. He had stopped off in the clubhouse to go to the toilet and a marshal offered him a lift to the next tee.

There's no way to do otherwise; you have to accept and do better next time. You have to conform; and, anyway, worse be if you go across the street and you no see the car.
Roberto de Vicenzo's response to Donald Steel when told how much he was admired for the dignified manner in which he had accepted losing the 1968 US Masters because of a scorecard error (*Golfer's Bedside Book*).

Thomson was trying to upset me, put me off, and I wasn't having any of that. We won't be getting on very well in the future but that doesn't bother me.

> **Peter Oosterhuis** on playing partner Peter Thomson after a rules query in the 1971 Carrolls International in Ireland.

That's his business. But to suggest I was trying to put him off is nonsense.

> **Peter Thomson's** reply.

I've never met a player yet who was happy with a two-stroke penalty.

> PGA European Tour referee **John Paramor** on being told Sergio Garcia was angry at the sanction imposed for making an incorrect drop. The penalty eventually cost Garcia victory in the 2001 Greg Norman Holden Classic.

That looks like a nimble bit of footwork which is not exactly kosher. But who am I to say?

> TV commentator **Peter Alliss's** remarks on television after observing a player treading down long grass behind the ball in the 1986 British Masters. The player was later disqualified.

Mr Witcher. If you play any more rounds in this tournament or any other tournaments in New Zealand, I will do something that will not be too nice.

> Unsigned **letter** pushed under American professional Chris Witcher's hotel room door during the 1976 New Zealand Open after nine of his club shafts had been bent. The culprit was never found but Witcher did not wait to find out. He left.

We made a mistake but we certainly aren't cheating.
Paul Azinger after a rules infringement was pointed out by opponents Seve Ballesteros and Jose Maria Olazabal during the 1991 Ryder Cup match.

It has nothing to do with cheating. Cheating and breaking the rules are two different things.
The **Ballesteros** response.

Would you mind not moving when I'm about to play?
George Burns to Sandy Lyle in an ill-tempered encounter during the 1980 World Match Play championship, which Lyle eventually won. In the same match Burns's driver snapped as he swung on the fourth hole. The American claimed that as it broke in his backswing, he had not made a stroke which is defined as 'a forward movement of the club with the intention of fairly striking at and moving the ball'.

You have to be drunk or sick to miss from three inches; though, of course, we have all seen those tiddlers missed in stroke play by somebody who carelessly flings a putter at the ball – which is exactly what Tony Jacklin did before anybody could say a word.
Jimmy Hitchcock explaining why he had claimed a hole from Jacklin in the 1965 Honda Foursomes, also admitting that he had recorded it as being halved on the scorecard before Jacklin needlessly tried a tap-in, which missed (*Master Golfer*).

I woke up to find myself the guy that everybody loved to hate.
Hitchcock's reaction to the widespread press criticism of his actions the following day.

I'm personally disappointed in a couple of people at that meeting. They know who they are. And whether some players like it or not, there are some people who came before them, who mean a hell of a lot to this game. It burns the hell out of me to listen to some of their viewpoints.

American Ryder Cup skipper **Ben Crenshaw** singling out Tiger Woods, David Duval, Mark O'Meara and Phil Mickelson for criticism after demands at the 1999 US PGA championship for payments to play in the Ryder Cup match.

I'm sorry he feels that way. I thought when we left that meeting everyone was on the same page. If I'm unpatriotic how come I'm the only player who did a clinic for the US troops?

Mark O'Meara's response.

The Ryder Cup is an enormous money-maker. Because of that, I think it's our right to give funds to help our communities.

Tiger Woods suggesting that the playing fee should go to each player's nominated charity or cause.

No matter which side you come down on, we should all be ashamed of ourselves for bringing this up now. This could all have been handled privately behind closed doors.

Tom Lehman's verdict on the entire wrangle.

There is doubtless joy in St Andrews; for the official announcement has gone forth that the Olympic tournament is off. It was announced that a number of British entries received at the offices of the Council were so confused they had to be returned in order that the particulars might be made clear. This not having been done by last Saturday only one entry which was in order remained, namely that of Mr George S Lyon, the Canadian champion, and it was, therefore, impossible for the contest to take place.

Report in *Golfing* magazine 1908.

It is the first incident I've faced on the tours. It was pretty hot for a while but then things calmed down.

Black golfer **Lee Elder** after being heckled during the 1969 Memphis Open.

He used to be my hero but not any more. I have no respect for him, not really.

Bernard Gallacher on Arnold Palmer. The American and Gardner Dickinson had claimed a hole during the 1971 Ryder Cup match in St Louis because of the conduct of a local caddie working for Gallacher.

What really aggravates me is that he didn't call it on me when it happened.

Jerry Pate on incurring a two-stroke penalty after playing partner Lon Hinkle reported him at the end of a round in the 1980 Byron Nelson Classic for breaking the rules by straddling the line of a putt.

Vot iss your name and number?

Official in the 1974 German Open at Krefeld who spotted British professional Peter Beames using a club towel to clean his golf shoes. (He was referring to the locker number.)

I didn't think about what I said at the time. It was just a slip. It was wrong but occasionally it happens in tournament rounds when friends are playing. No one should help in a round except you caddie, although you can compare yardage with another player.

Tom Watson on being overheard on a television microphone giving advice to playing partner Lee Trevino during the 1980 Tournament of Champions. Watson was penalised two strokes but still won the tournament.

I seem to be blamed for winning the Ryder Cup but I had eleven very strong individuals with me as well. It doesn't take an individual to win a Ryder Cup but I seem to be the cause right now.

Colin Montgomerie on being heckled by American fans during the 1998 US Open.

Nothing that a little filing will not put right.

Bernard Darwin's verdict after non-playing US captain Ben Hogan claimed on the eve of the 1949 Ryder Cup match at Ganton that the grooves on the faces of the British team's iron clubs were too deep and therefore illegal.

This is cheating and against the spirit of the game. I have to accept Mr Garland's decision and the rules of golf but I think it is wrong.

Korean Na Sin Park's **manager** after the golfer was disqualified for not informing his opponent, Christy O'Connor Junior, that he was playing a provisional ball in the 1992 Dunhill Cup. The point at issue was that Park could not speak English.

If it were a singles event I might feel differently. But this is a team event and I have a responsibility to the team. I'm only one-third of what happens here.

O'Connor's explanation.

🏌

I give you one job to do and you can't even get that right.
Ian Woosnam to his caddie after a two-stroke penalty cost him the lead in the 2001 Open championship at Royal Lytham when fifteen clubs – one over the permitted limit – were discovered in his bag.

🏌

I know you are pulling against me but at least give me a chance, give me the courtesy of putting. I don't call that very sporting.
Gary Player's controversial outburst to the crowd while national hero Tony Jacklin waited to take a putt in extra holes in the 1968 World Match Play championship. Jacklin missed and Player, who claimed he heard somebody say 'Miss it, miss it' as he faced his own stroke, was booed for suspected gamesmanship.

🏌

He made an overt gesture as if to say 'Okay, you idiot, pick it up'. That made me mad. I wasn't going to take that crap from anybody.
Open champion **Tom Lehman** after Nick Faldo conceded a putt in the 1995 Ryder Cup match.

🏌

If we allow these Americans to play after our members told us last year to stand firm, then we have broken faith. We would have to resign. The attitude of the Dutch officials gives us no place to go. We cannot play under these conditions.
Neil Coles, who led the players' strike against controversially imported competitors in the 1978 Dutch Open.

I would like to have one who knows the rules.

> **Jack Nicklaus** to referee Tony Duncan, who asked if
> he wanted a replacement after a dispute in the 1966
> World Match Play championship.

What other rules do you want omitted?

> Referee **joe Dey** to Ryder Cup skipper Eric Brown, who
> complained about a penalty he imposed during the 1971
> match.

Someone is walking round with an Australian Dot in his pocket.
If I find him, I'll kill him.

> **Ian Stanley** after being told that a spectator had picked up
> his ball in the 1975 New Zealand PGA championship.

I was crying like a baby. It's not a cross-country race out here.
We're playing golf.

> **Nancy Lopez** describing her reaction after being penalised
> two strokes for slow play in the 1985 LPGA championship,
> which she won.

I don't think TV has any business doing what it is doing. Putting
an official in the TV trailer is a cop-out.

> **Tom Kite** after a tournament official, designated to watch a
> television monitor, spotted an infringement during the 1991
> Byron Nelson Classic.

It surprises me that putts of that length were conceded.
Australian skipper **Terry Gale** after Greg Norman and Nick
Price both conceded each other's extremely missable putts in
an international match on grounds that they wanted to avoid
any Ryder Cup-style animosity.

If that's what the players saw fit to do, then so be it.
South African captain **Gary Player** on the same incident after
his team had beaten the Australians.

If I was trying to miss the cut then why did I go par, birdie, birdie,
par, par after the twelfth hole? I had both feet on the ground and
both hands on the putter. I was trying to make those putts.
Tom Weiskopf refuting allegations that he was not trying in the
1975 Tucson Open.

That was a bum decision. If Britain want the Cup this bad – why,
they can have it.
American **Ken Still** to the referee during the 1969
Ryder Cup match.

I thank God I have this gift to play golf. I've come from nothing,
eaten from paper-covered tables. This is our livelihood, we are
all tough pros. I got shook up and I'm real sorry.
Ken Still after the dispute with Brian Huggett and
Bernard Gallacher during the 1969 Ryder Cup.

Madam, I'd like to look in your handbag.
Bob Shearer to a woman spectator who had taken his ball
during the 1987 Queensland Open.

The fine came as a bit of a surprise and only two minutes after I learned of the robbery from my hotel room. I knew then the only way to make a profit was to go out and win.

Bernhard Langer winning the 1984 Spanish Open after being fined £100 for slow play and having £3,000 stolen from his room.

Take 'em.

Mark Calcavecchia handing his irons to a surprised golf course attendant after the second round of the 1991 Open championship.

The airplane. I've missed the cut.

Calcavecchia's reply when asked by the attendant what he would use the next day.

I feel bad about the tournament not because I did not win but because some people say I did not try to win. Of course I try.

Roberto de Vicenzo after missing a short putt on the last green of the 1971 Spanish Open.

Just call him a Scottish goalkeeper.

Raymond Russell after throwing his golf ball to his caddie to be cleaned during the 2001 English Open at the Forest of Arden and watching it roll into the lake beside the seventeenth green (costing him a two-stroke penalty) when the unfortunate man failed to catch it.

We are a little surprised as well as being flattered that eighteen Congressmen should be able to take time to help us operate a golf tournament.

Augusta National Chairman **Clifford Roberts** on receiving a telegram from the politicians demanding that black golfer Lee Elder be allowed to play in the 1973 US Masters.

The lightning knocked me to the ground. I rolled over and the eight iron in my hand was either knocked loose or I threw it. But whatever, it landed on the ground about twenty feet away. I got up and ran for about ten yards before I fell again. I got up again and I'm not afraid to admit it, I was hysterical. I didn't know what I was doing. Then the lightning started cracking again and again and again. I started running again but this time in a half crouch position like a soldier running between foxholes. I was really scared. I thought, 'Oh God, just let me live. Let me live.'

American golfer **Bobby Nichols** recounting to the *Cleveland Plain Dealer* newspaper how he was struck by lightning in the 1975 Western Open. Lee Trevino and Jerry Heard were also hit.

Since Tom's clubs are illegal and he used them to win the Masters and the British Open where I came second, does it mean I am now the winner?

Jack Nicklaus's jocular query after the discovery in 1977 that Tom Watson's clubs and those belonging to other players did not conform to the rules because of a manufacturer's admitted error (Renton Laidlaw, *World of Golf,* 1978).

I guess you could say he was a little rude about it. He said: 'I don't want you to wear that again.'

Pete Bender, caddie to Greg Norman, recalling an Augusta National member's reaction when he wore a Great White Shark motif on his overalls during the 1987 US Masters (Mark McCormack, *The World of Professional Golf,* 1988 edition).

I learned that if they want you to keep your mouth shut, you keep your mouth shut. I couldn't say what I wanted without being fined so I said the hell with it.

Bob Gilder in 1988 after being fined $1,000 by US tour officials for criticising their method of seeding competitors in a match play event.

I have never seen so many players collapse visibly when one man's name hits the top of the leader board.

Sir Michael Bonallack on Tiger Woods' runaway win in the 2000 US Open at Pebble Beach.

Every two years, when the times comes, whether we're at home or in Europe, it's like we're all constipated.

Former US Open champion **Jim Furyk** on American failure in the Ryder Cup matches against Europe.

11

'Someone to Spread the News': Or Just Prejudiced?

No contingent in the world of golf provokes more discussion and debate about its worthiness than the media, and in particular the print press. Everyone has a firmly held opinion about the purpose – or otherwise – it serves and will not be shaken from it. Such judgements, from performers who have found themselves in the spotlight for the wrong reasons, can be scathing and at times indignant.

But the vehemence of such views simply confirms the important role the media play in bringing the image of golf to a wider audience through its stars and their exploits. More to the point, the media can be critical, shape opinion and bring about changes for the good. And they can never be ignored.

Thus there have always been two main schools of thought. Bobby Jones's view was that there could be no fame without a media corps to spread the news. The counterbalance from Norman Von Nida held that in any press room there will be a mixture of honest, dishonest and prejudiced characters. Not much different, really, from life in general.

To gain any sort of fame, it isn't enough to do the job. There must be someone to spread the news. If fame can be said to attach to one because of the inconsequential performance of striking a golf ball, what measure of it I have enjoyed has been due in large part to Keeler and his gifted typewriter.

Bobby Jones paying tribute to Atlanta sports writer O B Keeler in his book *Golf Is My Game*.

Bobby Jones is the prince of golf but O B Keeler is his prophet and in the adulation of the prince, the prophet has too often been neglected. Jones would probably have become the prince of golf without the prophet but the royal purple of his robe would have lacked much of its illustrious sheen. While Jones composed his epics, Keeler sang them to the world and they seemed all the finer for the manner of singing.

H G Salsinger, *Detroit News*.

The game of golf is so rich in drama and glamour that a good golf writer, it has always seemed to me, must be a man who feels complete empathy with these qualities and has the ability to write about them with style and flair.

Bing Crosby writing the foreword to Herbert Warren Wind's *The Lure of Golf,* 1970.

Next time I come back as a golf writer. No three putts. Never miss a cut. And somebody else pays.

Open champion **Roberto de Vicenzo**, 1967.

My experience of newspapermen is that most are honest but some are prejudiced, some careless, and quite a few dishonest.

Australian golfer **Norman Von Nida** (*Golf Is My Business,* 1956).

I was born in South Africa, raised in Rhodesia. I have a British passport and I live in the US. You pick one.

Nick Price in 1988 when asked by the press to explain his nationality.

One day a deaf mute will win this thing and you guys won't be able to write a word.

Ben Hogan to American press at the US Masters.

These days I am a columnist, a technical term meaning a writer who hides in the mountains during the heat of the battle and then comes down to bayonet the wounded.

Peter Dobereiner.

The Open at Olympic is always barnacled with unknowns.

Jim Murray, *Los Angeles Times,* at the 1998 US Open.

Do that again and you'll wear my putter.

Australian **Bob Shearer**'s warning to a photographer whose camera clicked as he played a chip shot in the 1975 West Lakes Classic.

Most of the people who write, don't understand the game. They think they know but they really don't.

Tiger Woods to American columnist Art Spander.

While I enjoy playing, if I can find three companionable lunatics, I think that golf is essentially a silly game, especially in the light of the fuss and bother that are made over it, and the 'Whosis came thundering down the fairway, his mashie flashing like a gleaming sword, his shots cannonading into the cup' type of golf reporting has always made me a little ill.

Paul Gallico, *Farewell to Sport,* 1937.

If I wanted to know how I played, what heights I may have attained or failed to scale, I awaited the next day's account in *The Times* by its special correspondent. With what was therein written I was content, for here was the truth of things. I want nothing more than to be remembered by posterity in the words of Bernard Darwin.

J H Taylor, five times Open champion.

Rives McBee (Who He) Shoots 64.

Headline in the *San Francisco Chronicle* as the unknown took the lead in the 1966 US Open. But not for long. Billy Casper won the tile.

It's hot out there. You've been in here where it's air-conditioned and with all the damn beer you can drink. You go out there and you've got to save whatever you've got. You ain't got time to be clowning around out there. I'm 45 years old and it's tough. Look at you, you still smell good and everything.

Lee Trevino to a woman golf reporter who remarked that he was not his happy-go-lucky self during the 1984 US PGA championship.

Seventeen stone and a heart to match, scouring the links with tremendous ubiquity and bulging with notes of the play. Once, carrying an involuntary hod of snow on his hat, he went to the furthest point of the course, took four pages of notes on the shivering golfers and returned to the clubhouse to find that play had been cancelled.

> A **memoir** of *Daily Telegraph* golf writer Peter Lawless who later became a war correspondent and was killed while reporting on the first troops to cross the Rhine at Remagen in 1945 (Peter Ryde, *The Halford Hewitt*).

I ain't gonna tell ya.

> US Ryder Cup captain **Ben** Hogan's reply to a journalist who asked him to explain the reason for his pairings in the 1967 match.

Tom Watson is one of the few college students who can find splendour in the grass without smoking it.

> American columnist **Art Spander** recording how Tom Watson, then an undergraduate at Stanford University, led the regional qualifiers for the 1970 US Open (*San Francisco Examiner*).

Bernard Gallacher, a close friend, once cruelly commented that were I to hit my weight I would average a 400-yard drive.

> Television commentator and golf writer **Renton Laidlaw** in *The Golfers*, 1982).

If he can handle all the attention, all the pressure from you folks, Tiger can be as good or better than anybody who ever played the game.

> **Jack Nicklaus** on Tiger Woods at the 1996 US Masters before the prodigy had turned professional. A year later he won the Masters.

The media controls who is the superstar and who isn't. Me, I don't care but I think the media is an incredible factor. Greg Norman is a red-liner, no question. But up until last year nobody quite knew about him. I mean the media. Then he came on so strong it was like the second coming of God.

> American professional **Ken Green** (the *International* magazine, 1987).

He plays the game of golf as if he has a plane to catch. As if he were double-parked and left the meter running. Guys move slower leaving hotel fires.

> American columnist **Jim Murray** on US Open champion Corey Pavin (*Los Angeles Times*).

My reservoir of words to describe it is bone dry. What do you say? He's remarkable, he's unbelievable, he's incredible. None of those words are appropriate. We are the visual medium so you'd think the picture speaks for itself . . . In many ways I am thankful this is the last golf event of the year. I'm waiting for the football season to begin because I don't have anything else to say.

> CBS television commentator **Jim Nantz** in 2000 after Tiger Woods won the NEC Invitational.

It is on record that Mr Wolfe Murray once directed a letter to The Misser of Short Putts, Prestwick' and that it was taken straight to the right man – Tom Morris. If a communication had been thus addressed to Hoylake, one wonders how many people would have taken it silently away only to find it was meant for somebody else and to write exultingly across the envelope, 'Opened in error; try So-and-So'.

Sportsman magazine **report** on the 1906 Amateur championship.

Not true. I slept on the floor.

Fred Couples denying newspaper reports that he slept in the bath because his hotel bed was too soft during the 1991 Open championship.

I can but you can't.

Scott Hoch to the press at the 1995 US Masters when asked if he could ever get away from the memory of missing a short putt in a play-off to lose the 1989 event.

You think I play the hole the wrong way?

Seve Ballesteros to a reporter who asked why he took a four iron from the tee instead of his driver but still sank a putt of 40 feet for a birdie to take the lead in the 1991 Open championship.

There's one of them in there now.

The remark made by a Yorkshire **club official** who discovered Henry Longhurst writing his report in a small potting shed that had been allocated for the entire press corps during an English championship (*The Golfers,* 1982).

It's Monday, guys. Don't start overloading me on Monday. There's still two days of hype left.

Greg Norman to press during his preparation for the 1989 US Masters.

Her opponent, Martha Wilkinson, was a lovely swinger of the club – one of those juvenile sun-tanned products of the American conveyor belt who had played in 72-hole tournaments week after week through the summer.

Peter Ryde on Catherine Lacoste playing in the 1970 Women's World Team championship (*Golfer's Bedside Book*).

Any guy who would pass up the chance to see Sam Snead play golf would pull the shades driving past the Taj Mahal.

American columnist **Jim Murray** (*The Sporting World of Jim Murray*, 1968).

Never mind the bodyguards and police keeping fans at bay from Tiger, it was the galleries that needed protection from his errant shots.

David McDonnell (the *Mirror*) on the erratic last round of defending Open champion Tiger Woods at Royal Lytham, 2001.

Without you guys, there wouldn't be any tour.

Val Skinner dispensing champagne to the press after winning the 1986 Mazda Classic.

Duval's emotions never seemed to change and that was the sad thing. He never cracked a smile, furrowed a brow, pounded a club, pumped a fist or issued an expletive.

Chris Elsberry commenting in the *Connecticut Post* on David Duval in the 1999 Ryder Cup.

Never, surely, can Alliss's putter have extracted such obedience from the ball.

A **report** in *The Times* on Peter Alliss playing in the 1954 Penfold Match Play event.

I happened to be at the sixteenth hole at St Andrews in the year that the great Bobby Jones made his first championship appearance there and I saw him tear up his card, and afterwards reported that Bobby Jones considered the Old Links a 'cow pasture' and that he 'would never play there again'. But I also saw him in 1930, the year of his world record achievement when he won the Open and Amateur championships of Britain and USA.

Fred Pignon (*The Golfer's Year*, 1950).

It looks as though a squad of Marines ought to be raising a flag over it.

Charles Price describing the second green at Pine Valley which sits on a hill surrounded by waste land (the *International* magazine, 1987).

We were tossed around like a cocktail in a shaker. It was like falling in a giant lift when the cable had snapped.

Daily Express golf writer **Ronald Heager's** front page story when the plane carrying the entire 1959 Ryder Cup team to Palm Springs plunged 4,000 feet in turbulent conditions before the pilot could regain control.

Wee Woosie looks as though he ought to be playing miniature golf. Come to think of it, he does play miniature golf.

Columnist **Mike Downey** in the *Los Angeles Times*.

Massy's victory is a victory for golf as a catholic game, appealing not to one race alone but to any that cares to learn it. Scotsmen taught it to us and we have learned to beat them at it. Jersey has beaten both England and Scotland and now France has provided a pupil so apt as to beat not only Great Britain and Ireland but also the Channel Islands.

Comment in the *Manchester Guardian* on Arnaud Massy's 1907 Open championship win.

Being the son of the monarch means that when you raid your mother's possessions for something to present, there is little danger of coming up with a bashed-in pewter mug won at a fete.

John Hopkins in *The Times* on being told that the George III 1810 silver sugar bowl the Duke of York intended to offer as a prize in a junior golf event came from the Queen's vaults.

Fifty years of golf is a good round number to look back on. Those who can do so are now rather old and for the great majority of golfers of today 1899 is only a year in the record books in which are set down the deeds of half-forgotten champions. I wonder what somebody who, fifty years hence, writes a similar article will have to say about 1949. I must be forgiven if I doubt whether he will find greater or more picturesque heroes to chronicle than I have had.

> Extracts from a **Bernard Darwin** essay reviewing his half-century of golf writing (*The Golfer's Year*, 1949).

Let them come to me if they want to talk to me.

> **jack Nicklaus** declining to attend a press conference at the 1985 Open championship after missing the halfway cut for the first time in 23 consecutive events.

This is probably not the best time to ask this question and I'm not sure you would answer it anyway so I won't ask it.

> Irish golf writer to **Ronan Rafferty** during the 1989 Volvo Masters.

They wound up the Mechanical Man of Golf yesterday and sent him clicking round the East Lake Course.

> **Kerr Petrie** on Bobby Jones playing in the 1927 Southern Open (*New York Herald Tribune*).

Dutifully they have all bleated on about the privilege of taking part but the stony expression paraded by Michael Douglas, Kurt Russell and Kyle MacLachlan suggested this was a movie they would rather not be in and that they will certainly think hard before signing up for the sequel. So, too, Sir Steven Redgrave who has probably been at greater risk of drowning in this event than while winning his five Olympic golds.

> Golf writer **Alasdair Reid** on the pro-am style 2001 Dunhill Links Championship (*Sunday Times*).

Uncompromisingly fat.
  A **sports writer's** description of American golfer Bob Murphy.

🏌

We are delighted to learn that the only way he will visit us again
is in a box.
  Leonard Crawley, the *Daily Telegraph* golf writer, commenting
      in 1970 on Dave Hill's remarks that he would never go to
      Britain again unless he died and his body was shipped to the
                                                        wrong place.

🏌

They have, however, an exceptionally imaginative mind, and
can create several columns for their papers out of a few
questions and answers. It is amusing and a little alarming to
open the morning newspaper and find huge headlines
commenting on my arrival and giving exclusive accounts of
interviews which I had given.
  Harry Vardon on the American press during his 1900 tour.

🏌

If you gave the game up you could win the Open.
Sun sports writer **Jack Statter's** response to former English
amateur champion Gerald Micklem who claimed he played
better after a long lay-off.

🏌

As good a side as any that has ever played against Great Britain,
and probably better.
  Leonard Crawley, commenting in the *Daily Telegraph* about
                          the 1947 American Ryder Cup team.

🏌

I shot 80. Now haven't you newspaper so-and-sos got something to do out on the golf course? If it's too cold for you I'll be glad to lend you my jacket.

> Former champion **Tommy Bolt** at the 1970 US Open.

*

No Lullaby of Broadway this week.

> **Art Spander** on Andrew Broadway who scored 49 for nine holes but did not complete his card in the 1986 Open championship at Turnberry (*The Art Spander Collection*).

*

The man they call 'Superslob' yesterday took command of the Open and inspired every beer paunch in the land to sag with pride. Craig Stadler, looking like a failed weight watcher, spreadeagled the bronzed and muscular superstars with a dazzling display that smashed the Royal Birkdale course record and gave him a three-stroke lead.

> A **report** in the *Daily Mail* as the portly American took the first-round lead in the 1983 championship.

*

It's irritating to read such garbage but I'll survive. I've been called worse but never to my face. As much as that crap might bother me, it's a much more important nag that my driving and putting were crummy during the second round.

> **Craig Stadler**'s response the following day.

*

The tragedy was that one man had to lose. That man was Nicklaus. For the second time in the year, when it mattered Watson dented the image of a golfer who in any championship anywhere in the world was still accepted as the man the others had to beat.

> **Ron Wills** on the 36-hole duel between Tom Watson and Jack Nicklaus for the 1977 Open title (*World of Golf,* 1978).

You will be writing about me one day.
> **Wayne Grady,** then a 21-year-old unknown, talking to
> Australian golf writers a month before winning the 1978
> Westlake Classic.
> He went on to become US PGA champion.

He has as much chance of victory as most people have of
pronouncing his name correctly.
> **Mitchell Platts** in *The Times* on the encounter between
> Nigerian professional Peter Akakasiaka and Seve Ballesteros in
> the 1985 Dunhill Cup.

Sarazen licks Postage Stamp.
> **Headline** in a Scottish newspaper after Gene Sarazen, at the
> age of 71, holed in one at Royal Troon's 126-yard eighth
> during the 1973 Open championship.

Ooster Who?
> **Headline** in the *Atlanta Constitution* newspaper when Peter
> Oosterhuis held the lead going into the final round of the
> 1973 US Masters.

Sic transit Gloria.
> **Henry Longhurst's** reference to the defeat of Gloria Minoprio,
> the first woman to wear trousers on a golf course, in the 1933
> English Women's championship at Westward Ho!.

Sponsors Gruff as Golf Champs Puff.
Headline in a Melbourne newspaper after players were spotted
smoking cigarettes during the 1999 Victorian Open even
though the event had been sponsored by a government
agency set up to discourage the habit.

I certainly believe all of us have conscientiously observed the
no-smoking areas designated by the sponsors and the Victorian
Golf Association. In addition, I and my fellow players have made
every effort to avoid smoking in circumstances where the
activity might be captured by television cameras.
Australian **Bradley King** who was photographed smoking at the
event.

When little children come unto me it seems they suffer.
Daily Mail columnist **Ian Wooldridge** explaining how his
attempts to act as a baby-minder to ten-month-old Natalie
Faldo, while mother Gill watched Nick in the 1987 Open
championship, ended in failure and an SOS message on the
leader board when the infant began to cry.

The boy's game was perfect and chaste as Grecian statuary.
C B MacFarlane in the *London Evening News* on the 66
scored by Bobby Jones at Sunningdale in a qualifying
round for the 1926 Open championship.

It was possibly the most calamitous loss of nerve ever seen in a
major championship. Never was a shorter, easier putt for a
major championship missed.
David Davies in the *Guardian* describing the short putt Retief
Goosen missed on the 72nd hole for the 2001 US Open (even
though he won it in a play-off the next day).

She would come to the first tee, smile charmingly at her opponent when they met at the commencement of their game and then, almost as though in a trance, become a golfing machine.

> *Daily Telegraph* writer **Enid Wilson** on Joyce Wethered.

Hearing the ill-timed but quite spontaneous applause of the crowd at Miss Leitch's shot, a young horse standing in the road bolted and a stampede ensued. This probably accounted for Miss Titterton's failure to hole the putt and the pair tied at the eighteenth. Here MissTitterton was in the Swilcan, rebounded, hit the stone bridge and after all this, she succeeded in securing the match with a half in five and entered the finals.

> An **account** of the 1908 semi-final match in the British Ladies championship at St Andrews between the eventual champion and Cecil Leitch (*Golfing* magazine, 1908).

What has been questioned has been his desire to win, his determination to stamp his name on a game that could have been invented for him.

> **Bill Elliott** in the *Daily Star* on Sandy Lyle's 1985 Open championship win.

He knew how far he had come – back from the land of the fallen idols.

> Sports writer **Dan Jenkins** on the 1980 US Open victory of Jack Nicklaus (*Sports Illustrated* magazine).

I wonder what he's thinking in Spanish.

> Television commentator **Renton Laidlaw** on Seve Ballesteros.

A close finish adds to the fun but if the Ryder Cup depended on close finishes it would have died years ago. We may be in for another bad year but there have been a number of good ones lately and it would be absurd to talk in terms of ending it just because we may suffer a hiding. The occasion is the thing and the pride that even the most hard-baked, mercenary-minded professional feels when he stands up to play for his country.

Peter Ryde in *The Times* on the eve of the 1975 Ryder Cup match at Laurel Valley which the Americans won comfortably.

I wonder what it will be this time. God, peanuts or raisins?

Peter Dobereiner speculating on what 'secret' Gary Player would put forward for his spectacular 1978 US Masters win.

The difference between us and the pros is that we skull wedges and they wedge skulls.

Jack O'Leary, in the *Boston Herald,* after Ben Crenshaw threw his club in the air then needed three stitches when it struck him on the back of the head during the 1986 US PGA championship.

I sank a twenty-footer.

Joe Inman's reply to a reporter who asked him how he took nine strokes at the second hole during the 1985 US Masters championship.

Mase always did have a weak backhand.

Sports writer **Waxo Green** in the *Nashville Banner* after Mason Rudolph reached over to tap a short putt into the hole and missed during the 1969 US Open.

Greg Norman reminds me of the movies. Every time you think he's going to get the girl and ride off into the sunset, his horse breaks a leg.

American writer **Rick Reilly** on the Australian's succession of near-misses in major events.

Amazing isn't it? You give players hi-tech drivers and golf balls which go ever more ridiculous distances and the opportunity, if they so desire, to avail themselves of any drug known to any chemist. But stand them over an eighteen-inch putt to win a major and the game reverts to its fifteenth-century essence, the eternal puzzle of getting a little ball into a small hole.

Derek Lawrenson, in the *Daily Mail,* after Retief Goosen and Stewart Cink both missed short putts on the last green of the 2001 US Open (although Goosen went on to take the title in a play-off).

When he was on the green, the hole was never safe. Keeping his wrists unbroken and moving the club head more slowly under pressure than the game's case-hardened chroniclers had ever seen, Charles dropped putt after putt from any distance.

John Thicknesse on left-handed Bob Charles's 1963 Open championship win (*Sunday Telegraph*).

The best Good Friday Peter and Paul have had in 2,000 years.

Newspaper **headline** as Peter Butler and Paul Harney led the 1966 US Masters over Easter weekend.

Maybe I said too much to the press but I don't regret anything I've said to any of them. Over the years people have said to me, you say too much, you open up the book, you should close it a bit, let them wonder and think . . . but I'm not like that.

Tony Jacklin to Liz Kahn (*The Price of Success*).

Making this is the only thing that ensures that putter has a life after today.

Television commentator **Jim Belford,** watching Jim Thorpe pondering over a short putt in the Canadian Senior Open (*Golf Journal,* 2001).

A lanky figure moving down the fairways with the wide, clumping strides one usually associates with farm boys.

Herbert Warren Wind, in the *New Yorker* magazine, describing American professional Mark Lye during the 1984 US Masters.

Now there's this method to his madness, perfected by Nicklaus, who patiently waited for foes to draw the wrong club or the short breath. Jack was proud of how often he won and was just as pleased about how frequently he let someone else lose. Greatness means shifting the anxiety of the chase to those who are chasing. In a sport with no defence he compels others to err anyway.

American columnist **Bob Verdi** on Tiger Woods.

But is it legitimate to call a golfer the greatest athlete in the world? Is it acceptable to compare him to Muhammad Ali, Pele, Michael Jordan, Sir Steven Redgrave, Martina Navratilova?

Simon Barnes in *The Times* after Tiger Woods held all four major world golf championships.

Huish, Huish, whisper who dare, All Scotland is saying a prayer.
Local newspaper **headline** after North Berwick club
professional David Huish joined the leaders in the 1975
Open championship at Carnoustie. He faded over
the last two rounds.

Jimmy Demaret, a former US Open champion, has gone on
record as saying he was constantly amazed at the diatribes on
the golf swing which came from golfers whose remarks in his
company had never been more profound than 'It's your shot'.
World Sports magazine, 1962.

To see the old master, now 45, win with a flash of his old magic
when the chips were down, was worth getting soaking wet.
Michael Williams in the *Daily Telegraph* on Arnold Palmer's
1975 Spanish Open win in torrential rain.

The man who once rolled it as smoothly as Bob Charles is
presently putting more like Ray Charles.
Mark Reason on Jose Maria Olazabal in the *Sunday
Telegraph.*

COCKY DOODLE DOO! Walter Hagen, boastful American
champion, is boyishly confident of winning the British Cup
which only once in its history has ever left British shores. Hagen
says that no golfer should ever be over 72 around Deal. He
intends to show us how to play the game and he prefers to pitch
to the flag so close he doesn't have to putt.
Daily Mail **report** before the 1920 Open championship
which so angered the American that he successfully
demanded a retraction, but he failed to win the title.

Fire away – and use real bullets.

> **Tony Jacklin** to the press after losing to Jack Nicklaus in the 1970 World Match Play championship.

𝍏

I felt pissed out on that hole but I played steadily and putted well.

> **Bill Longmuir,** as quoted in *Golf News* magazine after a double-bogey six in the 1986 Kenya Open.

𝍏

If Norman had been born with dark hair (which presumably he was not) the world would not have taken half as much notice of him.

> American columnist **Dan Jenkins** on Greg Norman.

𝍏

Apparently he was trying to attack the pin that was stashed real back.

> A **description** in *Golf News* magazine on the 1986 Kenya Open.

𝍏

And sod, Mrs Beck, good luck and bring back to Britain that coveted trophy.

> **Misprint** in *Fairway and Hazard* magazine as the Curtis Cup squad left for the United States in 1954.

𝍏

Wow! How did you come back?

> **Tiger** Woods's response to a journalist who asked what he would say to the legendary Bobby Jones (died 1970) if they met in the Augusta National clubhouse, after Tiger's US Masters victory in 2001 which earned him all four major world titles.

Then it was time for tea.

    Allegedly part of **Bernard Darwin's** report after watching only
two holes of Henry Cotton's record-breaking 65 in the 1934
Open championship.

I was sick with nervousness that had my stomach gripped in a
vice. I could not sit still and my legs shook when I tried to walk.

    Atlanta golf writer **O B Keeler** on his feelings as Bobby Jones
faced a play-off for the 1923 US Open.

Unfortunately a non-golfer was at the other end to take down my
message. Stymie, chip, bunker, dormy were Greek to him and all
the time the voice of the French telephone operator, at first
polite, then insistent, then furious, buzzed through my ears,
'*Etes-vous fini, Madame*?' It seemed as if I would never finish.
And then in the middle . . . silence. We were cut off and an
apologetic postmaster explained that there was a very important
conference twenty miles away at Boulogne and perhaps Mr
Lloyd George was wanting to talk to London. The lesser must
sometimes interfere with the great.

    Eleanor Helme on dictating her report to *The Times* from the
1920 French Ladies championship at Le Touquet.

Faldo to World Tour: Bugger Off.

    The **headline** in the *Mainichi Daily News,* 1994, when Nick
Faldo declined to join a proposed breakaway golf circuit.

I didn't write it, boys. You're the ones who buried me and I appreciate it. Now I understand why athletes don't talk to you guys.

    Fuzzy Zoeller after his remarks on Tiger Woods caused
widespread condemnation.

I'd played in three Ryder Cups before a golf writer even condescended to speak to me. Now they are giving press conferences twice a day.
Peter Alliss to Ian Wooldridge (*Daily Mail*).

Mr 'Feel for the Game' believed it was appropriate at a golf event for the future President, George W Bush, to read out the last thoughts of the lieutenant-colonel commander of the Alamo as he is surrounded by 1,000 Mexican troops. In capital letters the soldier's despatch finishes: Victory or Death.
Golf writer **Derek Lawrenson,** in the *Daily Mail,* reviewing US skipper Ben Crenshaw's account of the 1999 Ryder Cup match.

Jones had the best that life could offer and took it with great grace and then he had the worst and took it in the same way.
Herbert Warren Wind on golf legend Bobby Jones, who was confined to a wheelchair for the latter part of his life.

Cotton knocked on the door and walked in. Harry Vardon was still in his bed. Cotton gave him the trophy without speaking, and Vardon looked at it and began to weep. Perhaps it was the joy at meeting an old friend, for this trophy had been his for six years and nobody bettered that record. Perhaps too the trophy was a reminder of glories past, of the great names that had been part of his life, of his own talent on which the modern game was based, and of the infirmities which now trapped him. Cotton wept too.

For him it was a beginning. And Vardon knew that too.

From **Sir Henry Cotton's** account of his visit to bed-ridden Harry Vardon soon after he won the 1934 Open (*Great Moments in Sport: Golf*).

Gary had, or thought he had, dysentery and asthma. At the Portmarnock Golf Club he collapsed before the opening round. A doctor gave him a shot and he staggered to the first tee. At last report, his card for that round was still under glass in the clubhouse, a course record 65.

Columnist **Red Smith** in the *New York Times* on Gary Player in the 1960 Canada Cup.

The news item reported that I'd said 'British golfers are lazy.' What I had actually said was that Britain's lack of good pro golfers was due to the very little practice they could get on their home links.

Walter Hagen, following the 1923 Open championship.

He has words and wit, a pleasant discursive style and thankfully does not drive us to near narcolepsy with protracted analyses of swings and putting styles.

Ian Wooldridge in *The Daily Mail* on TV commentator Wayne Grady at the 2006 Open Championship.

In sport's cynical and coarse age, there are still some authentically beautiful scenes, and Nicklaus bowing out on the 18th at St Andrews surely qualifies among the finest.

Sports writer **Graham Spiers**, *The Herald* newspaper, at the 2005 Open Championship.

12

'Standing Outside Myself, Looking On': The Mind Game

There is a mystical aspect to golf that every competitor experiences at some time or other, although some refuse to openly acknowledge its existence. Whether it is caused by the sheer loneliness of the endeavour, which leaves a player with only his or her own psyche for company during play, remains a mystery.

But there have been too many instances from credible witnesses of impeccable honesty for the phenomenon to be ignored. Bobby Jones was aware of a governing force beyond him, but certainly taking care of him during his 1930 Grand Slam year. Marley Spearman, the British champion, admitted to an out-of-body experience in a moment of extreme pressure.

Moreover, there is a curious ability to read the future. Johnny Miller revealed he could see things that were going to happen as he played. Gary Player revealed that he saw his name on the winner's scoreboard before he won the 1965 US Open. Jack Nicklaus knew – absolutely knew – that a putt from 30 feet was going to drop before he played it in the World Series.

All of it suggests more than the confidence-boosting mind games that all top-class competitors follow dutifully to ensure they are at their best for the fray. Such moments are of crucial importance and mark the difference between winners and losers. There is, after all, more to golf than hitting a ball.

It's like a Western. I want another notch on my gun. I must accept the challenge. Just as I have in the Open in the past from Arnold Palmer, Gary Player, Lee Trevino and Johnny Miller.

Jack Nicklaus before his epic duel with Tom Watson for the
1977 Open championship at Turnberry – which he lost.

Seve has the charisma to dominate you. When he walks on to the course he looks as though he owns the place. And when he holes a good putt he makes you think he's unstoppable. So I decided not to watch him. I looked at the trees, the spectators, the planes flying in and out of Heathrow, anywhere but at Seve. It enabled me to concentrate on my own game and it paid off.

Australian **Rodger Davis** on how he beat the Spaniard
7 and 6 in the 1986 World Match Play championship.

Why don't You come down and fight like a man?

Simon Hobday's outburst towards heaven in a crowded
Royal Birkdale clubhouse after missing crucial putts
during the 1983 Open championship.

Instead of knocking again, I just kicked the door in.

Fulton Allem on winning the 1986 Charity Classic.

I heard voices in my head saying: 'Look how good Doc is playing.' We all have our doubts. That's not abnormal. What you have to do is say: 'I hear you but I don't believe you.'

Joe Inman on beating Dr Gil Morgan in the 1998 Pacific Bell
Senior Classic.

We are playing for our souls.

Ben Crenshaw, the 1999 US Ryder Cup captain, defining
his team's attitude to the match against Europe having lost the
two previous encounters (Art Spande in the Ryder Cup
magazine).

I played with Carol Mann when she won her first tournament
and I didn't think she was going to get off the last hole. I
remember she asked me if I had an air sickness bag. She didn't
even know where she was.

Judy Rankin on US Women's Open champion Carol Mann
(*Golf Digest Annual,* 1977).

Every day I went down to the practice tee where they had a
scoreboard with all the past Open champions' names on it
and I stood there and visualised my name etched on the
scoreboard.

Gary Player on his positive attitude when winning the 1965
US Open championship.

I meant to tell Lee Trevino not to be too despondent. This cup is
going to change hands quite often in future. He will not be the
last losing American captain.

Tony Jacklin, the European skipper, following the American
defeat in the 1985 Ryder Cup match.

But the bottom line is, no matter what, even if I shoot 90
tomorrow, I'm going to enjoy it. Maybe people will say 'Oh he
blew it' or whatever. Maybe I'm going to blow it, it's the first
time I've ever been there. What do you expect? You know I'm
not number one in the world. My knees are going to touch each

other on the first tee tomorrow. But let me tell you, I'm going to enjoy it.

French professional **Jean Van de Velde** before the final round of the 1999 Open championship, in which he eventually squandered a three-stroke lead on the last hole then lost the title in a play-off.

Whether I am playing for £1 or £41,000 makes no odds. I don't need any inspiration.

Mark **James** on winning the Desert Classic in Dubai (Tim Glover, *Volvo Tour Book,* 1989).

You see those golfers practising over there? They've all got golf swings good enough to win this tournament. The only trouble is those golfers are more afraid of winning than they are of losing. Now when I got off the plane I told everybody I was gonna win this British Open. I didn't say it just once. I said it a hundred times and if you keep saying something you get to believe it. And once you believe it, it comes as no shock when you are out there leading the tournament. You then take victory as your right.

Lee Trevino at the 1971 Open championship (*Golf Illustrated* magazine, 1972).

No one deserves a victory more than I do. I didn't come here to be second.

Colin Montgomerie on winning the 1995 German Open.

When I stood up to it, I had the feeling that something had been taking care of me through two matches that I very well might have lost, and that it was still taking care of me. I knew that however I struck that putt, it was going down.

Bobby Jones describing a crucial putt on his way to winning the 1930 Amateur championship in his Grand Slam year (*The Bobby Jones Story*).

When I won, it was as though I were standing outside myself looking on. That's always the feeling – win or lose. I never sit down and think 'Me, I'm champion golfer of Britain.'

British champion **Marley Spearman** (*World Sports* magazine, 1963).

We must always talk about winning. Never losing. We must never give up. That is too easy. When I play with Jose Maria Olazabal there are no 'sorrys' between us if either of us hits a bad shot. We just make sure we get the next one right.

Seve Ballesteros on the secret of his successful Ryder Cup partnership with his fellow Spaniard (*Daily Mail*, 1993).

When you finish second seven times in a season all sorts of terrible things go through your mind and that word choker would be top of the pile. You wonder if you will ever win, you wonder what you did wrong, whether it was your bad golf or someone else's brilliant golf.

Padraig Harrington after winning the end-of-season Volvo Masters (*Guardian*, 2001).

I can't guess how good they're going to be out there. But I'll gladly tell you the message I've just given my boys in the locker room – and that is there aren't ten golfers from the whole world who could possibly beat us right now.

> US skipper **Arnold Palmer** talking to the British andIrish press before the 1963 Ryder Cup match (Mark Wilson, *Golfer's Bedside Book*).

Before, when I played in the Ryder Cup it had been in the company of [Tom] Watson and [Jack] Nickiaus. You felt two down as soon as they walked into the same room. This time it was different. The Americans had nobody with that charisma.

> **Howard Clark** at the 1985 match won by Europe.

It wasn't that I played many bad rounds. I was just too often ruined by one bad hole. Hagen used to tell me: 'Gene, you waste 'em. I save 'em.'

> **Gene Sarazen** on the short-game problems that led him to invent the original sand wedge (the official US Open magazine 1979).

I want to make a good living from golf with as little publicity as possible.

> **Bob Gilder** on winning the 1980 Canadian Open.

It's like a colour movie. First I see the ball where I want it to finish. Then the scene quickly changes and I see the ball going there. Then there is a sort of fade-out and the next scene shows me making the kind of swing that will turn the previous images into reality.

> **Jack Nickiaus** on his pre-shot preparation 1992.

Excessive golfing dwarfs the intellect. And is this to be wondered at when we consider that the more fatuously vacant the mind is, the better for play. Alas! we cannot all be idiots. Next to the idiotic, the dull unimaginative mind is best for golf.

Sir Walter Simpson.

To end up beating him is beyond what I can comprehend. The fans were pulling for their hometown hero. Heck, I was pulling for him too.

Dana Quigley on beating Tom Watson in Kansas City for the 2000 Waterhouse championship.

If you think positively and keep your mind on what's right, it gives you a better attitude. If you moan and groan and are disgusted, you play miserably too.

Bernhard Langer after winning the 1997 Benson and Hedges International Open in bad weather.

I knew I was going to make that putt. Why miss it after I'd gone to all that trouble to get there?

Jack Nickiaus reflecting on his putt from 30 feet for his par five after hitting into trees, taking a penalty drop, hitting behind another tree then finding the green with his fourth shot in the 1975 US PGA championship, which he went on to win.

Any time you win is special. To win in Scotland is special and to win against this quality of field is special too.

Tom Lehman on his 1997 Loch Lomond World Invitational victory.

Be patient. You know exactly how to play this course. You are the greatest golfer in the world.

The note that **Seve Ballesteros** wrote to Jose Maria Olazabal before the final round of the 1994 US Masters championship, which he went on to win.

I was confident about winning here and even had my speech made out on Saturday night.

Isao Aoki at the Sunday prize giving of the Coca-Cola Golf Classic (which he won in 1989, Melbourne, Australia).

Not yet.

Nick Faldo's reply when asked at the 1990 Open championship whether he was beginning to look invincible. He went on to win the title.

I like to come from behind because I can play aggressively and go for broke. I have nothing to lose.

Karrie Webb on her last-round charge which included six consecutive birdies to win the 1997 Komen International.

When you've had a three-year dry spell, fear is always around the corner.

Sandy Lyle returning to form to win the 1991 BMW International.

I finally realised you don't win anything when you keep knocking the ball into the rough.

Richard Boxall on becoming 1990 Italian Open champion.

It was just one of those days. I had the feeling that no matter what the distance might be on the greens, I had the line right and I had nothing but good positive thoughts. I can understand better now how the great players manage to keep their game going on a high, how when you watch them, they never seem to get out of the groove.

Rodger Davis after scoring 62 to win the 1986 New Zealand Open.

It was a feeling of enormous strength and confidence he was never able to explain. He felt caught up by a spirit and power greater than himself, and that day he demonstrated many times that he was, as it were, simply the instrument of this greater force.

Max Faulkner on winning the 1951 Open championship (*Great Moments in Sport: Golf,* 1971, by Michael McDonnell).

He'll probably have a good night's sleep, all two and a half hours of it.

Johnny Miller on Peter Oosterhuis, who led the 1973 US Masters with one round to play.

Some of the players told me not to expect too much this week. They said I'd come down out of the clouds. But it worked the opposite for me. I stayed in the clouds.

Sherri Turner, winning the Corning Classic a week after capturing the 1988 LPGA championship.

Far be it from me to assume the least of poking fun at our sedate and altogether sportsmanlike British cousins, but in the light of Miss Joyce Wethered's recent victory in the British Ladies golf championship at St Andrews, the suggestion forcibly obtrudes itself that they might do a lot worse than induce Miss Wethered to enter the next British Open championship which the American forces have been capturing with such monotonous regularity since 1920.

American sports writer **O B Keeler** in 1929.

We've allowed ourselves to become intimidated by American self-confidence. The main challenge is one of psychology – breaking down the European reserve and inferiority complexes before we meet the millionaire superstars.

European team captain **Tony Jacklin** before the 1983 Ryder Cup match.

Don't anybody feel sorry for me. It's not the end of the world. I've had a great year. I lost a chance to win a great title but I've proved I can play with anyone in the world. I've proved I'm a contender. I'm going to benefit from what happened to me here.

Paul Azinger after losing the 1987 Open championship to Nick Faldo.

In a way, I like the underdog role. I like to be afraid of everybody. It's a mind game, a challenge to me. I have to prove something.

Ken Green talking to sports writer Kaye Kessler after scoring a surprise win against the established stars in the 1986 inaugural International championship.

With a sore eye and nearly having pneumonia I win the English Open. When I am healthy next week, I start missing cuts again.

Irish professional **Philip Walton,** 1995.

Can you imagine Jack getting beat by a guy smoking a pipe?
Arnold Palmer on Brian Barnes, who defeated Nicklaus
twice in one day during the 1975 Ryder Cup.

I just throw some junk in the air and hope it stays out of the
rough and eventually gets to the green.
US Open champion **Julius Boros** describing his own game.

I know that I have had previous lives from experiences in my
therapy and in my dreams. I have had some of my most vivid
dreams of fighting in the Civil War – in and around where this
course is now.
Muffin Spencer-Devlin after winning the 1986 United
Virginia Bank Classic in Virginia.

At the top of the backswing you feel – I do anyway – 'Please,
please make sensible contact with the ball' and hopefully it will
go somewhere straight.
Colin Montgomerie on Ryder Cup team pressures.

It took seven holes, but You still recognised me!
Simon Hobday, who claimed he was wearing a sombrero to
disguise himself from the Almighty, after taking three putts.

You figure it out. I can't. I've been struggling for four years to win
a tournament and then the weakest part of my game becomes
my strength when I needed it and I win. It's a crazy game.
Bill Ray Brown referring to his phenomenal putting spell
as he won the 1991 Greater Hartford Open.

I told my caddie 'Let's get 30 under.' As long as I'm living a fantasy I might as well take it all the way.

Robert Wrenn on winning the 1987 Buick Open.

I guess I'm just reaching my potential. They always told me I had potential to be a great player. And I'm messing around winning one tournament a year.

Johnny Miller, 1974.

I think the PGA championship changed me as a person. When I won, I felt maybe I was selling myself short a little bit. That I wasn't as bad a player as I had always told myself I was.

David Graham on winning the 1980 Memorial Tournament.

Why should I play with the flat-bellies when I can play with the round-bellies?

Lee Trevino confirming his intention to leave the main US Tour and join the senior circuit in 1989.

I asked myself: 'What would Tom Watson do in this situation?' Well, I know Watson would just grind away and that's what I did.

Mark O'Meara on winning the 1986 Australian Masters.

You're trying to make great strategists out of us and we're just a couple of old golfers.

US Ryder Cup skipper **Jack Nicklaus** with European counterpart Tony Jacklin on being asked by the press to explain his batting order before the 1987 match.

I just turned away and waited for the crowd to tell me what happened.

Bruce Lietzke after hitting a 25-yard putt which eventually dropped at the fourth play-off hole to earn him the 1977 Tucson Open.

So when I entered the Inverness locker room – the first time the pros were offered this privilege – there was The Haig in all his glory, hearty and smiling and surrounded by admirers. I couldn't help thinking he looked like a maharajah. Somebody introduced us and he was pretty casual about it, I don't remember exactly but he said something like 'Hi, kid' and went on with his conversation.

Gene Sarazen recalling his first meeting with Walter Hagen, who was to become his great friend and rival, at the 1920 US Open (the official US Open magazine, 1979).

I played that final round all night long. I was disappointed when I woke up at dawn and found I hadn't already won.

J C Snead, who in fact went on to win the 1976 San Diego Open.

Hanging on to anxiety as if it were a family heirloom.

Sports psychologist **Alan Fine's** verdict on David Feherty before the Irishman won the 1986 Italian Open.

I was paired with Tony Jacklin. 'I don't want to talk today,' he said. I said: That's OK. You listen. I'll talk.' I figure you are going to be out there four hours and if you keep your mouth closed for four hours you get bad breath.

Lee Trevino recalling his encounter with Jacklin in the 1972 World Match Play championship.

I want you guys to stop referring to me as a cowboy. I'm a rancher now.

George Archer after winning the 1972 Greensboro Open.

I'm not like Fuzzy Zoeller and some other guys. I am not able to laugh and slap my knee when I'm going around out there. I needed to get off by myself. I had to go somewhere and collect myself. In this case it was the Port-A-John.

David People explaining why he retreated to a portable toilet during a delay in the final round of the 1991 Southern Open, which he won.

Which one of you is going to be runner-up?

Walter Hagen's remark to Leo Diegel and other professionals on the eve of the 1925 US PGA championship which Hagen went on to win.

Behold the champion of all Spain! Kneel, you bastards, kneel!

Eddie Polland's light-hearted greeting to his fellow professionals the week after winning the 1976 Spanish Open.

When I get it going it's like I'm in a trance. I know what's going on around me but I can black out everything. It's like I'm hypnotised. I can see the things that are going to happen. I feel like I'm going to birdie every hole.

Johnny Miller explaining his brilliant form at the 1975 US Open.

A year and a half ago when I really didn't feel I could win again I wondered whether I really needed to stay out here any more. I resigned myself to either get more prepared and get in shape or quit playing golf.

> **Nancy Lopez** after her comeback win in the 1997 Chick-fil-A Charity championship.

We all know that Jack Nicklaus thinks better than anyone else under pressure, and that makes him so great.

> Australian **Graham Marsh**.

I think you have some who remember it as a lucky chip-in or whatever, and I'm sure at times that got under my skin a little bit but it doesn't any more because I won the tournament and it's as simple as that. It isn't a one-hole golf tournament. I hit a heck of a chip to win.

> **Larry Mize** to golf writer Lauren St John on holing a chip shot from 100 feet to beat Greg Norman in a play-off for the 1987 US Masters.

> The Ball no question makes of Ayes and Noes,
> But Here and There as strikes the Player goes;
> And he that toss'd you down into the Field,
> He knows about it all – He knows – HE knows!
> **Edward Fitzgerald,** *The Rubaiyat of Omar Khayyam.*

You have to be able to leave this game behind. The last thing you want is to be sitting in the cinema watching a film and find you're thinking about golf.

> **Padraig Harrington** after winning the 2006 European Order of Merit.

You have nothing to fear. Make today the best day of your life. You were born to do this job. This is what we practise for. This is what we live for. Now go. Go and do it.

Ryder Cup captain **Sam Torrance**'s advice to his team before they won the crucial last day singles series and the match in 2002.

13

'Hit 'em a Bloody Sight Harder, Mate!' Helpful Hints

Sir Henry Cotton identified the common factor that all great golfers share in their technique as the unerring ability to make the clubface meet the ball squarely time after time. How that is achieved is another matter, of course, because body movements vary with each physique. But the moment of impact remains identical.

Sir Michael Bonallack, at one time the best amateur golfer in the world, confessed that his style resembled a drunk shovelling coal. Gay Brewer looked like he was trying to kill snakes. Miller Barber had the look of a man who had caught his club in a clothes line. Hubert Green had the style of a drunk trying to find a keyhole in the dark. And Ralph Guldhal was said to take on the appearance of a man squirming into a phone box with a load of parcels in his arms.

Whatever else, though, they were all champions. Not one of them was obsessed with finding a textbook swing; instead they made sure that what they had been born with worked properly. It is a question of recognising one's strengths and playing to them, while ensuring that one's weaknesses remain well hidden.

And now I too have been in the game for so long, and have learned from a life that has passed all too quickly that to play good golf rests entirely on the ability to find the back of the ball with the club head square.

> **Sir Henry Cotton** (*Thanks for the Came,* 1980).

Of Vardon, we heard it said that the strength of his game lay in the fact that all his shots are tee shots, meaning that he hit every ball irrespective of its lie as well as if it had been teed. And in truth he was hitting marvellously clean, marvellously far and steadily.

> *Golf Illustrated* **account** of Harry Vardon's 1899 Open victory.

A quiet, almost dull, man with big hands and feet who never seemed to hit the ball but just swung at it.

> Boyhood reflections of J H Taylor's son **Jack** on Harry Vardon.

When Harry wrapped those hands around the handle there was no daylight between the fingers. You could see the club was a prisoner. He was a wonderful judge of distance and was never influenced by the club he used. He had a silky sway and flail swing. Only Vardon could control a sway.

> **George Duncan,** the 1920 Open champion, on Vardon's playing style (*Golf Monthly,* 1961).

He has the long, upright, graceful swing to my short, flat one. He's more elegant. I'm a bit of a plodder.

> **Sandy Lyle** contrasting his golf swing with that of Nick Faldo (David Davies, Ryder Cup magazine, 1987).

In his physical make-up he quite accidentally combined all the necessary qualities of perfect co-ordination, sense of rhythm, balance and timing that are needed to play the exasperating and elusive game of golf with anything approaching perfection.

Paul Gallico on Bobby Jones (*Farewell to Sport,* 1937).

Hit 'em a bloody sight harder, mate!

Ted Ray's brusque advice when asked how to get more distance on tee shots.

The guy can scramble and win more tournaments than most guys playing at their very best.

Bill Rogers on Tom Watson winning the 1980 Byron Nelson Classic.

At his peak he was probably the best amateur golfer in the world despite a golf swing that, of his own admission, resembled a drunk shovelling coal.

From a **profile** on five times Amateur champion Sir Michael Bonallack (*Golf Journal,* 1983).

I've always held the bel ief that you've got to make the best of what you've got. I decided early on to get the best out of the swing I had instead of searching round – and wasting time doing it – for a good-looking action. There are plenty of players with beautiful swings who never win anything.

Neil Coles (*World Sports* magazine, 1962).

He has the ability to do things no one else can do and yet has a short game where, if he makes mistakes, he can correct it. That's what's so phenomenal about him.

Jack Nicklaus on Tiger Woods at the 1999 Memorial
Tournament.

Those short putts! Put him twelve feet from the hole and not a better holer-out could be named. But with eighteen inches or two feet as the measure to be negotiated – it were kinder to allow the figure of aposiopesis to come to the rescue.

Reflections on the putting problems of Old Tom Morris
(*Golfing* magazine, 1906).

How does a seagull fly? How does a centipede get all those legs working at once? I've been playing this game of golf for more than twenty years. I just do it. I don't question it.

Billy Casper, US Masters and Open champion, in 1972 on his
attitude to technique.

I have come to the conclusion that I enjoy nothing more than the sight of Braid getting out of the rough. The choice may not indicate a Christian spirit but the best – or worst – of Braid in the rough is that it generally means no punishment at all to him. It is a real treat to watch him playing a shot in an extremely difficult position. He has no equal at it.

Harry Vardon on James Braid (*How to Play Golf,* 1912).

I became the best in the world and I thought I had to change everything to stay the best. I tried to change my swing and that was a load of rubbish. I went to a sports psychologist and that was a load of crap. I'm a natural.

Ian Woosnam after winning the 1996 Heineken Classic.

His swing is beautifully under control and he hits the ball with that nip – that element of resolution – which counts for so much in the execution of a shot.

Harry Vardon on J H Taylor.

His swing looks like a drunk trying to find a keyhole in the dark.

American columnist **Jim Murray** on US Open champion Hubert Green's playing style (*Los Angeles Times*).

I'm only 61. What's so tough about swinging a golf club?

Sam Snead on finishing runner-up in the 1974 Los Angeles Open.

It's kind of disjointed. My boss told me I shouldn't take it out of town because if it broke down I couldn't get the parts.

American golf writer **Kaye Kessler** talking to Ben Hogan about his own golf swing (*Golf Digest* magazine).

The loose, slashing style known as the St Andrews swing, in which the player seems to twist his body into an imitation of the Laocoon, and then suddenly to uncoil, is the perfection of art. It is a swing and not a hit; the ball is met at a certain point and swept away with apparent abandon, the driver following the ball and finishing with the swing over the shoulder in what is almost a complete circle.

(***Scribner's Magazine***, 1895).

The rapidity of his swing is such as to excite wonder among those who cling with affectionate superstition to the time-crusted maxim of 'slow back' and aphorisms of similar import.

A **description** of Scottish professional Wiliie Campbell's style
(*Golf Illustrated,* 1900).

If he ever grows up, he'll hit the ball 2,000 yards.

Sandy Lyle after being beaten by diminutive boyhood rival Ian Woosnam (5ft 4in) in the final of the 1987 World Match Play championship at Wentworth (*Daily Mail*).

The way he was hitting it, I didn't want to watch.

Robert Gamez on being asked on which hole playing partner Seve Ballesteros had hurt his back and was forced to withdraw from the Players championship in 1996, having taken 41 strokes for the first nine holes.

Before each shot, Ronnie goes through a series of seemingly odd contortions. These are his father's idea. He believes that the muscles have to be 'reminded' of their role before each shot. Young Shade can be observed standing away from the ball posing in the top of the backswing position and flicking his hips. This is to 'remind' his hips to move first. His most usual pose is the follow through which he performs and holds three times before each strike.

The pre-shot routine of Scottish golfer Ronnie Shade as described by ***World Sports*** magazine, 1962.

Given a strong pair of lungs, firm muscles upon the legs and a healthy desire to emulate others in physical exercise, a man may become a golf player. Without these he had better stay out of the sport for no man who cannot run several miles without stopping can make any kind of a respectable appearance in the game.

Part of an **essay** on the sport in the *St Louis Globe-Democrat* newspaper, 1889).

Pavin's swing must be the swing of the future because I sure as hell haven't seen anything like it in the past.

American writer **Charles Price** on US Open champion Corey Pavin's individualistic style.

He felt the secret of golf was ten secrets: work, work, work, work, work, work, work, work, work and work. It was a silent perseverance.

Mac O'Grady on Ben Hogan (*Golf World* magazine, 1997).

I'm not the prettiest golfer in the world but when it counts I knuckle down and get the job done. I've got flaws in my swing but I just try to get by on what I've got.

Craig Parry after winning the 1996 Australian Masters.

Playing technique of the professionals didn't show any particular developments during the year with the possible exception of the increasing trend towards Mangrum's straight-arm method of putting. Mangrum unquestionably is the most competent 'scrambler' in American golf. He can stray from fairways and turn pars into birdies by marked finesse in his approaching and putting.

Herb Graffis on Lloyd Mangrum's style (*The Golfer's Year,* 1949).

I have never met any player, amateur or professional, who hasn't benefited from going slightly slower than that which seems natural to him. The reason I got a rather laborious swing, or developed one, was that my first hero was Cyril Tolley and my next was Bobby Jones. Both swung the club slowly and whenever I have been out of form myself, I have always gone back to the practice ground and made myself swing slower.

Former English champion **Leonard Crawley** quoted by Donald Steel in *The Golfers,* 1982.

There was the man who seemed to be attempting to deceive his ball and lull it into a false sense of security by looking away from it and then making a lightning slash in the apparent hope of catching it off its guard.

P G Wodehouse (*Heart of a Goof,* 1923).

Coats should be cut loose without being baggy and are better cut without a flap at the back. Shoulder strapping, gussets, pleatings and belts are the inventions of the tailor prompted by the Devil. Sleeves should be loose without being baggy and should be cut well up under the arms. Breast pockets are best cut inside the coat and the ordinary outside pocket should have flaps. Coat collars should be cut so that they can be buttoned when turned up.

Sartorial tips for golfers from **Major Guy Campbell** (*Golf for Beginners,* 1922).

When Barber swings, it looks as if his golf club gets caught in a clothes line.

Ben Crenshaw on the playing style of Miller Barbe (*The Sporting News,* 1984).

Peculiarly low down, like someone strangling a turkey.
Australian cricketer **Keith Miller** describing the golf swing of
British sports cartoonist Roy Ullyett.

He swings the club in a figure eight. If you didn't know better,
you'd swear he was trying to kill snakes.
Dave Hill on US Masters champion Gay Brewer Junior (*Teed
Off*, 1977).

My own view is that it's cheating to use it but so long as the
authorities say it's completely legal it will stay in my bag.
Mike Clayton referring to his long-handle putter, with which
he won the 1994 Heineken Classic.

I noticed that my second putts are shorter than before which
means I wasn't missing my first putts by as much.
Ryder Cup golfer **Steve Pate** on trying the long-handle putter
(*Golf World* magazine, 2001).

I don't care what it looks like. We don't get paid for looking
good. We get paid for getting the job done.
Bernhard Langer on winning the 1996 Asian Masters with a
long-handle putter.

I've learned the more you play with the top players, the more
you realise how many bad shots they hit. They're only human
too.
David Gilford on winning the 1991 English Open.

It must be very pleasant to hit the golf ball as Mr Edward Blackwell hits it, not only because it must be such a delightful sensation but also because it must make the subsequent problems after the tee shot so much more simple. It is by happy dispensation that Mr Blackwell is not a very good iron player. If he were, driving as he does and putting as he does – for he is not a bad putter, although his putting does not compare with his driving for their respective qualities – there would be no holding him at all.

Horace Hutchinson (*Country Life,* 1906).

Two tin legs do not provide the happiest base upon which to build a game. Yet for years after the war, with his flying honours thick upon him, Douglas contrived to play golf, with infectious enthusiasm, to a single figure handicap displaying in the process rare strength in hands, wrists and forearms.

P B 'Laddie' Lucas on his brother-in-law, Group Captain Douglas Bader, who lost both legs in a flying accident yet still became a renowned Second World War fighter ace (*The Sport of Princes,* 1980).

Seldom does Woods ask Williams to read putts, subscribing to the school of thought that the last thing you want on a putt is a second opinion.

Golf World magazine describing the working relationship between Tiger Woods and his caddie Steve Williams.

Still, some men like to play with shafts made of their old billiard cues, and since this wood is sure to be well seasoned the conceit is harmless.

Horace Hutchinson on choosing clubs (*Golfing* magazine, 1898).

I should have kept my mouth shut.
> **Lee Trevino** ruefully reflecting on earlier advice to Jim Dent about taking more time over his putts. He did, and beat Trevino in a play-off for the 1997 Hope Depot Invitational.

And above all the pace of the takeaway, the completely unhurried start of the downswing and the constancy of arc. Watching him can be almost hypnotic. Beauty is an ephemeral quality; rarely in a golfer has it been more constantly expressed.
> **Pat Ward-Thomas** in the *Guardian* on former US Open champion Gene Littler (1969).

In the practice rounds Gene Littler asked me to help him with his swing. That's like trying to tell Stradivari how to play the violin.
> **Miller Barber** at the 1988 Memorial Tournament.

Aesthetic purity has been sacrificed to the cause of eliminating unwanted movement with the intention of creating a more reliable mechanism. Some of the fluid grace has gone, replaced by a greater impression that the ball is being hit with every ounce of his 180lb frame.
> **Richard Williams** (*Guardian*) on Tiger Woods at the 2001 Open championship.

I took a bigger club and aimed at the back of the green. Luckily it hit someone.
> **John Fourie** on his shot to the last green over water to win the 1973 Transvaal Open.

It was like Jack and the Beanstalk and I'm Jack. But I was able to tackle the monster.

> American professional **Mike Reid**, a modest hitter, on how he
> tackled the massive Kemper Lakes course to share the first-
> round lead in the 1989 US PGA championship.

Watch Braid on the links. There is no ponderous cogitation over the lie of the ball, no elaborate waggle preparatory to hitting it. He just walks up to where it is lying, looks at it carefully, calculates the distance to the hole, selects his club and makes his shot with calmness and precision.

> ***Golfing*** magazine on James Braid, 1906.

He defies so many of the accepted principles of the game, he is so very nearly a complete set of laws unto himself. He is the master of the knack of recovering the right position at the moment of impact after having moved his head and body during the backward swing that would spell disaster for almost anybody else. As he brings the club down, you feel he is either going to make an extraordinarily good shot or an extraordinarily bad one.

> **Harry Vardon** on Ted Ray.

A Scottish newspaper critic of the Amateur championship is 'down' on Mr Harold Hilton for his method of putting with one hand – an experiment which the writer mentioned stigmatises as a dismal failure. The same article conveys the suggestion that Mr Hilton's novel style was adopted to court notoriety. Such a totally unjustifiable charge will be warmly resented by all right-minded golfers for, whatever Mr Hilton's little mannerisms on the course may be, no one could accuse him of not taking the game seriously, particularly in such an important event as the Amateur championship.

> Editorial **comment** in *Golfing* magazine, 1907.

I think he is very mechanical. Hogan was mechanical. The mechanical golfer – and Faldo may be the exception – is probably going to get beat by a feel player.
Jack Nicklaus on Nick Faldo.

To me, only three players have ever looked entirely natural swinging a golf club – Christy O'Connor, Roberto de Vicenzo and Neil Coles. Christy flows through the ball like fine wine.
Lee Trevino.

The waggles are many but the shots are few.
Comment of unknown origin on Sandy Herd's golf style.

My eyes go out of focus and my brain kind of goes out of a little focus too. So I don't get hung up on trying to hit anything on a perfect line. It's hard to explain. I kind of let my eyes go into a blank stare.
Loren Roberts explaining his putting style after winning the 1995 Nestle Invitational.

That was the championship in which Hezlet's uncommonly wide straddle was given to the world as the 'Cape to Cairo stance'.
Frank Moran commenting on Irishman Charles Hezlet losing in the final of the 1914 Amateur championship at Sandwich (*The Golfer's Bedside Book*).

When a guy hits a green in regulation he should be rewarded, not have a 50-footer. No wonder pros complain about their putting on some courses. But I keep going back to what Ben Hogan said of those complaints: 'Did you ever consider getting closer to the hole?'

Johnny Miller, 1974.

A fine steely spring is what the golfer wants to feel, a spring that will bring the club back, quick as thought, to the straight. Then it feels, in his hands, like a living thing, full of energy, of controlled obedient energy – to do his service.

Horace Hutchinson quoted in *Golfing* magazine, 1906, on the qualities of a good club.

When I hit a bad shot before, it would be awful. Now it usually stays where I can get at it. That's the difference and I suppose you'd have to call that experience.

US Open champion **Gene Littler**, 1971.

I don't know how he can keep going. If I played like that, I'd have to go away and sort it out and if I couldn't sort it out, I'd pack up.

Ian Woosnam, quoted in the *Daily Mail,* 2001, on the poor form of Seve Ballesteros.

Mr Hilton's driving is not unusually long but is fully long enough and only the 'slashers' out-drive him at all considerably. On the other hand he has the advantage of any of them, and of almost all the world, in consistent straightness.

Horace Hutchinson on Harold Hilton, 1899.

Palmer's style is a false style, a contrived method which depends solely on his capacity for producing physical power. And while that capacity remains unimpaired Arnie will be good. When it goes, he'll go too.

Neil Coles in *Golf Annual,* 1965.

When you haven't won for five years some very strange things start going through your mind when suddenly you get into contention. I decided the best thing to do was keep the ball in play on the fairway. It may not have looked all that pretty but it worked.

Mike Clayton on winning the 1989 Victorian Open.

Whitcombe changed his club to a one-iron and standing well ahead of his ball, seemed to swing directly down in such a manner as he might were he attempting to drive it into the ground. The shot, however, was one for the book. The ball scarcely left the tee level, flying almost with a straight trajectory to the green and stopping almost instantly when it came in contact with the turf.

Worcester Telegram's description of Charles Whitcombe
hitting into a headwind from an elevated tee during 1927
Ryder Cup practice.

Havers, the youngster of the team, has the push-iron shot down to perfection and in fact uses it on the tee and off the fairways. His swing is such that he eliminates the follow-through almost entirely, the club head seldom reaching beyond twelve inches of the point of contact before markedly losing much of its momentum.

The *Telegram's* description of Open champion Arthur
Havers's swing at the inaugural Ryder Cup match
in 1927.

I loosen my girdle and let the ball have it.
American professional **Babe Zaharias** on the secret of her long
hitting.

If God had wanted man to play golf He would have given him
an elbowless left arm, short asymmetrical legs with side-hinged
knees, and a trapezoid rib-cage from which diagonally jutted a
two-foot neck topped by a three-eyed head.
Alan Coren in *The Times,* 2001.

On the sodden greens their approaches pitched past the pin, sat
down and then, as a rabbit temporarily stunned, scuttled back,
often fifteen feet before lying dead.
Leonard Crawley commenting in the *Daily Telegraph* on the
short-game skills of American Ryder Cup golfers during the
1947 match.

I have to be honest. I look at his swing and it's got faults. Under
the severest pressure will it hold up? It's way too loose.
Nick Faldo on Greg Norman.

As smooth as a man lifting a breast out of an evening gown.
American entertainer **Phil Harris** describing the gentle bunker
play of Johnny Miller (*The Art Spander Collection*).

The image of his swing, surely the strangest that modern first-
class golf has known, remains clear in my mind to this day. He
drew the club back outside the line of flight and turned his wrists
inward, to such an extent that at the top of the swing the club

head would be pointing in the direction of the tee box. It was then whipped, no other word describes the action, inside and down into the hitting area with a terrible force.

Pat Ward-Thomas on the unorthodox technique of Irish amateur Jimmy Bruen.

He was 72 and I was 17. I was out-driving him by 100 yards. He'd take a spoon [three wood] or a brassie [four wood] and I'd be hitting a niblick [five iron] but you know what? It was my turn to putt first every time.

Max Faulkner recalling a match against 1902 Open champion Sandy Herd, as told to John Hopkins (*The Times*).

Guys like me who are thick around our legs and hips can't swing as well when it's cold.

Lee Trevino.

Grip fast, stand with your left leg first not farr; Incline your back and shoulders, but bewarre You raise them not when back the club you bring; Make all the motion with your bodies swinge And shoulders, holding still the muscles bent.

From the 1687-88 diaries of Edinburgh golfer **Thomas Kincaid** and thought to be among the earliest printed golf instruction.

Learn the Fundamentals of Golf. SWINGING. SWEARING. CHEATING. Practice balls – 5 shilling a bucket. Some of them round.

The sign on the door of **Dan Soutar's** pro shop at Manly Golf Club in Sydney (Tom Ramsey in the *International* magazine, 1987).

Whenever golfers gather and begin talking about one of the game's most popular topics, 'Who is the best player ever?', it is certain that before many minutes have passed the name of Joyce Wethered (now Lady Heathcote-Amory) will be mentioned. I do not think a golf ball has ever been hit, except perhaps by Harry Vardon, with such a straight flight by any other person.

Sir Henry Cotton (*This Came of Golf,* 1948).

Therefore, in spite of its lack of grace, and partly by reason of its lack of grace, it is a peculiarly fascinating style to watch. This sounds a paradox; but there is a special delight in seeing the kind of divine fury with which he 'laces into' the ball and yet the wonderful accuracy with which the club meets the ball.

Horace Hutchinson on James Braid (*The Book of Golf and Golfers,* 1899).

He splits his hands on the shaft, spreads his legs and hunkers over the ball like a chicken laying an egg.

Dave Hill on US Open champion Hubert Green's putting method.

I hit it as far as most of them. On my day I fancy my chances against any of them.

Laura Davies on competing against men professionals.

There is nothing of the firework character in his game, it is true scientific golf, the result of an unerring eye, of a good touch and of an ideal temperament for the game; and I for one consider that he deserved to win at Sandwich.

Harold Hilton on Walter Travis, who beat him in the 1904 British Amateur championship on his way to becoming the first American to take the title.

I don't watch him much. Sometimes he hits shots that nobody else in the world can. You have to learn to play with him and I am fortunate to have done that. Then you get used to those 250-yard three irons and drives that go 340 yards into the wind because your game can get dragged down by watching somebody that impressive.

Thomas Bjorn on Tiger Woods before beating him in the 2001 Dubai Desert Classic.

I have never seen a player whose hitting was such a pleasure to watch, such a beautiful exhibition of grace and power, showing such ability to concentrate in a moment, and on a spot, all the muscular power that a human frame was master of.

Horace Hutchinson on John Ball, Open champion and eight times Amateur champion, 1899.

I have never really been wild about his swing. And he's so fast. He doesn't look great but, boy, he does the same thing every time.

Jack Nicklaus on Jose Maria Olazabal.

Ian Woosnam has got a beautiful swing. There's nothing mechanical about Woosnam at all and he's about as smooth and flowing a player as I have seen in a long time.

Jack Nicklaus.

There is a great deal of body swing in his driving stroke. It is a rather slow swing, the kind of swing that permits a man to use a rather supple club. Tom's clubs are supple and flat in the lie and his swing is a flat one, rather of the 'auld wife cuttin' hay' style, according to Bob Martin's description of his own fine driving manner-generally sending the ball away with a fine flat trajectory that gives it a good run.

Horace Hutchinson on Old Tom Morris, 1899.

Peter said I'd get better results if I flattened the face of the club. So I gave it a bash against the nearest tree, which must still bear my autograph.

Tony Jacklin on how Peter Oosterhuis advised him to alter his sand wedge before the 1975 Lancome Trophy.

Of course the crowd were much interested in the style of putter he was using in the final and doubtless there will be a demand for the pattern he manipulated then, a species of insanity that shows ignorance of the fact that it is not the putter but the man who holes the putts.

Report in *Golfing* magazine on E Lassen's 1908 Amateur championship win.

His wriggling at the address has been likened to a man squirming his way into a telephone box with a load of parcels in his arms.

Ralph Guldahl's technique (*The Encyclopedia of Golf,* 1975).

First, second, first in the last three majors. What's why.

Tiger Woods' reply in 2005 when asked why he had made fundamental changes to his golf swing.

Every golfer who has ever won at St Andrews has been a good thinker. That's all I really ever has as a player.

Peter Thomson, five times Open Champion 2005.

14
'Selfish, Pig-headed and Conceited': An Alternative View

Not everybody falls head over heels in love with the royal and ancient game: there is a view that its popularity as a solo pursuit has robbed sport of its team spirit and had wider repercussions for society in general. Be that as it may, the game stirs strong opinions both from outsiders and those within.

And the tendency to speak out critically is not confined to those who argue for or against the merits of the sport. At times its leading performers feel moved strongly enough to target their distinguished colleagues. Thus, one of the most sporting gestures in the history of golf, when Jack Nicklaus conceded Tony Jacklin's putt and allowed the 1969 Ryder Cup match to be tied, took on a totally different meaning when viewed by his disgruntled teammates. Nicklaus's captain, Sam Snead, declared that they came over to win, not to be 'good ol' boys'.

Such criticisms are calculated and considered, not heat-of-the-moment stuff. Thus they carry weight and are worthy of deeper consideration. A classic case was when Jack Newton criticised the media for labelling Seve Ballesteros a lucky player, and reminded them after the Spaniard won the 1980 US Masters that they had a superstar on their hands – and for a long time too.

The moments of retaliation to criticism also remain a delight. When the distinguished architect Robert Trent Jones was criticised by players for making a US Open venue too tough, he retorted that all they wanted were flat greens, flat fairways, little rough and few traps: 'you could order it from a Sears-Roebuck catalogue'. Nevertheless, it remains a tribute to the game that people care enough to get angry about it and with each other.

The sooner it is realised that golf is merely a pleasant recreation and inducement to indolent people to take exercise, the better. Golf has none of the essentials of a great game. It destroys rather than builds up character, and tends to selfishness and ill temper. It calls for none of the essential qualities of a great game, such as pluck, endurance, physical fitness and agility, unselfishness and esprit de corps or quickness of eye and judgement.

The present tendency is undoubtedly towards the more effeminate and less exacting pastimes, but the day that sees the youth of England given up to lawn tennis and golf in preference to the old manly games (cricket, football, polo etc.) will be of sad omen for the future of the race.

An extract from a letter to *The Times* in June 1914 from **B J T Bosanquet,** inventor of the 'googly' ball in cricket.

Golf should not be taught in schools. It encourages children to be selfish and makes them pig-headed and conceited.

Cyril Stafford-Northcote, headmaster of St Bede's School in Staffordshire, quoted in the *Sun*, 1971.

I remember when I used to win a match in Britain, people would cheer me. The Ryder Cup isn't like that any more. Make a birdie now and they boo.

Lee Trevino (*Daily Mail,* 1993).

But the Englishman did not accept the game as an inheritance with all its traditions. He took it up rather as a parvenu who has purchased a house from aristocratic owners. He came in with the spirit of cricket possessing him and plays golf with less than Scottish solemnity. He is known to laugh when his adversary makes a bad stroke – he sometimes plays in flannels and takes his coat off – he often runs after the ball, frequently shouts at it and almost invariably counts his score.

Horace Hutchinson (*Golfing* magazine, 1898).

I've read some of the newspaper articles this week and, you know, it's almost as though you guys are waiting for Seve to blow up. I've also heard some pretty snide, completely uncalled-for remarks from some of the players, that say he's lucky and a one-putt Jessie and all that crap. America's considered to be the tops in professional golf and here comes a young 23-year-old and he's taken some of the highlight away from your superstars. But, you know, the guy's a great player and the sooner Americans realise it, the better.

Jack Newton who finished runner-up to Seve Ballesteros, tackling the media during the 1980 US Masters.

Caterpillars were turning into butterflies in the time it took him to play some of his shots and he even tossed up bits of grass to check the wind before he disappeared into the trees for a call of nature.

Sports writer **Martin Johnson** commenting on the slow play of Belgian professional Nic Vanhootegem at the 2001 European Tour qualifying school (*Daily Telegraph*).

The US players had worked their tails off to get into that position and then Nicklaus gave them a tie. I think most of the players were very upset. I would like to have seen Jacklin hole that putt and earn it outright.

Billy Casper commenting on the decision by Jack Nicklaus not to ask his opponent Tony Jacklin to hole a putt on the last green, thereby allowing the entire 1969 Ryder Cup match at Royal Birkdale to be tied.

When it happened all the boys thought it was ridiculous to give him that putt. We went over there to win, not to be good ol' boys. I never would have given a putt like that – except maybe to my brother.

US skipper **Sam Snead** on the same incident.

Jacklin couldn't have missed that putt in a hundred years. Since we were going to retain the Ryder Cup it didn't matter one way or the other whether he made it or missed it. Tony was the hero of Britain at the time. He had just won the British Open and I didn't want to give him the chance to miss it and cost his team the Ryder Cup outright. I just thought it was the right thing to do and in the spirit of what the matches are about.

Nicklaus's reply to Peter Farricker in the Ryder Cup magazine 1995.

Golf is a first-class game and, in my opinion, second only to cricket. It must be admitted that it fails in one important particular, namely that each player strikes his own ball only and never plays a stroke with the direct object of embarrassing his adversary.

Ernest Baggally, Metropolitan magistrate (*Golfing* magazine, 1907).

When we complain about conditions, we're just bitches. But when the men do it, people think, 'Well, it really must be hard.'

Betsy King on the state of the 1991 US Women's Open venue.

Say what you like about the Scots but they recognise tripe when they see it.

Golf writer **Derek Lawrenson** explaining the absence of spectators at the inaugural pro-am style 2001 Dunhill Links championship (*Daily Mail*).

When Phil and I got to the first green we were shocked. We could see our own reflections.

Colin Montgomerie on how he and Phil Mickelson reacted to the controversial glassy greens in the 1999 Players championship.

The game of golf is in a fair way of becoming unplayable in America on account of the amazing and unconscionable slowness of American players. The prevalent idea that the American is a bom hustler is sadly belied on the golf links. It may be that because he has learned to travel in express subway trains, the American has forgotten how to walk on the golf links. But that is not the only reason why he takes such a long time to get round the course. Because Walter Travis takes a practice swing before most shots, the beginner appears to think he cannot become a good golfer unless he does the same. So he takes a preliminary swing, and then waggles his club needlessly over the ball or crouches over it with glaring eye as if by sheer hypnotic power he would compel it to fly. As a result it is almost impossible to get round a crowded golf links in less than two hours and a half.

Outing magazine, 1910.

If I counted as do some of these others or violated the rules as many of them do, I could beat all my old championship figures.

Davie Brown, the 1886 Open champion, on the manner in which some of his contemporaries disregarded the rules (*The American Golfer,* 1925).

The Road Hole is the most famous and infamous hole. As a planner and builder of golf holes worldwide, I have no hesitation in allowing that if one built such a hole today, you would be sued for incompetence.

Peter Thomson on the seventeenth hole of the Old Course at St Andrews (*Golf Digest,* 1984).

Perhaps they should add a couple of windmills and a dinosaur.

Laura Davies on the venue for the 1999 Tournament of Champions.

You have to land it in a tea-cup.

Laura Davies's comment on the small size of the greens.

There was a lack of real greatness about the golf; and one feels more and more every year that something has gone out of the game since the disappearance of the gutta-percha ball.

Comment in the *Sportsman* on the 1908 Amateur championship.

Goddammit Jay, I can hole them from past the hole but I can't hole them from short.

Lanny Wadkins to foursomes partner Jay Haas in the 1975 Walker Cup match at St Andrews after Haas left yet another of his putts woefully short (David Davies, *Guardian*).

Of 1,750 clubs in the British Isles whose co-operation we invited, only 216 have accorded help. It is a deplorable reflection on the attitude of the average golfer towards the game.

We fear it must be held to afford definite evidence that the oft-repeated slur against the pastime that most of its players are selfish possesses a good deal of truth.

A *Golf Illustrated* **editorial** on the difficulties in raising £3,000 by public donation in 1927 to send a team across the Atlantic for the first Ryder Cup match.

The modern American professional has no character and no crowd appeal. He just goes on and on playing what a famous cricketer called the business shot.

Correspondent in *The Times* previewing the 1939 Ryder Cup match, which was subsequently cancelled because of the outbreak of war.

I don't think you should have a sudden-death play-off to decide a national championship. It's a little too much merely to accommodate television.

Jack Nicklaus on losing the 1975 Canadian Open in extra holes to Tom Weiskopf.

I couldn't make a living doing anything else except maybe pumping gas. A lot of guys on tour gripe about the travel and the food and the laundry. Well, no matter how bad the food may be I've eaten worse. And I couldn't care less about the laundry because I can remember when I only had one shirt.

Lee Trevino.

When I started, the professional tour was like a travelling circus, a nomadic village. Players, officials and the press travelled and worked together, ate and drank together and even played golf together on practice days. Each was a specialist within the Big

Top. But that has all gone and now even the community spirit among players is breaking down.

> Golf writer **Peter Dobereiner** in *The Golfer's Companion* magazine, 1988.

Everyone is talking about the new stars we have on this tour and he's dusted them twice. If people don't change their opinion of Fleisher, shame on them. He's still the sheriff in town.

> **Dana Quigley** in 2000 on fellow senior professional Bruce Fleisher, who had just scored his ninth win in fourteen months.

Some genius has suggested that, when the Olympic games are decided in London next year, golf should be included in the programme. As the games will be decided within an arena of limited area, it is difficult to see how the thing can be done.

> ***Golfing*** magazine, 1907.

You can be friendly with them another time. For one week we are trying to beat these guys.

> **Raymond Floyd's** remark to partner Fred Couples, who complimented his opponents too frequently on their good shots during the 1991 Ryder Cup match. (Ryder Cup magazine, 1995).

If you built the kind of course the pros would really like, you would have dead flat greens, dead flat fairways, very little rough and very few traps. That kind of course wouldn't require an architect; you could order it from a Sears-Roebuck catalogue.

> **Robert Trent Jones** replying to the pros' complaints about Hazeltine golf course at the 1970 US Open.

Slow play is a disease. It's the price you pay for modern golf. You could make the course less severe and turn it into a putting contest but I'd rather have par mean something.

Jean Van de Velde on the six-hour rounds during the 2000 US PGA championship.

To begin with, we regret to say that the St Andrews club seems indifferent to the position of guardian of the traditions of the game with which other clubs have shown their willingness to entrust it. Let us hope St Andrews will awaken to a sense of its responsible position. If it does, there are some points on which it would require to legislate in the interests of golf in general and some points, which for local purposes as well, might with advantage be made more clear.

Sir Walter Simpson, the captain of the Honourable Company of Edinburgh Golfers, urging the Royal and Ancient Golf Club of St Andrews to exert its powers of law-making (*The Golfing Annual,* 1888).

Most tournaments have become a test of who can hit the ball longest, whether they are straight or not. You might as well put us on a driving range and the fellow who hits it the farthest in any direction is the winner.

Gary Player, 1969.

The modern tournament golfer becomes accustomed to blithely whaling at his tee shot because the penalty for missing fairways is hardly ever severe in the weekly Tour events. In the Open he hesitates and often drives with an iron or a fairway wood because he lacks confidence in his ability to hit the driver straight enough.

Robert Sommers in the official US Open magazine, 1990.

The seventeenth is just a way to get from the sixteenth green to the eighteenth tee.

      Jack Nicklaus's withering comment on the penultimate hole at Olympic Club during the 1998 US Open.

I prefer it when people are punished for missing a fairway. This course has been set up for tournament professionals. We go to too many courses where the members have just finished playing when we turn up.

      Colin Montgomerie on the Forest of Arden venue for the 1996 English Open.

Do not treat your club professional as if he was on the same level as the man you employ to roll your greens. If you invite him to your club to take part in a tournament, do not place him on the same level as the sheep; in other words to be allowed to wander as they graze over the land but to be rigorously excluded from the clubhouse. If you are too poor to pay a professional properly don't have one. If you have one, be satisfied to see him reap the benefits which are legitimately his by virtue of the position he occupies.

      Unknown **ex-professional** writing in *Golfing* magazine, 1906.

Ye've got the same bloody bad temper your grandfather had and it'll do ye no good. I suggest ye take a hold of yourself.

      American writer **Patty Fisher's** memories of the Scottish-born Charlie Thorn, long-serving professional at Shinnecock Hills in New York, and his method of dealing with one troublesome pupil (Walker Cup magazine, 1977).

Nothing changes. It's nice to come back and see how bad greens can be.

> **Sergio Garcia's** verdict on Loch Lomond during the 2001 Scottish Open (for which he was fined by the PGA European Tour).

I just don't get the recognition he does. I feel I've been underestimated.

> **Ian Woosnam,** winning the 1991 US F&G Classic, referring to Nick Faldo.

The man who designed this course had the blueprints upside down.

> **Dave Hill** on the Hazeltine course where Tony Jacklin won the 1970 US Open.

We pay you to express your supposedly expert opinions, for which we are paying you quite generously, not those of various golf professionals of questionable intelligence.

> The terse message sent from **Sir Gordon Newton,** editor of the *Financial Times,* to his distinguished columnist Ben Wright during the 1968 US Masters (the *International Edition,* 1988).

I have seldom used inverted commas since.

> **Wright's** response.

Who wants to know what Faulkner says? My readers want to read my view of things.

> Golf essayist **Bernard Darwin** on being told that Max Faulkner, the new Open champion, was ready for his press conference in the interview room following the 1951 championship.

I've just got to chat to you. I don't like you throwing your clubs down like that. I used to do it and, as you can see, it never got me anywhere.

> **Gerald Micklem's** advice to a young Nick Faldo (*The Sunningdale Centenary*, 2000).

In many respects the Amateur championship of 1906 has been the most unsatisfactory and, to some extent, the poorest in the history of the contest. Certainly there was a lot of luck about and a lot of lack of head and a lot of lack of heart.

> *Golfing* magazine **report** of the event at Hoy lake, won by James Robb.

They cater for foreign players and that stinks. They fail to realise it's our tour, our Masters. To most foreign guys, it's just the US Masters. To them, it could be the British Masters or the Scandinavian Masters or the Malaysian Masters. They don't care.

> US professional **Billy Andrade** criticising Augusta National officials for issuing special invitations to overseas players (*Golf World* magazine, 2001).

If you used these pin placements on a Saturday afternoon with municipal players, they'd be out here for two weeks.

Lee Trevino on the course set-up for the 1983 Isuzu-Andy Williams San Diego Open.

Some guys will say winning 700,000 dollars means you've had a great year but you can win that much without winning a tournament. Some guys are happy with that but I think you've got to play to beat each other. You've got to win.

Nick Faldo at the 1991 US Masters.

They all travel with their wives and kids. They go out and play their round of golf. Then they beat balls for six hours. Then they work out in the [fitness] trailer for four hours. Then they go back to their rooms and read the *Wall Street Journal* and telephone their accountants. Some of them, for God's sake, even eat green vegetables.

Lee Trevino bemoaning the lack of characters among the new generation of US tournament professionals (Bob Green in the *International* magazine, 1987).

Despite his stunning achievements, Guldahl was labelled 'phlegmatic, unglamorous, solemn, colourless, sluggish, methodical, deliberate'. It was also written that he was 'devoid of showmanship and didn't know what the crowd wanted in a champion'.

American writer **James Gaquin** on the harsh criticism handed out to Ralph Guldahl, who won successive US Opens and a US Masters (the official US Open magazine, 1978).

The Americans used to have first-class treatment while we flew out in the back of the airplane. They made more money, even had better shoes.

> European captain **Bernard Gallacher** before the 1991 Ryder Cup match (Mark McCormack, *The World of Professional Golf,* 1992.

I'm not crusading to get a black into the Masters. I'm just tired of them making it sound like it has been our inability to play the game that has kept us out of the Masters. If I were qualified or invited I would play for two reasons. It would be an honour to be the first and I would like those who come to the Masters to see a black play golf.

> US tour professional **Lee Elder**, 1971.

It does not make any difference whether I am paid or not. When people ask you to come and play, you have to perform.

> **Greg Norman** answering criticism that he had been paid appearance money equal to the entire prize fund of the 1996 South Australia Open – which he won.

The rough is impossible – impossible to stay out of, impossible to play out of. But I guess I'd rather be in it 40 yards ahead of everybody else.

> **Jack Nicklaus** at the 1968 Open championship in Carnoustie.

If it weren't for the greens, this course would be nothing.

> American amateur **Steve Scott** on Augusta National after scoring 79 in the 1997 US Masters to miss the halfway cut.

I'd rather putt on a motorway – yes, with all the traffic – than on those greens.

Tony Jacklin at the 1974 Italian Open.

I love Arnie to death but it's time for him to surrender. I know he still loves to play golf but there's no point in being out there if you shoot 83 or 84.

Mark Calcavecchia after Arnold Palmer, nearing 70, missed the halfway cut in the 1999 US Masters.

It's like a cheap public course. Riviera was once great but today it would make a good runway.

Mac O'Grady to Shav Glick in the *Los Angeles Times* in 1986.

I believe they can read English. They will see it in the papers.

Seve Ballesteros explaining to the press why he would not write a letter of complaint to officials about the severe condition of Turnberry for the 1986 Open championship.

It's a pretty silly course. It's almost sacrilege but I don't like it. You can stand on the tee and hit it anywhere you want as hard as you want.

Tournament professional **Russell Claydon** on the Old Course at St Andrews during the 1990 Open championship.

It was a stab in the back. When you win three major championships, the third is no fluke.

Larry Nelson after his 1987 US PGA championship win, refuting suggestions in a magazine that his major victories were flukes.

The worst display of ball-striking I have ever seen. He was like a 24-handicapper out there.

Mark McNulty on playing partner Nick Faldo in the 1999 South African PGA championship.

A millionaire on his golf earnings alone, he is so austere in his personal life that by contrast a Franciscan monk looks like a swinger.

Writer **Robert Jones** on US Masters and Open champion Billy Casper, 1969.

The Lytham greens are harder to read than *Finnegans Wake*.

Mark Reason (*Sunday Telegraph*) on the 2001 Open championship at Royal Lytham and St Annes.

Can you hear them calling? They're starving for water out there.

Payne Stewart to a green-keeper on the condition of the greens during the 1995 Players championship.

The committee has noted that the standard of dress has deteriorated and has decided that ragged jeans, denims, bomber jackets and other way-out gear are not permitted.

Notice in the clubhouse during the 1977 Martini International in Blairgowrie.

They make a lot of money and don't have to go and scratch for it like I did.

Arnold Palmer on modern tournament professionals.

How is it, then, that in the vast majority of professional tournaments and inaugural exhibitions, match play is neglected and medal play favoured? The answer, I am afraid, must be that the modern golfer looks on golf as a game of strokes rather than of holes.

Saxon Browne in *Golfing* magazine, 1907.

Jimmy Hitchcock is my bad sportsman of the week.

Columnist **Frank Butler** in the *News of the World* after the golfer was accused of failing to concede Tony Jacklin's three-inch putt in the 1965 Honda Foursomes and then claiming the hole when he missed.

The problem was in this tournament I had most of the young players beaten before they stepped up to the first tee. I don't ever go into a tournament thinking I am playing for second place and I'd like to see all the young Australian pros do the same.

Greg Norman after winning the 1988 Tournament Players championship in New South Wales.

Why don't you dig them up and pour in concrete?

Kerr Petrie of the *New York Herald Tribune* to an official who ordered a heavy roller to be used on Oakmont's greens in order to make them faster for the 1935 US Open.

People have been saying all year that they didn't think I could win again but I didn't care what people thought. I knew what I thought.

Amy Alcott after winning the 1989 Boston Five Classic.

It is almost an insult to give such a ridiculously small sum of money to some of the world's best golfers. You've got to pay if you want the best.

> **Henry Cotton** on receiving the equivalent of a £52 cheque
> for finishing runner-up in the 1936 French Open.

The greens need a rest. I have never seen the greens bumpier. They're in good condition considering. It's just that they run people through here like a bunch of cattle.

> **Johnny Miller** referring to the condition of Pebble Beach
> before the 1985 Bing Crosby Pro-Am.

Why is the media press trying to call off these matches? Has everyone forgotten what this is all about? The two nations send their best players to have a friendly go at each other. It's the comradeship, the friendships, the memories and the experiences that count. It's not a bloody war!

> **Brian Barnes** on the eve of the 1975 Ryder Cup match.

To me it's sad what he has done with his career, with his ability. He came along, won the Open, and if you had to pick a person to win that title, you couldn't have picked a better person because he had the charisma, the looks, everything going for him. But I never saw a man go from so high to so low.

> **Gary Player** on Tony Jacklin's decline (Liz Kahn,
> *The Price of Success*).

We are both champions. I said after the Masters when I lost, that sudden death was unfair and I still say it now. I have won but it's like tossing a coin and guessing which way it will fall.

Seve Ballesteros having defeated Ian Woosnam at the first extra hole of the 1987 Suze Open a week after losing the American title in similar fashion.

𝕗

It is sad not to be able to congratulate the ITA on their coverage. I fear I must go further and say that, as a public performance, it was pathetic. As it is only once in four years that we have the pleasure of seeing these great players from America, surely the time has come when the organisers should consider very carefully to whom the coverage on television should be entrusted.

Duke of Norfolk's letter to *The Times* concerning commercial television's coverage of the 1973 Ryder Cup match.

𝕗

It was noticeable that many of his approach putts were short. This, a rare fault with Jones, caused an American friend to say to him that he had never seen a hole move to meet a ball, while a little later Jones said: 'I'm sticking to my guns but they won't shoot.'

The *Guardian* on Bobby Jones during the 1926 Open, which he won.

𝕗

Thanks for telling us your troubles but do you realise nobody here really cares?

Peter Thomson's locker-room response to Maurice Bembridge after the Englishman complained about his bad luck.

𝕗

Did you remember to bring your clubs?

> US Ryder Cup captain **Ben Hogan's** crushing reply to
> Arnold Palmer, who asked for a supply of smaller British-size
> golf balls before the 1967 match in Houston, Texas.

There is an unwritten rule among golfers that you always defend
the title.

> **Bernhard Langer** on being told that Seve Ballesteros
> would not compete in the 1987 British Masters he
> had won a year earlier.

Today we have played with pin positions which show Australian
officials have no respect for the players. This is the only country
where they set the pin positions a week before the .event and
they never take into account the possibility of bad weather.

> **Greg Norman** after winning the 1985 Australian Open.

Every man and dog has been on my back. I didn't ask to play in
the World Cup and I was picked because I won the PGA title last
year. I wish they'd get off my back and let me play golf.

> **Billy Dunk** responding to criticisms of his selection for
> Australia's 1972 World Cup squad.

And things have come to such a pass because of the vain-
gloriousness of second-rate professionals and amateurs, who
annually encumber the field, that the qualifying test which it was
recently decided shall be set for entrants for this year's contest,
has been rendered necessary.

> **Comment** in the *Golfing Annual on* the 1906 Open
> championship at Muirfield.

I just don't care for the weather or the type of courses they play. I don't enjoy playing that type of golf. I've seen times when you hit a good shot and it turns out bad, or worse, than if you hit the same shot over here. And Ben Hogan went over there one time, won, and didn't go back.

Scott Hoch, to *Golf Digest* magazine, on his reasons for not playing in the Open championship.

This course is set up perfectly to destroy a golf swing.

Peter Oosterhuis at Royal St George's during the 1975 PGA Championship.

If an architect had designed it, they'd have asked for their money back.

Sir Henry Cotton on the seventeenth – the Road Hole – at St Andrews.

Our officials are setting up the courses too easy. Instead of making it a test of a player's ability, they turn it into a putting contest. I feel like we're on the ladies' tour.

Tom Weiskopf before the 1974 US Open at Winged Foot.

They have watered the greens, not watered the fairways and cut the rough. It's not the same course. You have players who can't break par shooting 62s and 63s.

Seve Ballesteros complaining at the way European Tour officials had set up Royal Pedrena, his home club, for the 1988 Spanish Open.

He is so extraordinarily quick that it is very hard to tell how he executes his shots. The ball is on the ground and he is addressing it; a moment later, while you are still waiting to study his movements, the ball is hurtling through the air and he is off for the next stroke.

Harry Vardon on George Duncan's breathless pace of play, 1912.

He is a very exciting player but unfortunately some of his worst days have been the most highly viewed in the history of sport.

Mark McCormack on Greg Norman (*Golf Digest* magazine, 1998).

The only hope I can see for Jacklin, if he is not to become a puppet golfer dangled incessantly and ineffectually from one tournament and one business meeting to another, is to separate both mind and body, Jacklin the businessman and Jacklin the golfer.

Henry Longhurst in the *Sunday Times* after the Englishman's 1970 US Open triumph.

For a great many years of his golfing career Mr John Ball was a disappointment – both to his friends and to himself. He played extraordinarily well at Hoylake, went round in wonderful scores, beat anyone who dared to play him; but when he went away from this, his native heath, he always failed to do himself anything like justice.

Horace Hutchinson in 1899 on John Ball who won eight Amateur championships and the Open.

Some of what he does seems too obvious. Moving next door to Nicklaus. Tying their boats up together. 'Design my back garden, Jack.' But when he's playing with Nicklaus he's always saying stuff like: 'Watch this, I'll fly Jack here. No problem.' I don't know if that's how you treat a friend.

Nick Faldo on Greg Norman.

Why is Royal Sydney staging this Australian Open? There are more do's and don'ts at this course than a kid would find at his first day in school.

Bruce Devlin, 1969.

Those cats at Royal Sydney, what a snob mob. Every time I got to the eighteenth green and looked up at those towers I felt like a Mexican bandit about to attack the castle.

Lee Trevino at the 1969 Australian Open.

A man who complains about gamesmanship is a sissy. One of the reasons I admire Jack Nicklaus so much is that he never looks for excuses when he loses.

Gary Player, from his autobiography.

He has as much personality as a glass of water.

Dave Hill, in his autobiography, on US Open and Masters champion Billy Casper.

You know, if I get me some black shoe polish I could do well here. Of course I wouldn't need all that much.

Lee Trevino's wry comment in 1980 on the local black caddies-only policy (since changed) operating at the US Masters.

He is the most violent, ugliest, most rude human being on Earth. The verdict of an **air steward** on Australian Open champion Wayne Riley, who was accused of air rage on a flight to Perth.

Why doesn't he just play the bloody game and leave the rest of us alone?

Alexander Walker reviewing Robert Redford's film *The Legend of Baggar Vance.*

I just have no interest in playing golf at this speed. I waited on every shot and I've no intention of continuing in this way.

Guy Wolstenholme explaining his withdrawal from the 1969 Caltex event in Australia because of the slow pace of play.

Ever since Massy defeated Braid at Deal, certain writers have been putting forward excuses which, to say the least of it, are scarcely dignified in explanation of the Scotsman's failure. In one quarter it is gravely stated that Braid was suffering from an attack of liver. This may of course have been the case but at least it was not Braid himself who advanced the plea. Neither was it Braid who said that what some individuals called a flukey holing-out shot, by which Massy secured the first hole in the afternoon, decided the fate of the match.

Whatever our opinions as to the respective merits of Braid and Massy, it would certainly have been more generous and dignified to give the Frenchman his just due as the better player in the match at Deal than to hunt about for excuses because his British opponent failed to beat him.

Comment in *Golfing* magazine, 1908.

At no time have we Americans been admitted to the clubhouse not even to pick up our mail. At this particular time, I'd like to thank you all for the many courtesies you've extended to us. And I'd like to invite you all over to the pub where we've been so welcome so that all the boys can meet you and thank you personally. If the committee likes, they can present the trophy to the new champion over there.

Walter Hagen's speech following the 1924 Open championship at Troon.

Can't we get back to old-fashioned, non-manured fairways during the summer on all courses? What is more fun than the old-fashioned run-up or chip-and-run shot to the green as it used to be played in Scotland and is now quite neglected in England?

Letter from **Sir Hugh Rhys Rankin Bt** to *Golf Monthly*, 1968.

I think he's just another person and not a particularly nice one at that. He certainly doesn't go out of his way to improve his image with other people.

Tony Jacklin after playing with Ben Hogan (Liz Kahn, *The Price of Success*).

Anyone who says this is fun is joking. This is not fun and this is not enjoyment. This is a job and a horrible one.

Colin Montgomerie on competing in the 2004 Open Championship at Royal Troon.

Golf is what I do. It is not who I am.

American professional **Patricia Meunier-Lebouc** on beating Annika Sorenstam by a stroke for the 2003 Kraft Nabisco Championship.

15

'No Pub Un-stoned': Memories of a Good Life

It is a measure of the sport that it provides a feast of fond and imperishable memories for its devotees whatever their ability: not simply the moments of triumph or miraculous strokes, but the shared experiences that bring a reflective smile and prompt thoughts of fellow travellers from the past.

Gene Sarazen recalled the 1920s as a 'nice slice of the century to be young in' because 'the parties were frequent, the girls were pretty and the drinks were long'. For Densmore Shute the 1937 Ryder Cup was remembered for the bus journey which took the team to Scotland and stopped at so many hostelries that they left 'no pub un-stoned'.

Lean times, too; Jimmy Demaret admitted deliberately hitting into the orange groves of Florida to collect enough fruit to sustain him through the day because he could afford no other food. Golf was to change his fortunes dramatically and make him very rich.

But such memories will never fade. Nor will the thoughts of the sacrifices they made, the self-doubts they overcame to achieve their rightful place in the history of the game. Above all it was the love of golf that kept them going when perhaps good sense told them to stop. How smart they were.

Life of the whole had been kind to me and enviable. I had achieved a certain notoriety both in writing and broadcasting about golf, and most people who remembered the frightful things I had done and said in the course of the past 40 years were no longer with us to recall them to a later generation.

Sunday Times golf writer **Henry Longhurst**.

It will be remembered by those who have seen Tommy at golf, that when playing a teed ball and sometimes through the green, his Balmoral [bonnet] fell off behind him and was picked up by his caddie or himself, but this did not seem to inconvenience him in the least. There was also a general concurrence of opinion among those who knew his play, that he could make more of a bad lying ball than any player they had ever known.

Profile of Young Tom Morris in *Golfing* magazine, 1905.

I saw a stocky figure emerge from the back seat of the car wearing a stetson and cowboy boots and could hardly believe my eyes. Frankly I thought he was a nut case.

Caddie **Willie Aitchison** on his first meeting with Lee Trevino, with whom he won two Open championships.

For me, of course, winning at St Andrews was the last ambition. I had won all the championships; they no longer inspired me. But I wanted the Walker Cup because it had eluded us for so long and we had won it only once in all the years since it began in 1922. During the riotous celebrations that evening, I felt a kind of emptiness. It was a personal conclusion. I had climbed the mountain and there was nothing left to do. But it was an imperishable moment too. We all shared in it. I think we will be linked by it for the rest of our lives.

Sir Michael Bonallack on leading the Great Britain and Ireland Walker Cup team to victory at St Andrews in 1971 (*Golf Journal,* 1979).

Ray with his long stride and imperturbable manner and inevitable pipe and Hagen, the greatest showman and money player on the American links proved too great an attraction. The spectators noticed especially the different manner of dress in the two teams. The English players were attired in rather drab and sober outfits of grey made the more noticeable by the gayer costumes of the Americans. There was no swelling crescendo of tumult, only ripples of applause following the particularly brilliant shots. Even the clouds were apparently affected by the evident tension as they hung motionless like irregular rings of smoke.

Worcester Telegram account of the 1927 Ryder Cup.

I can remember him telling me: 'We've got them on the run, Guv'nor. Go on, you can beat this boy.' You felt you had to win for Max. I'll never forget his contribution that afternoon.

Ken Bousfield talking to golf writer Gordon Richardson about the supportive role played by Max Faulkner, even though he had been dropped from the side, during the famous 1957 Ryder Cup victory over the United States (Ryder Cup magazine, 1987).

You couldn't help recognising them as part of the early tradition, especially the way they dressed. Out on the course, they both wore tweed jackets and felt hats.

Gene Sarazen's reflection on his US Open debut in 1920 when he saw Harry Vardon and Ted Ray for the first time (the official US Open magazine, 1979).

We were all club professionals. When the Ryder Cup matches ended, we all went back to selling sweaters in our golf shops.

Peter Alliss on his early days of team golf (Ryder Cup magazine, 1995).

We left no pub un-stoned on that ride.

Densmore Shute recalling how Walter Hagen hired a bus after the 1937 Ryder Cup to take the American team to Scotland for the Open championship so they could make frequent stops en route.

I played Tommy Armour at Wentworth in 1926, a year before the official match was started. I beat him mentally. The fact is he had a couple of extra drinks and that was no good at all. I could keep my mind on the game but he couldn't. He got mad and you only have to get mad twice in a round of golf and you've had it. I beat him 2 and 1.

Aubrey Boomer talking to the *Daily Mail* before the 1989 Ryder Cup match.

He wakes up early and then it's full speed. At least he took care of the kids some and then he was chasing the nannies the rest of the time.

Jesper Parnevik on having fellow professional Sergio Garcia as a house guest (*Golf World* magazine, 2001).

She played with her sleeves rolled up, to the mild shockment of some people. She certainly brought a spirited goodwill into the hitting of the ball.

Eleanor Helme's account of Gladys Ravenscroft in the 1909 Ladies championship at Royal Birkdale.

How on earth any of us managed to hit a ball in the outrageous garments which fashion decreed we should wear, is one of the great unsolved mysteries. I wore all grades of stiff collar, first the plain stand up, then the double collar, highly glazed and as deep as possible. Often one got a raw sore neck all around the left side after playing in those monstrosities.

Veteran golfer and journalist **Mabel Stringer.**

I consider that the thoughtful and appreciated gesture of bringing their own food (meat and butter) with them was noted by us all, particularly as many Britons, including the home team, were invited to share.

Henry Cotton, captain of the losing 1949 Ryder Cup squad, commenting on the American decision to avoid rationing in post-war Britain (*The Golfer's Year*).

When Horace was at his best there were far fewer first-class amateurs than there are now. They could easily be counted on the fingers of two hands – Horace himself, John Ball, Johnny Laidlay, Alexander Stuart, Leslie Balfour, Mure Fergusson, A F Macfie – as a result they met oftener in hard matches than our leading amateurs do now and were often perhaps a little jealous of one another.

It was, as I fancy it, rather a hard fierce school and Horace could be a fine fierce match player, especially when he could work himself up to a kind of cold anger. Though a kindly man, as well it befits me from experience to say, he was not by nature a notably patient one; but he could control and take an iron grip on himself and in that mood he was a formidable fighter.

Bernard Darwin on Horace Hutchinson (*The Oxford and Cambridge Golfing Society 1898-1948*).

I can remember that the toughest job I had when I won the British and US Opens, was not thinking about the prize-giving ceremony and receiving the trophy – not letting my mind wander ahead.

Tony Jacklin to author Liz Kahn (*The Price of Success*).

At last, yielding to temptation, he squirms his feet firmly into the sand and lashes the ball up over the water, over some distant fishing boats, over a quay, over two gaping brothers and into a far wooded hill. The soles of your feet tingle as you watch and when he grins you suddenly share in the feeling: the pure joy of hitting a ball.

Dudley Doust's account of watching Seve Ballesteros, then aged twenty, practising on a beach in northern Spain (*Sunday Times,* 1977).

I have never stopped looking back on it, not only because the match changed me from a good junior into a good golfer but also because the whole week at Muirfield – the preparation for the match as well as the match itself – personified sport at its best, people at their best, the world at its best.

Jack Nicklaus writing about his debut in the Walker Cup match in 1959.

How straight it flew, how long it flew,
It clear'd the rutty track
And soaring, disappeared from view
Beyond the bunker's back –
A glorious, sailing, bounding drive
That made me glad I was alive.

The first stanza from **John Betjeman's** 'Seaside Golf, read by Sir Michael Bonallack at the memorial service for *Daily Telegraph* golf writer Michael Williams at St Bride's church in 1997.

Churchill and Lloyd George often played together in those pre-war days. On one occasion, the Reverend Borlase assures us, they arrived on the eighteenth green with their match undecided. 'Now,' said Churchill, 'I will putt you for the Premiership.'

An incident in 1911, described in the commemorative **booklet** *Walton Heath Golf Club 1904–1979,* when Churchill was Home Secretary and Lloyd George was Prime Minister. As Churchill did not become Prime Minister until some 30 years later, it is safe to assume he missed the putt.

When he holed a putt on the last hole that was as long as the O J Simpson trial, Hale took off like a possessed teenager at a disco. He slapped his hands with the gallery, running round the eighteenth green giving low, middle and high fives.

American television commentator **Jack Whitaker**'s recollections of Hale Irwin forcing a play-off in the 1990 US Open before winning the title (the centennial US Open programme, 1995).

Among others, I was shown one particular set of golfers, the youngest of whom was turned four-score. They were all gentlemen of independent fortunes who had amused themselves with this pastime for the best part of a century without having felt the least alarm from sickness or disgust; and they never went to bed without having each the best part of a gallon of claret in his belly.

A description of Leith golfers from **Tobias Smollett**'s 1771 novel *The Expedition of Humphrey Clinker.*

The perimeter of the camp was protected by a high, double-stage, barbed wire fence. Any attempt to climb this could be met with a bullet but inside the main fence was a strip of no man's land bordered by a low trip wire. Entering this area was forbidden but so many balls from incessant games went in that the Germans provided a few white jackets. Donning one of these was tantamount to giving parole that no attempt to escape would be made and the balls could be retrieved.

Pat Ward-Thomas on playing golf in a prison camp during the Second World War (*Not Only Golf*).

But over the years, so many have claimed they actually saw it happen, I estimate there would have had to be 10,000 in the gallery. Actually there were probably about twenty, including fellow competitor Hogan, and our caddies, Bob Jones standing behind the green and a handful of sportswriters.

Gene Sarazen reflecting on the second shot he holed on Augusta's par five fifteenth en route to winning the 1935 US Masters (the official US Open magazine, 1979).

Long before Cotton made his appearance on the first tee this morning, a crowd of three or four thousand were lining the fairway up to the first green. Cars clustered in the parking places like great shining black beetles. Cinema cameramen mounted their talkie machines on the tops of their vans and laid long wriggling cables across the tee.

Guardian **report** on Henry Cotton's first Open win in 1934.

At one time I had fifteen clubs. When we left the fifth green, Nicklaus couldn't find his putter. He had put it in my bag. I told him I'd take the two-shot penalty if he didn't use the putter for the rest of the round.

Lee Trevino recalling a mix-up with Jack Nicklaus during the 1974 US PGA championship.

Dad and he never got on well.
> **Jack Taylor** talking about the relationship between his father, J H Taylor, and Walter Hagen.

One of us would take careful aim and shoot into the trees. The shot would go out of bounds and cost a stroke but it was a necessary sacrifice. On the pretext of hunting for the ball (a valuable item in 1934) we would forage in the orange grove, filling our stomachs and even our golf bags with the wonderful fruit. Often this was next morning's breakfast as well as the evening's dinner.
> **Jimmy Demaret,** US Open and Masters champion, on his early days (*My Partner Ben Hogan*).

I'm sitting there with the press, all pleased and comfortable, and when Arnie holes the 30-footer they leave me like I've got the pox.
> **Ken Venturi** recalling Arnold Palmer's putt to win the 1960 US Masters.

When one sees Palmer striding down the fairway today, a folk-hero in his own time, it is hard to believe that he was ever just another 'promising young player'; that, however, was the extent of his celebrity in the years between 1955 and 1958, his first three as a pro, and Arnie's Army in those days was about as multitudinous as the Andorra Navy.
> **Herbert Warren Wind,** 1966.

I have always loved the isolation of the early mornings on golf courses. Everything smells clean and fresh and the grass squeaks underfoot. The course seems to be much more alive to me then, almost as if it is breathing.

Dexter Westrum (*Elegy for a Golf Pro*).

On the European tour of the early 1980s we didn't play for a lot of money. We played just to win – all of us. We played purely to beat each other.

Nick Faldo, 1991.

Sammy Torrance offered me a lift to the course in his car. Then he told me I was playing him and he intended driving to London so that if neither of us turned up he would get a half-point. That was the kind of fun we had.

Lee Trevino on the spirit between the teams in the 1981 Ryder Cup match at Walton Heath.

Lady Margaret started with a great advantage. On the course in Stowell Park, an excellent nine-hole green, she played golf constantly with her father and brothers, from a child. The links was at the door of her home, she began at the right age, all her practice was with those who were likely to begin with greater natural aptitude for games than herself. They took up the game in the proper, correct spirit, trying to play it as well as they could – a spirit in which country-house golf is often lacking.

Horace Hutchinson in 1899 on Lady Margaret Scott, who won the Women's championship three years in succession then never competed in it again.

Our daughter Natalie woke up crying in the middle of the night in a Dublin hotel during the Irish Open two years ago. I took her downstairs so that all the players on our floor could get some sleep. Bernhard Langer was in the next room and he was leading the tournament. He needed his sleep. So did Nick. So we sat downstairs and the night porter fed Natalie her bottle because I dozed off.

Gill Faldo (*Daily Mail,* 1989).

The match had not been going for very long before I realised that here was a player who was something far above the ordinary. His placidity, his coolness, the unruffled nature of his game were such as to unsettle a much less nervy player than me.

J H Taylor on being defeated 8 and 7 by Harry Vardon in their first encounter which took place in 1896 at Ganton.

I stayed awake all night as the train sped north to Scotland but it was not the prospect of the Old Course in the morning that kept me from sleep. There were no sleeping compartments available and I had to sit bolt upright until dawn.

Former English Amateur champion **Gerald Micklem**.

So off I went to play golf while all the other poor sods had to polish their boots and clean their brasses.

Sir Michael Bonallack on being excused an army parade to compete in the English Amateur championship.

We played bridge into the miserable twilight of the empty Friday and there might never have been an Open championship at stake. The calculated risk of his bidding, the hard concentration of his play, his obvious enjoyment of competition and the challenge of the game itself were as revealing of his nature as the tremendous unforgettable quality and power of his golf. A great champion.

> **Pat Ward-Thomas** on Arnold Palmer the night before the final round of the 1961 Open championship, which he won.

Are they your old school colours or your own unfortunate choice?

> **Bernard Darwin** to a member of the 1954 Canadian Commonwealth team wearing a lumberjack-style shirt at St Andrews.

Who is doing a highland reel on my green? I've left my dinner to see what's going on.

> **Captain Paddy Hamner,** Muirfield secretary, on catching Ben Crenshaw, Tom Kite and others playing at dusk with hickory clubs a few hours after the 1980 Open. It had been won by Tom Watson who also played – but got away.

At dinner in a Southport hotel one night a member of our party, a slightly fey woman with a Greer Garson complex, picked up a carnation from the table decoration and sent a waiter with it to Bywaters who was sitting at a nearby table. He acknowledged it with an extravagant bow, dunked it into his claret and ate it with obvious relish.

> **Peter Dobereiner's** reflections on Major John Bywaters, secretary of the Professional Golfers Association.

I first knew Valentine Castlerosse when we were both freshmen at Cambridge. He asked me to play golf at Bishop's Stortford. We went to Cambridge station in the Pitt Club car and caught the

London express which stops at Bishop's Stortford. When we got there, there was another limousine car waiting to drive us to the golf links which are only a few hundred yards from the station. I said to Valentine: 'How clever of you to have ordered a car; it seems a very nice one.' He said: 'Oh, I had it sent out from Cambridge.'

Oliver Lyttleton's memory of Lord Kenmare, bon viveur and one of the first newspaper gossip columnists (*The Oxford and Cambridge Golfing Society 1898–1948*).

When I was three, my father put my hands in his and placed them around the shaft of a cut-down women's golf club. He showed me the classic over-lap or Vardon grip – the proper grip for a good golf swing, he said – and told me to hit the ball. 'Hit it hard, boy. Go find it and hit it again.'

Arnold Palmer with James Dodson, *A Golfer's Life,* 1999.

Nervousness is shown in various ways depending upon the temperament of a person. I do not know how many girls noticed this during that short ride but it was apparent to me. Some were talking incessantly, others not saying a word. The majority of us were yawning, a true sign of nervousness. I dare say none of us were quite sure what we had for breakfast.

American **Virginia Van Wie** recalling the bus ride to Wentworth for the 1932 match against Great Britain.

He had no money and little prospects and after the Armistice he seemed no better off, writing slogans for a New York advertising agency. 'All I lived for was to save up enough money to visit her.' When he did so he found much of her time was taken up by another suitor, a personable young golfer named Bobby Jones. For a time he feared she would marry Jones.

> The early romance of American novelist F Scott Fitzgerald and his wife-to-be Zelda, described by **Sheila Graham and Ceroid Frank** (*Beloved Infidel*).

It was a nice slice of the century to be young in. The times were good, the parties were frequent, the girls were pretty, the drinks were long, and the stock market was as strong as an ox.

> **Gene Sarazen** recalling the 1920s before the Wall Street crash.

It's tough when you are playing a real good friend. And I'm smoking the cigars he's brought me up here this week.

> **Darren Clarke** on halving his Ryder Cup singles match with Davis Love after being two down with three to play at Oakland Hills, 2004.

I can listen to my wife now because I'm done with golf. She's charge.

> **Jack Nicklaus** after playing in his last Open championship. St Andrews, 2005.

Bibliography

Betjeman, John, *Collected Poems,* John Murray, 1959.

Boswell, Thomas, *Strokes of Genius,* Simon & Schuster, 1987.

Cotton, Henry, *This Game of Golf,* Country Life, 1948.

Cotton, Henry, *Thanks for the Game,* Macmillan Publishers, 1980.

Davies, David & Patricia, *Beyond the Fairways,* HarperCollins, 1999.

Dobereiner, Peter, *Dobereiner on Golf,* Aurum Press, 1998.

Gallico, Paul, *Confessions of a Storyteller,* Gillon Aitken Associates, 1961.

Gallico, Paul, *Farewell to Sport,* Gillon Aitken Associates, 1937.

Jenkins, Dan, *The Dogged Victims of Inexorable Fate,* Little, Brown & Company, 1970.

Jones, Bobby, *Golf is My Game,* Doubleday, 1960.

Keeler, O B, *The Bobby Jones Story,* W Foulsham & Co, 1953.

Kahn, Liz, *Tony Jacklin: The Price of Success,* Octopus Publishing Group, 1979.

Ryde, Peter, *The Halford Hewitt,* Public Schools Golfing Society, 1984.

Ryde, Peter (ed.), *Mostly Golf: A Bernard Darwin Anthology,* A&C Black, 1976.

Ferguson, Duncan & Wilson, John (compilers), *The Suggestion Book,* Vertue Publishing, 2001.

Simms, George (ed.), *World of Golf,* Queen Anne Press, 1978 & 1979.